ANCESTRAL LINES

ANCESTRAL LINES

THE MAISIN OF PAPUA NEW GUINEA
AND THE FATE OF THE RAINFOREST

JOHN BARKER

Teaching Culture: UTP Ethnographies for the Classroom

UTP

for Anne and Jake

Previously published by Broadview Press 2008
Library and Archives Canada Cataloguing in Publication
Barker, John, 1953–

   Ancestral lines : the Maisin of Papua New Guinea and the fate of the rainforest / John Barker.

(Teaching Culture: UTP Ethnographies for the Classroom)
Includes bibliographical references and index.
ISBN 978-1-44260-105-5

   1. Maisin (Papua New Guinean people). 2. Maisin (Papua New Guinean people) — Social conditions. 3. Maisin (Papua New Guinean people) — Social life and customs. 4. Maisin (Papua New Guinean people) — Economic conditions.
I. Title. II. Series.
DU744.35.M32B37 2007   305.89'912   C2007-905748-9

We welcome comments and suggestions regarding any aspect of our publications — please feel free to contact us at the addresses below or at news@utphighereduation.com

North America
5201 Dufferin Street North York, Ontario, Canada M3H 5T8
2250 Military Road, Tonawanda, NY, USA 14150
Tel: (416) 978-2239; Fax: (416) 978-4738
email: customerservice@utphighereducation.com

UK, Ireland, and continental Europe
NBN International, Estover Road, Plymouth, UK PL6 7PY
Tel: 44 (0) 1752 202300; Fax: 44 (0) 1752 202330
email: enquiries@nbninternational.com

www.utphighereduation.com

Higher Education University of Toronto Press acknowledges the financial supports of the Government of Canada through the Book Publishing Industry Development Program (BPIDP) for our publishing activities.

Edited by Betsy Struthers.

Designed by Chris Rowat Design, Daiva Villa

This book is printed on paper containing 100% post-consumer fibre.

PRINTED IN CANADA

Contents

List of Illustrations

FIGURES

PLATES

Preface

Like many books written by academics, this one emerged out of my experience teaching anthropology to undergraduate students. For most students, an introductory course may be the only experience they have of the hugely diverse and lively discipline of anthropology. In North America in particular, instructors tend to use large introductory textbooks usually accompanied by a volume of readings and/or a book-length ethnographic study of a single people. There are excellent books that serve one or another of these purposes. Yet, more often than not, they fail to match up with each other. Most ethnographic monographs, even those explicitly written for undergraduates new to anthropology, are not designed with introductory textbooks in mind. They focus upon an aspect of the culture under study of particular interest to the author, thus only dealing with one or two of the general topics covered in the accompanying textbook, or they are written more or less as autobiographical accounts, forcing students to sift out general themes from the personal stories.

This ethnography provides an introduction to the cultural and historic experience of the Maisin people of Papua New Guinea, organized around the theme of tapa cloth (pounded and decorated bark cloth), with the ultimate aim of understanding why the Maisin made the fateful decision in the early 1990s to ban industrial logging on their ancestral lands. It includes personal vignettes: anthropologists love to tell stories from the field; when told well, they enliven lectures and convey important truths about the nature of learning about foreign cultures. Much of the text, however, follows the conventions of traditional ethnography in seeking to provide readers with a general sense of the way of life in a remote Melanesian village and an interpretation of the key values and orientations that provide the basic frameworks that govern its people's lives. I have deliberately constructed this book in a way that conforms to the general categories found in most introductory textbooks. Hence the chapters of this study deal with, in turn, fieldwork, economics, social organization, religion, political and legal organization, and globalization. While the chapters do build upon each other, I have written them so that an instructor, if she or he chooses, can easily stretch out the

1

reading of the book over an entire term or quarter, in tandem with a textbook. Rather than dealing with a new culture with each new topic, then, students return to a culture that becomes increasingly familiar over time as they study it from successive angles.

Because the primary audience for this book is students taking an introductory course, I have worked to keep specialized language and references to a minimum. Today's textbooks and readers, often accompanied by a specialized website, provide students with a huge list of recommended sources and references that can be daunting. I see no reason to add to this. Thus, I have tried to limit references to those directly relevant to this work, along with some to guide students with particular interests in Melanesia or just curious about the Maisin and their neighbours. Students wishing to learn more about, say, legal systems or art will find plenty of excellent references in their textbooks and from their instructors.

This book is also intended for students taking courses on the cultures of the Pacific Islands, on Indigenous people's art, and on the environment in an age of globalization. Using tapa cloth as a metaphor for culture, this study examines a small society that is facing challenges common to all of us. The Maisin provide a fresh perspective and, to borrow the words of environmentalist Dr. David Suzuki, "good news for a change" (Suzuki and Dressel 2002) in a world very much in need of it.

Finally, but certainly not least, this book is intended for the Maisin of today and future generations. This is not the kind of book a Maisin would write and, I hope, one day soon will write. This is an outsider's account, yet one based upon a long acquaintance and respect for the Maisin people. I hope, in a small way, it will contribute to their struggle to maintain control over their lands and honour the ways of their ancestors. At the very least, it provides a record of their society as I observed it during the late twentieth century, a time of momentous change.

The fieldwork on which this book is based has been financially supported over the years by several agencies: the Social Sciences and Humanities Research Council of Canada, the National Geographic Foundation, the Wenner-Gren Foundation for Anthropological Research, the Overseas Ministries Study Center in New Haven, and the Hampton Fund of the University of British Columbia. In Port Moresby and Popondetta, I received much practical support from the Australian National University, the Institute for Papua New Guinea Studies, the Anglican Church of Papua New Guinea, the University of Papua New Guinea, the Institute of Papua New Guinea Studies, and Conservation Melanesia. My thanks as well to the very helpful research staff members of the Australian Museum in Sydney, the New Guinea Collection at the University of Papua New Guinea, the National Library of Papua New Guinea, and the National Archives of Papua New Guinea.

While in Papua New Guinea, I enjoyed the hospitality and benefited from the sound advice offered by many people. I wish to thank in particular Archbishop David Hand, Bishop Isaac Gadebu, Archbishop George Ambo, Sister Helen Roberts, Bishop Paul Richardson, Father Timothy Kinohan, Paul Sillitoe, Andrew Strathern, David and Betty Buchan, James and Achsah Carrier, Maev O'Collins, Father Wellington Aburin, Father Giles Ganasa, Sian Upton, Gary Trompf, and Dr. John Waiko.

My wife, Dr. Anne Marie Tietjen, was my companion in 1981-83, conducting pioneering research on developmental and social psychology in a Melanesian society. She appears several times in this account, including in a return visit we made to Uiaku with our son, Jake, in June 2000. Less visible, but no less real, are the results of Anne's careful reading of the manuscript. Her insights and suggestions — and corrections to my sometimes creative memory — run through this book.

Many colleagues have contributed to my understanding of the Maisin, Melanesia, and anthropology. I wish to acknowledge in particular Kenelm Burridge, Cyril Belshaw, John LeRoy, Martin Silverman, Bill McKellin, Dan Jorgensen, Bronwen Douglas, Ann Chowning, Joel Robbins, Anna-Karina Hermkens, and Lafcadio Cortesi. A warm thanks to Bruce Miller, who more than once saved my sanity during the Maisin-Stó:lō exchange in June 2000. I owe a special debt of gratitude to Roger Lohmann and Joel Robbins who painstakingly read through the manuscript and offered many excellent suggestions for improvement.

Thanks as well to my students, both undergraduate and graduate, who have listened with patience to my stories from the field. Your enthusiasm, challenging questions, and endless curiosity are very much part of this book.

My greatest debts are to the Maisin people — my friends, my teachers, and my adopted family. Many of those we sat with and learned from in earlier years are now departed, but fondly remembered. I begin by recalling three men who were more than key informants, insisting that I call them my fathers: Adelbert Sevaru, Frank Davis Dodi, and Jairus Ifoki. I am also grateful to all those who worked as research assistants and translators, particularly MacSherry Gegeyo and Roland Wawe. It is not possible to thank all of those who assisted me over the years, but I do want to mention George and Mary Rose Sevaru, Franklin Seri, Romney Gegeyo, Father Kinsley Gegeyo, Lester Seri, Julia Seri, John Wesley Vaso, Gideon Ifoki and Frieda Numa, Sylvester Moi, Rebecca Gegeyo Moi, Agnes Sanangi, Lambert Gebari, Deacon Didymus Gisore, Deacon Russell Maikin, Copland King Ganeba, Nigel Bairan, Macdonald Rarama, Holland and Maggie Kania, Naomi

Sakai, Guy Kimanu, Frederick Bogara, David Beyo, and Ross Kania. In Sinapa, I'm grateful to Christian Karebi for friendship and guidance; likewise to Andrew Ofare in Yuayu and Cephus Dave in Airara. To all the others who have shared their lives with Anne and me over the years, I say: *Au natofo, tekyu bejji.*

All royalties from this book will be donated to the Maisin to be used for the benefit of students in the Airara and Uiaku community schools.

CHAPTER ONE

Fieldwork among the Maisin

August 14, 1982. We expected a small farewell party. We had been living in Uiaku for almost nine months and had reached the dreaded moment when my wife Anne's leave from her university job ended, requiring her return to Canada. Anne would return to the village for three months at the end of the school year, but that was a long eight months away. Romney Gegeyo, the village councillor, had told us that the people were organizing a goodbye dinner. We had been to many community gatherings and had a pretty good idea of what to expect. Late in the afternoon, women gathered by the shelter near our house with baskets of food, firewood, and blackened clay cooking pots. Young boys husked and scraped coconuts while the women sat peeling taro. They filled the pots to the brim with large chunks of the grey tubers along with plantains, squash, sweet potatoes, pork, and fish, topped by edible greens. They then poured in water sweetened by squeezing it through coconut shavings. After placing banana leaves as lids, they laid out the pots in a long line upon piles of firewood. As the food cooked, the men sat on the shaded platform of the shelter, chewing betelnut,[1] smoking, and discussing the events of the day.

Anne came attired for the occasion in a tapa cloth skirt and blouse that the church women's group, the Mothers Union, had made for her. While I took pictures, Anne pitched in to help the women, who greeted her with a satisfying chorus of jokes and laughter. Eventually, we were requested to sit at the place of honour on a large, gorgeously designed tapa cloth at the head of the shelter. Women forked food into bowls and then climbed onto the shelter, crossing the platform on their knees to place the food before the seated men. Once the deacon had said the grace, Anne rejoined the women on the ground and we all tucked in. After the feast ended and the women had cleared the bowls away, the senior men made speeches thanking us for our work in the community. There was a pause for more betelnut chewing. An elder called out to the crowd around the shelter, "Has anyone gifts to give

Figure 1.1 The farewell party, August 1982. Anne is greeted by Ilma Joyce Gombi and a little girl. Note the line of women waiting to present tapa cloths. (Photo by J. Barker)

our sister?" Then the most amazing thing happened. As Anne sat on a low platform, women, children, and men came forward to place shell ornaments around her neck and flowers and fragrant leaves into the coconut husk bracelets adorning her arms and legs. They brought tapa cloths, opening them with a flourish before placing them before Anne or over her lap. The tapa piled up, more than 50 pieces in all. We knew, if we had any lingering doubts, why Uiaku was so famed in Papua New Guinea for its traditional cloth.

This event marked one of those moments that occur periodically in the course of anthropological fieldwork: an instant that serves to define a culture, that gives a sense of what makes it special and unique. Over the course of five visits extending over a quarter century, I have come to think of the Maisin-speaking people who inhabit Uiaku and neighbouring villages as "tapa people" because their distinctive, beautiful cloth figures so centrally in their history, interactions with each other, and dealings with the outside world. This book is about how the Maisin make a living, organize their social interactions, meet the opportunities and tragedies of life, and conceptualize the spiritual world. It is also about the ways they have adjusted to the incorporation of their communities into larger colonial and post-colonial worlds. Not least, it is about the fateful decision the Maisin made in the early 1990s to refuse commercial logging on their ancestral lands.

Much has changed over the years, not least during recent times when the Maisin have faced grave threats to the rainforest and waters that sustain their lives. Maisin tapa cloth, adorned with bright red geometric swirls and curls, has also sustained the people. It connects them to a still vital ancestral past; it defines gender roles and the modes of local sociability; it provides income where there are very few opportunities to make money; and it stands as an iconic symbol of identity within the cultural mosaic that is Papua New Guinea. It is appropriate, then, to approach Maisin culture and history through the medium of tapa.

Tapa is the common name for cloth made from the pounded inner bark of certain trees. Prior to European colonization, most of the inhabitants of the South Pacific Islands manufactured some sort of bark cloth, ranging from the delicately coloured *kapa* worn by nobility in the Hawaiian Islands (from which we get the word "tapa") to simple unadorned loin cloths worn by men in parts of Melanesia (Neich and Prendergast 2005). Across the region, local people experimented with a wide variety of trees, dyes, tools, and techniques, resulting in a kaleidoscope of styles as varied and distinctive as the cultures themselves. Tapa served many purposes: clothing, wealth, a symbol of authority and divinity, a canvas for decorative designs or the face of an ancestor. Early European visitors admired tapa for its beauty and practicality. The incorporation of the islands into global commercial networks, however, opened the door to the import of cheap and durable mass-manufactured cotton and, later, synthetic cloth, hastening the demise of tapa. Today, tapa is regularly made in only a few places such as Samoa, Fiji, and Tonga, chiefly for the tourist trade and for ceremonial purposes (Kooijman 1972). Where tapa has survived, and often where it has not, it has become tightly associated with people's sense of cultural identity in an increasingly mobile and interconnected world (e.g., Small 1997). The Maisin are one of those people.

The people of Uiaku and neighbouring villages call themselves the Maisin (pronounced, "My-seen"). Numbering around 3,000, many of whom now live in distant towns, the Maisin form one of the more than 700 linguistic groups who make up the nation of Papua New Guinea. The cultural diversity of Papua New Guinea has long made it a beacon for anthropologists. Although the land and population are small (today around 5 million people), few places have been as intensely studied or as well-documented by ethnographers—leading to the old joke that the typical New Guinean family consists of a husband, wife, children, a pig, and an anthropologist. Anthropologists originally went to faraway places to document exotic cultures before they were transformed by the juggernaut of Christianity, commerce, and Western "civilization." It cannot be denied that the area continues to exert a romantic tug, but most anthropologists today working in Papua New Guinea go there not so much to document the past but to examine the present. What we find is that we have much to learn from people like the Maisin, not just about the range of cultural diversity but also the ways in which people in the far corners of the globe are dealing with problems that today confront us all. This book is concerned with two of those challenges in particular: first, how a people can retain a sense of cultural identity in the face of the homogenizing influences of the global system that has so greatly eased the mass movement of people, products, and ideas; and, second, how to create and maintain a decent standard of living without destroying the environment on which all life is ultimately sustained. Tapa figures prominently in the ways the Maisin have dealt with such challenges.

All people face similar challenges, but the stakes appear far more consequential and stark for some Indigenous cultures due to their small size, lack of economic and political clout, and, in many areas, direct dependence on the natural environment for their survival. By the time that Anne and I arrived late in 1981, Maisin culture had already been inalterably transformed after more than a century of interaction with colonial agents. A school and church had existed in Uiaku since 1902. All of the people were Christian, all had attended at least the village school, and a quarter of the population now resided permanently outside the rural villages. Yet for all of the changes, Uiaku and other Maisin villages retained a strong connection to a distinctive ancestral past, including the use of their own language, a commitment to several key rituals, extensive mutually supportive kinship networks, and, not least, a sense of pride in their cultural achievements, most notably tapa cloth. It seemed to us that people had found a balance — not perfect by any means, but one that combined some of the best features of the old and new. The balance, however, was fragile. Most villagers considered themselves very poor indeed and eagerly sought means of earning money. In the early 1980s, the best option to many appeared to lie in selling off timber rights to the nearby rainforest. The cleared land would be replaced by profitable commercial plantations of oil palm, providing the people with a steady income. Many people were aware of the risks; even at that early date, word of the environmental damage caused by industrial logging elsewhere in the country, and the corrupt behaviour of some of the logging companies, had reached them. Yet people felt that their isolation from markets and shameful poverty left them with little choice.

Many Indigenous peoples have made such choices or, more often, simply had their lands and resources taken from them in the name of "development." Knowing this, Anne and I left Uiaku in July 1983, quietly lamenting

8

that even if the opportunity arose to return, the village we had come to love might well be changed beyond recognition. But the people had a change of heart. Doubts about the wisdom of clear-cutting the rainforest had, by the mid-1990s, hardened into a determination to keep out commercial loggers and a growing suspicion of all large-scale development projects. Villagers resisted a series of projects foisted upon them by the national government in cahoots with logging companies, eventually besting their adversaries in a landmark case in the National Court. Their quixotic campaign attracted the attention of international environmental organizations and, soon after, museum curators and the media. Maisin delegations visited North America, Australia, and Japan to promote their cause. Maisin tapa was exhibited in art galleries in Berkeley, New York, Philadelphia, and Tokyo.

I had the good fortune to return to the Maisin villages in the midst of these developments for a couple of brief visits in 1997 and 1998. In July 2000, Anne and our (then) 12-year-old son, Jake, came as well. We were met with a joyful celebration in which Jake was taken through the first stages of the initiation ceremony for a first-born child. Physically, the villages and their surroundings looked much the same as in the early 1980s. The changes that had occurred were less visible but perhaps more significant. More people could speak English, and villagers appeared more affluent. They had better clothes and owned more store-bought goods. There was now a bi-weekly market at which people sold garden produce for cash. As we met with old friends and got to know younger folk who were babes-in-arms or not even born during our first visit, we detected a remarkable sense of confidence that had largely replaced the self-deprecatory attitudes of earlier times. People spoke with pride of their ancestral traditions and contrasted their subsistence way of life favourably against that enjoyed by relatives working in the towns. They eloquently told of the need to preserve both their distinct traditions and the environment for future generations. Tapa cloth has become the key symbol of that determination.

Tapa also provides the inspiration for my approach in this book. Ethnographic fieldwork is based largely upon participant-observation or, as anthropologists occasionally joke, "deep hanging out." One learns not just through asking questions or observing but by getting involved directly, trying things out oneself. Making my own piece of tapa enabled me to better appreciate the skills involved and the wider significance of the cloth to the Maisin. Making a tapa involves several discrete stages, each building upon the other while employing distinct techniques and procedures. A human culture is a bit like that. You encounter a way of life as a seamless whole at first, but in time you learn to distinguish among the general processes and domains that sustain it. Each chapter of this book thus opens with a short section concerning

9

tapa cloth as an introduction to differing facets of the society as I observed it during the latter decades of the twentieth century. The introductory sections of Chapters 2 through 4 trace the making of a piece of tapa from the cultivation of the tree that provides the bark to the finishing application of red dye. These sections, in turn, introduce three of the fundamental domains of social life: economic activities, social organization, and religion. Chapter 5 opens with a survey of the various ways Maisin use tapa, both for community purposes and as a source of income. This leads into a discussion of the legal and political aspects of community life. Thus, the first five chapters focus mostly upon the enduring fundamentals of Maisin society. Chapter 6 brings us closer to the present. It opens with the visit by a four-man delegation from Uiaku to the Berkeley Art Museum in California to open a major exhibition of Maisin tapa cloth. While Maisin culture retained its distinctive shape, the events of the 1990s — most importantly, the decision to reject commercial logging — significantly increased the involvement of Maisin with outside agencies. These entanglements, in turn, have caused the Maisin to rethink their relationship to their own ancestral roots and the world outside their villages.

Before turning to these topics, it will be helpful to provide some background, beginning with an account of how Anne and I came to live and work with the Maisin. I then turn to the physical world within which Maisin live and finish with an overview of the historical changes that have occurred in the area since the moment of first contact with European colonials back in 1890.

FIELDWORK IN UIAKU

As is the case with most anthropologists, the path that led us to Uiaku passed through the circumstances of our lives and studies, intense background research, and dumb luck. I first became interested in the South Pacific Islands while studying for my BA in anthropology at the University of Western Ontario. I was fortunate enough to land a Commonwealth Scholarship that took me to Victoria University of Wellington in New Zealand for graduate studies under Ann Chowning, one of the great figures in Melanesian anthropology. I was very excited about my proposed project: a study of the impact of multinational corporations upon the self-image of Pacific Islanders. Unfortunately, like a lot of great projects, this turned out to be impractical, given my tiny research budget and the difficulties of gathering scattered information in the days before the Internet. I spent my mornings in the Alexander Turnbull Library perusing newspapers from its marvellous collection of Pacific Islands documents, my spirits steadily sinking as the impediments of the project became more and more obvious. From time to time, my attention wandered to the old books in the collection, many of which had been written by pioneering missionaries in the period prior to formal colonization. I soon was captivated. The books were not the stiff-necked "preachy" tracts I had expected (although they contained many expressions of piety and more than a little ethnocentrism) — they were more like the Victorian adventure stories by the likes of H. Rider Haggard, the author of *King Solomon's Mines*, which I had enjoyed as a child.

In the end, I wrote a social history of three missions that operated in southeast Papua New Guinea between 1871 and 1930 for my MA thesis (Barker 1979). This in turn led me to my topic for my PhD research. I had read widely in the anthropological literature on Papua New Guinea and other Melanesian areas by this point and was surprised by how little attention anthropologists paid to the impact of the missions and the presence of Christianity (Barker 1992). The most recent national census figures from the country indicated that an overwhelming majority of the people, more than 90 per cent, considered themselves Christian.[2] Yet you would never know this from anthropological works, which focussed almost entirely upon indigenous religious practices and ideas. What happened when people became Christians? I had some ideas from the research I had done for my MA thesis, but almost all of the assessments had been done by European missionaries writing decades earlier. I wondered what Papua New Guinean Christians themselves made of their Christian faith and its relationship to their ancestral cultures.

To pursue this topic, I decided that it would be best to study a community where the church had become an accepted part of ordinary life, where the people were second- or, better, third-generation Christians, and missionaries were a fading memory. This limited my choices to a coastal area. I also wanted to work in the southeast of the country so I could make good use of the historical research I had already done. Of the three missions I had studied, I was most intrigued by the Anglicans who, in contrast to the stereotypes most of us hold about missionaries, had been ardent defenders of many village traditions and often fiercely critical of industrial society (Wetherell 1977). This narrowed my search to the northeastern coast of the island of New Guinea where the Anglicans had worked exclusively for most of the colonial period.

At this point, I returned to Canada to take up PhD studies at the University of British Columbia under Kenelm Burridge, another great Melanesianist scholar best known for his writings on cargo cults and, more recently, missionaries. I had about 500 kilometres of coastline to consider for possible field sites. Two events led me to the Maisin and Uiaku village. The first was meeting, falling in love, and marrying Anne Marie Tietjen. Trained as a developmental psychologist at Cornell University, Anne had a strong interest in cross-cultural research, having carried out her dissertation fieldwork in Sweden. She developed a project to study the development of social

11

cognition and behaviour that required a village with lots of children (Tietjen 1986). I came across an old census of the region and found that the two largest villages along hundreds of kilometres of the coast lay within 12 kilometres of each other on Collingwood Bay: Wanigela and Uiaku. The second event was the arrival of the Right Reverend David Hand, then the Archbishop of the Anglican Church of Papua New Guinea, on a fundraising tour that took him through Vancouver. When I caught up with him after a service, Bishop David was immediately supportive. Before I had a chance to tell him of the villages we were considering, he recommended that I work among the Maisin in Uiaku. He had begun his missionary career in 1946 working as the priest-in-charge for the area and had retained a fondness for the Maisin, who he considered to have achieved a remarkable balance between ancestral traditions and modernity.

Bishop David gave me the name of the Papuan priest, Father Wellington Aburin, who served the Maisin and their immediate neighbours to the west. I dutifully wrote, outlining our research plans. I didn't receive a reply. This was a worry, but meanwhile Anne and I pushed on, writing grant proposals and applying for research permits from Papua New Guinea. Soon everything was more or less in place. In October 1981, visa in hand, I set off ahead on a route through New Zealand and Australia, where I would carry out archival research, eventually arriving in Port Moresby, the capital of Papua New Guinea, where Anne would catch up with me about six weeks later.

At the time of my departure, all I really knew about the Maisin was the names of some of their villages, the size of their population a decade earlier, and some aspects of their language. I reasoned that they shared cultural features and a similar experience of colonization as better documented coastal peoples, but it was disconcerting to be going in so blind. Once in Port Moresby, I managed to pick up some details about Uiaku. I met my first Maisin — Father Kingsley Gegeyo, then a chaplain at the University of Papua New Guinea. He was friendly and encouraging, praising the village way of life and making suggestions on where we might stay until we arranged to have a house built. Anne flew in from Canada. We stocked up with provisions before flying to the capital of Oro Province, Popondetta, to meet with government and church officials and to buy more supplies. We then flew out in a tiny prop plane, passing over seemingly endless forest, mountains, and swampland before circling around the cloud shrouded peak of Mount Victory, a dormant volcano, and landing on the grass airfield at Wanigela. We were accommodated there by Sister Helen Roberts, a missionary nurse who had lived in Wanigela since 1946. She was a font of information on the local people, who held her in the highest regard, and quickly became a close friend. We also met David and Betty Buchan, a New Zealand couple running a small rubber plantation about five kilometres inland from the airstrip on the lower slopes of Mount Victory, who also became fast friends during our stay.

Within a few hours of arriving at the airstrip, Anne and I trekked down a dirt road to the beach where we gazed southwards towards the area we thought Uiaku would be. When we returned to Helen's house, she introduced us to several women who had come up from the Maisin villages to sell tapa. They told us that the people had already prepared a house for us on the "mission station" at Uiaku and inquired, with some delicacy, if we were connected to the Summer Institute of Linguistics, a huge missionary organization dedicated to translating the Bible into different vernaculars. A couple of days later, Father Wellington appeared. He had received our letters as it turned out and told us that we had been expected to arrive two weeks earlier. He was friendly enough, but quiet, and I worried that this was less from shyness than annoyance with our tardiness. Father Wellington returned to Uiaku in the afternoon. We really did not know what to expect at this point, but the next morning several young Maisin men appeared at the mission house ready to take us and our gear down to the beach to be loaded on a dinghy for the trip across Collingwood Bay to Uiaku. We had reached the final stage of our journey.

As the dinghy swung out from the beach at Wanigela and headed into open water, we were dazzled by the dramatic scenery — the broad sweep of rainforest rising from the coast, the immense mountain wall to the south, and the line of volcanic peaks to the west. An hour later, we approached Uiaku itself. The boat operator pulled the little outboard motor up and we surfed across a low sandbar into the mouth of a broad river, shaded on the southern side by high coconut palms. We landed at what we were told was the "mission station." Father Wellington was there along with the community school headmaster and dozens of curious children. Father Wellington took us up to his house — a commodious, cool building constructed of bush materials, with a broad verandah looking out over the river. It had recently been built to serve as an office and a home for a radio-telephone promised by the Bishop. When we materialized instead of the radio, the leaders decided to add a kitchen extension and give it to us for our use. The house was small, but more than suitable, with a kitchen, a bedroom just large enough for our mattress and mosquito net, two small offices with rough tables, and an alcove that we adapted for a bucket shower and wash area. As we approached our new home, we were relieved to find a group of men hard at work constructing a latrine on the east side (we had been contemplating the station latrines with some dread — they were little huts built over the river at the end of long rickety bridges).

During our short stay in Wanigela, Betty and David had given us a kitten that we had dubbed "The Reverend A.P. Jennings" after the only European missionary to have lived, if only briefly, with the Maisin, some 60 years earlier. Holding "Appy," we walked through the nearby part of the village. We felt a bit like royalty on parade, with people lining the sides of the path to see us and the children calling out "hello, hello" and breaking into hysterical giggles every time we replied. White people rarely visited the area, and so we were quite a novelty—so much so that the smaller tots burst into terrified screams at our approach. In the late afternoon, we returned to the house and began setting up our new home. Around dinnertime, Gideon Ifoki appeared at the door. He along with Ilma Joyce Daima, both of whom were around our age, would help us over the first month or so as research assistants and language teachers. At the moment, however, Gideon was leading the first of several women who appeared over the next two days with string bags full of garden produce, which they dumped just inside the entrance to the house. These, we were told, were gifts. We should not pay cash for the food.

We could hardly have dreamed of a more welcoming reception, with a house, food, and research assistants all pre-arranged by the people themselves. We were grateful but also overwhelmed. Why were they doing this? What did they expect of us? The morning after we arrived, Father Wellington introduced us to the community after the church service. I took the opportunity to give an explanation in simple English of our research goals and to invite questions (all this was translated for the congregation by Gideon). Later I repeated the speech at a community meeting called to discuss our project. In succeeding weeks and months, as I made the rounds of the villages, I found myself returning to this speech. I think that most people understood the basics of what we said we were up to; they simply couldn't credit that white people would come all that way to live among them just to study their culture. Many people hoped that we had come to translate the Bible, while others worried that we were missionaries from one of the newly arrived Christian denominations seeking to challenge the long-established Anglican Church. Some villagers hoped that we would make use of our (supposed) connections to "American businessmen" to bring "development" to the area. Many years later, we learned that there had been hopeful whispers among some of the old people that we might be ancestral spirits returning in a new form to our old home.[3] I doubt that we were able to entirely scotch the rumours and hopes that attended our arrival, but after a time when nothing miraculous happened, most people seemed to accept that we really were who we said we were.

Living in Uiaku required adjustments on our part as well. First of all, there were the physical discomforts. We had arrived at the start of the wet season, and the combination of heat and high humidity left us exhausted by the end of the day. We found it impossible to remain clean for long. During the day we had to slather ourselves repeatedly with strong insect repellent to fend off swarms of tiny sandflies that rose daily from the sandy grounds of the village as the air heated up. In the evenings, we lathered on more repellent and donned extra clothes despite the heat to protect ourselves from the anopheles mosquito, the carrier of malaria. Grit got into everything — our clothes, our skin, our hair. At first, the lack of running water and electricity seemed romantic, rather like camping out. The novelty wore off quickly. Everything took longer: finding kerosene for the lamps, hauling water for washing up, boiling drinking water or catching rain water from a tarp, and so on and on. We never entirely got used to the climate or environment, but we acclimatized, adjusted, and learned. Soon things settled down into a daily routine of housekeeping. Fortunately, we liked the local food. The main staples of taro, sweet potatoes, and cooking bananas were starchy and bland, but there was plenty of fruit from the gardens, and we had brought along spices and tinned sauces to add some variety. Periodically, people brought fish or game. This was always a treat.

The lack of privacy in the village posed another challenge. The thin sago ribbed walls of the houses do little to muffle sounds and so we, along with everyone else, got to listen in whenever voices became raised. We ourselves were objects of intense curiosity, especially to children, who often hung around and under our house, hoping to catch sight of us. It is rather unnerving to glance down and see a pair of young eyes staring at you through a crack in the floor boards. After a time, we put together scrapbooks of pictures of animals and places around the world cut from magazines and invited the children into the house, where they sat mesmerized for hours at a time. The kids closest to our house soon got used to us, but whenever I ventured to the further reaches of the village or to neighbouring villages, I would be followed by curious children, shouting out "Bye! Bye!" or "Bariyawa!" (Whiteman) and squealing with laughter whenever I replied.

Ethnographic Fieldwork

Anne and I arrived in Uiaku with specific research projects in mind. We knew, however, that the path to learning about the contemporary religious ideas and the psychological development of children ran through the culture as a whole. We would not be able to gain more than a superficial understanding of our research topics without the broadest possible understanding of Maisin historical experience and cultural orientations. Ethnographic research draws on a holistic perspective, a basic assumption that "the various parts of a culture must be viewed in the broadest possible context to

15

understand their interconnections and interdependence" (Haviland *et al.* 2002). Compared to the typical research strategies pursued in the social sciences, ethnographic research tends to be intimate and slow. To fully understand the impact of Christianity on the Maisin, I would need to become familiar with the language, daily routines, social organization, and care of the young and elderly — the minutiae of life. I would be witness to crises and conflicts, celebrations and debates, all of which would shed light on deeper social patterns. Through this, I would gradually enculturate, become increasingly familiar and comfortable with Maisin ways and expectations. The more we learned, the more our initial projects developed in new and often unexpected directions. They became less our own and more the shared endeavour of ourselves and our Maisin hosts.

Over many years, anthropologists have made ethnography into a fine art. I had previously taken courses on ethnographic fieldwork and studied many methodological textbooks. It was exciting moving from theory to the real thing. Although I knew that the fieldwork would take unexpected directions, I came prepared with a detailed research strategy, which I immediately put into action.

Our most immediate need upon arriving in Uiaku was to learn how to interact properly with our new neighbours. We had read extensively about Melanesian societies prior to coming and knew that reciprocity would play a central role in local relations. This was confirmed rather directly shortly after we first stepped out of the boat at Uiaku by the school headmaster, who cautioned us not to pay money for any services or food. "We live by the 'Melanesian Way,'" he exclaimed, which, he further clarified, meant that people should help each other without expecting payment (see Narakobi 1980). Things turned out to be somewhat more complicated than our reading or the cheery advice of the headmaster prepared us for. Intellectually understanding a social system and practically dealing with it are two very different things. This became clear that first afternoon in Uiaku as we watched the pile of garden produce deposited in the centre of our tiny new "living room" climb. It was far too much for our use, and how were we supposed to reciprocate? By the afternoon of the second day, the taro, bananas, sweet potatoes, and squash were beginning to rot, but still people kept bringing us more. What should we do? If we refused these gifts, wouldn't the people be insulted? Yet throwing it out would be equally bad. We decided to consult privately with Father Wellington, who we noticed had been eying the food on his frequent visits to our house. His whispered suggestion was simplicity itself: "Give it to the priest." So, under the cloak of darkness, he sent his children over to the house to relieve us of our burden. Later I learned that within the hour, the food had been redistributed across the station, to the three teachers and Deacon Russell, with the excess eventually returning to families in the village. Thus, we learned our first practical lesson about exchange networks.

We were at the beginning of a process of cultural immersion that anthropologists call "participant observation." The basic idea behind participant observation is that one can learn a great deal about a community by joining in ongoing activities. Fieldwork for me has involved garden work, making tapa cloth, tying roof thatch, traditional dancing, regular church services, and endless hours chewing betelnut on verandahs while sharing the gossip of the day. "Being there," however, is not always very pleasant. Whenever I try to work with Maisin, I am inevitably brought up by my physical weakness and incompetence at even the most basic tasks. Anne and I faced numerous obstacles, beginning with the language but also including Maisin assumptions about proper behaviour. We made mistakes and, hopefully, learned from them. The Maisin were gracious, although we certainly must often have tested peoples' patience.

Over time, we learned. I suspect that the Maisin were just as unsure of how to deal with us as we were with them. In the early days, people continually brought us food whether we needed it or not and, just as insistently, requested things from us. We knew that they were treating us as one of their own, but we did not have gardens and realized quickly that we had to pace our gift-giving of tobacco, rice, and other goods carefully both because of the expense and the difficulty of getting new supplies.[4] Eventually we worked out a balance. People brought a more reasonable amount of food, and we learned that we could negotiate on a more balanced rate of return in store goods. Perhaps the most welcome and useful thing we did was to provide some basic first aid for our neighbours. Each morning began with Anne treating a line of men, women, and children with bandages for cuts and scrapes and care for other minor ailments.

If participant observation only involved direct involvement in the flow of daily activities, however, fieldwork would amount to little more than adventure tourism. Anne and I immersed ourselves as much as we could into community life with a serious purpose in mind—to further our research. This required maintaining good fieldnotes. I carried a small notebook everywhere I went, jotting down reminder notes during the day and typing up much more detailed accounts during the evenings. These scratch notes could often be very detailed, especially when I observed community meetings and ritual occasions, like funerals and end-of-mourning ceremonies. I also kept a daily journal for more personal reflections. Systematically recording observations allowed me to begin the process of making sense out of the culture both by revealing patterns and by suggesting new questions and avenues of research.

We used participant observation in conjunction with a variety of other research methodologies. The day after we arrived, I walked the length of the village with Gideon, drawing a rough sketch map indicating the location of houses and major features such as the mission station and the two creeks and river that formed natural divisions. Where I saw uneven lines of houses stretched along the shore, Gideon identified clusters belonging to different clans and separated by boundaries subtly marked by trees or bushes. A couple of weeks later, I devised a basic household census. Gideon translated the questions into Maisin for me, and, with his help as a translator, I proceeded to visit all of the houses in the village. The census provided information about household composition, education, marriage, languages spoken, and a variety of other basic matters, giving me a good overview of the social organization of the village. I practised my small Maisin vocabulary, to the great amusement of the villagers, and got to spend some time with almost everyone. Census work could be tedious, but I was surprised by how much I enjoyed myself. The questions often led to more detailed conversations on the people's lives or aspects of Maisin culture and history, rapidly filling my notebooks. The work progressed at a leisurely pace. I gave participants gifts of packaged rice and oily tobacco sticks. Interviews always ended with smoking, in which I did not indulge, and a chew of betelnut, for which I rapidly developed a fondness.

Before completing the census, I arranged group meetings with members of the different clans occupying Uiaku to record genealogies. While not without their difficulties—few Maisin it turned out remembered their ancestors back further than two to three generations—the genealogies provided further information on kinship relations and marriage alliances, the basics of the local social system (described in Chapter 3). Later, I conducted other surveys to probe understandings of death, attitudes towards leaders, the frequency and contents of economic exchanges, and understandings of Christianity. In my second year, I conducted a census and other inquiries in the Maisin village of Sinapa, a coastal village about six kilometres to the east, to broaden my knowledge of the Maisin beyond Uiaku.

Most days, I set up interviews with elders to discuss a wide range of subjects, with a particular focus upon spiritual matters. I became an enthusiastic audience for Maisin oral traditions, both clan histories and stories told for amusement. I tape-recorded over 100 of these, translating them as time allowed with the help of a research assistant. Over time, I carried out other surveys on topics such as explanations for deaths, daily records of exchanges, ideas about leadership, and understandings of Christianity. I tried to engage with as wide a circle of people as I could on most matters, but inevitably I found myself frequently consulting a small number of people who were espe-

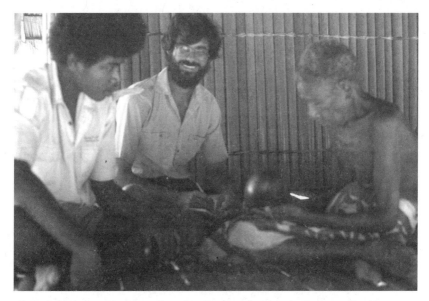

Figure 1.2 Conducting an interview with Nita Keru (holding the lime gourd), with my research assistant, MacSherry Gegeyo, in 1983. (Photo by A.M. Tietjen)

cially knowledgeable and helpful. In anthropological parlance, such people are known as "key informants." The term does not adequately describe the reality. I first visited elders like Adelbert Sevaru, Frank Davis Dodi, and Agnes Sanangi intending to interview them as they were very active in the church and respected for their knowledge of Maisin traditions. It didn't take long for them to define our relationship. They were the authorities, the elders, the teachers. They listened patiently to my questions but more often than not talked about what they knew to be relevant. Eager to get on with my work, I was at first impatient. With time, I calmed my urge to direct the flow of conversation and just sat, hour upon hour, listening quietly, asking the occasional question. I dimly realized I was being offered a gift. My "informants" became my mentors and, as my knowledge grew, my collaborators. At the most intimate level, as trust grew, they drew Anne and me into their families.

The work was not without frustrations. A few people were suspicious or scared and refused to talk with me. More often, villagers were too busy with gardening or other chores to bother with my seemingly endless questions. We had a hard time finding and keeping good research assistants. Some got bored with the work, but most quit because they couldn't cope with endless badgering on the part of relatives who assumed, because I was paying them for their time, that they must be amassing a fortune. Most frustrating was the sheer difficulty of making sense of what was going on around us. I felt this especially during the early months. Yet even at the end of my fieldwork, I was acutely aware — perhaps more aware than ever — that there were key questions I had not thought to ask, many aspects of Maisin experience that remained a mystery to me. I had amassed several thousand pages of notes, hundreds of hours of interviews and stories on tape, and countless photographs and films of people engaged in ordinary activities and ceremonial events. Twenty-five years and four visits later, I feel that I'm still scratching the surface.

Departures and Returns

Most of the time, Anne and I loved living in Uiaku. We learned to cope with the difficulties, and each day presented something new and remarkable. While we had our separate projects, we compared notes during the evenings and were encouraged that we were discovering the same basic cultural and social patterns. We became very close to some people, who insisted on treating us as family. In August 1982, Anne returned to Canada while I remained in the village. She returned to a boisterous welcome the next May for three final months of fieldwork. We were by this time relaxed and comfortable with the culture and our surroundings. It was a very productive time but also one that brought us ever closer to our friends. Finally, the time came to depart. We spent a day visiting, finally reciprocating for that huge gift of food that welcomed us by dividing our gear amongst different families. There was a farewell feast, followed by a dance, for which both of us were decorated in traditional finery. With many tears and regrets, we left as we had come, by dinghy early the next morning. It was July 1983.

Three years later, I returned on my own for two months to research tapa cloth and women's facial tattooing. I found that our neighbours had torn down our old house right after our departure and taken an axe to the surrounding coconut palms, basically treating our departure the way they would a death. The return trip was very productive, but perhaps its main importance was to establish for Maisin as well as ourselves that our mutual bonds would not be broken so easily. As it turned out, however, this was the last fieldwork I was able to carry out in Uiaku for some time. I moved from a post-doctoral position at the University of Washington that allowed abundant time for research to a teaching post at the University of British Columbia. Soon after this, our son Jake was born, and I looked for fieldwork possibilities that would not require long absences from home. I began to work with the Nisga'a and Nuxalk First Nations of British Columbia on different projects.

Of course, we did not forget about the Maisin. We continued to publish papers based on our research, sending back copies as well as tapes and other materials we had recorded in the 1980s. We received the occasional letter in response, informing us of deaths and other events. Then, out of the blue, Franklin Seri, then the village councillor and a dear friend, wrote to me late in 1994. He and four other men were travelling to Berkeley, California to put on a museum exhibit of tapa cloth and talk about the rainforest. This is how I first learned about the Maisin's decision not to allow commercial logging in their territory and their alliance with Greenpeace, which had co-sponsored this trip along with the Berkeley Art Museum. Anne, Jake, and I went to Berkeley where we had a wonderful reunion with the Maisin delegation. Franklin stayed behind to live with us for two months during which time we produced a reader of stories, in Maisin and simple English, to be used in the village schools.

This event renewed our ties to the Maisin. I returned to Uiaku in February 1997 for five weeks to study the community's attitudes towards rainforest conservation and the impact of their partnerships with national and international environmentalists. My role was now changing. In the past, I had studied the community while remaining somewhat detached from it. People greatly appreciated the record I made, especially of traditions that were fast disappearing. But now I wanted to make a more direct contribution to the needs of the community. My knowledge of Maisin history and culture proved to be useful to some of the non-governmental organizations (NGOs) working with the people, for whom I served as a consultant. And then I came up with my own project. I returned briefly in 1998 with two Canadian filmmakers to discuss the possibility of setting up an exchange of delegations between the Maisin and the Stó:lō First Nation in British Columbia. The visits would be made into a documentary to highlight the Maisin's fight to save their rainforest from commercial loggers and to witness two very different Indigenous peoples trying to work out their own solutions to common problems. The concept intrigued Bruce Miller, a colleague in my department with long experience working with First Nations communities in southern British Columbia and Washington State, including the Stó:lō, and he agreed to join the project. Following a frenzy of fundraising, recruiting, and planning, Bruce, five Stó:lō delegates, and I finally arrived to a glorious welcoming ceremony in Ganjiga village. The film crew had already set themselves up for the shoot and for the next two weeks proceeded to document the exchange.[5] While exhilarating, dealing with the all-too-often conflicting needs of the delegation, the film crew, and the Maisin left me exhausted. It was with some relief that I travelled to Port Moresby to see Bruce and the Stó:lō off to Canada (the film crew had already departed) and to greet Anne and Jake, who had arrived on the same plane. We now made the return trek to Uiaku, for Anne's wonderful reunion with old friends after a 17-year absence and Jake's initiation celebration.

Anne's and my association with the Maisin now stretches back more than 25 years. Most of the elders we knew in the early 1980s have died, and many aspects of the culture that they related to me exist only in my notebooks. We are now referred to as "mother" and "father"—and even "grandparents"—by the majority of the rapidly growing Maisin population. A great deal has changed in the last quarter century. The Maisin villages are not nearly as isolated as they once were. It is now possible to reach the village via satellite phone, and I am able to correspond with some Maisin in the towns by e-mail. Yet, despite the lessening of distance, much in the local communities remains the same—the subsistence basis of life, adherence to Christianity, strong kinship ties, and an ethic of moral egalitarianism—values all exemplified by that central emblem of Maisin identity, tapa cloth. Above all, through determined resistance, the Maisin have so far been able to protect the forests and waters that sustain them.

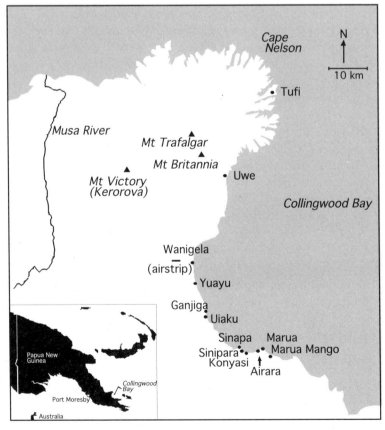

Figure 1.3 Location map of Collingwood Bay and the Maisin villages.

THE PHYSICAL SETTING

The Maisin live in a breathtakingly beautiful place. From a canoe or small boat in the midst of Collingwood Bay, the southern shore sweeps out in a vast arc. There are few obvious signs of human habitation. The coast is outlined by a dark green line of mangrove swamps. Behind this, dense forest climbs upwards, interrupted in places by small mountains, until it reaches the mountain wall of the Owen Stanley range, about 20 kilometres inland. In the early morning, before heavy clouds shroud the peaks, one can often see right to the peak of Mount Suckling (Gorofi), at 3,676 metres one of the tallest mountains in the country. The mountain wall is torn at places by the scars of massive landslides and broken by waterfalls plunging from high basins. From the beaches of the Maisin villages, one has a clear view of the western edge of the bay, which is dominated by the peaks of Mount Victory (Kerorova), a dormant volcano which last erupted shortly before European contact, and the older volcanic ridge of Mount Trafalgar.

As one approaches the Maisin villages from the sea, houses slowly take shape as glimmering brown aggregates of cubes suspended between the line of the sea and the dark green mangroves behind. Drawing closer, the cubes separate and take on sharper outline, and the groves of coconut palms marking village sites emerge into focus. Finally, a grey beach comes into view, lined by greying outrigger canoes of varying sizes and the occasional aluminium dinghy. The Maisin villages tend to be long and rather narrow, situated on sand bars between the surf and swampy ground behind. They are vulnerable to erosion and flooding. The Vayova River that runs through Uiaku, for instance, has broadened and shifted in the past 20 years, forcing some of the villagers who used to live on the south side to relocate their houses to the north.

A few iron roofs have begun to appear in parts of the villages, but most houses are built entirely of materials gathered from the nearby bush and forest. They are simple in design but very attractive. All are built on posts, rising one to three metres above the ground, and many have broad open verandahs where people share food and socialize. In most villages, the houses are arranged in an uneven parallel line, facing across an area of bare packed earth that serves as both central path and plaza. In a few places, the houses spread apart to enclose much broader plazas, usually to the side of the main pathway through the village. The ground under and about the houses, as well as in the plazas, is kept completely bare of grass. One often wakes up in the morning to a gentle rhythmic swish, the sound of women and girls sweeping up dead leaves, twigs, and bits of refuse. The Maisin plant areca palms, small shade trees, and flowering plants around their homes. In general, the villages are clean, open, and breezy, forming an attractive contrast to the contorted tall grasses, areca and coconut plantations, and jungle that commences immediately behind the interior row of houses.

At the geographical centre of Uiaku lies a large grassy sports field bordered by neat croton-lined paths. Classrooms, the church, houses for the priest and teachers, shelters for visitors and special occasions, and, since 1986, market stalls line its edges. Graceful mango trees planted a century ago by the first Melanesian teachers provide shade near the original site of the first church. Although decades have passed since the last Anglican missionary worked in the region, Maisin still refer to this space as the "mission station."

Maisin have only a single word for a settlement (*wa'ki*) but they nonetheless recognize several encompassing levels. At the broadest level are four village clusters, which the Maisin refer to by the "big name" of the largest named settlement. These are, going from the north to the southeast, Yuayu, Uiaku, Sinapa, and Airara. The last three are made up of smaller villages. The Uiaku cluster is composed of Ganjiga on the northern side of the Vayova River and Uiaku on the south. Uiaku proper is further divided into Vayova, Maume, and Yamakero. Two of the villages making up the Sinapa cluster are composed of single clans. Everywhere else, however, the villages are multi-nucleated, occupied by two or more clans each with its own named area. These are often contiguous, although everyone knows where the boundaries lie.

Beyond the swampy area behind the village houses, lies a zone of secondary forest radiating out four or five kilometres; this is where people make their gardens and harvest sago. Further inland, one finds areas of extensive grassland and dense primary rainforest. The lush jungles, swamps, grasslands, and forests of the Maisin environment nurture a rich diversity of flora and fauna. The forest canopy provides a home for a profusion of birds: cockatoos, hornbills, birds of paradise, and guria pigeons, among many others. Hunters find bandicoots, wallabies, cassowaries, and wild pigs in the bush and grasslands. Giant pythons, large monitor lizards, and dangerous saltwater crocodiles thrive in the low-lying swamps and rivers. Insects of all descriptions, even the rare Queen Alexandra butterfly—the largest in the world—thrive in the area. As in other parts of Papua New Guinea, the lands around Collingwood Bay have proven to be rich breeding grounds for the anopheles mosquito, the carrier of malaria. The dark sands around the villages provide a home for billions of sand flies, infinitesimal insects which, until the invention of Deet-based insect repellents, probably did more than anything to discourage anthropological research along these coasts.[6] Finally, the shallow waters and coral reefs of southern Collingwood Bay teem with a diversity of marine life.

When breezes fail to blow in from the bay, the combination of hot tropical temperatures and high humidity can be oppressive, even for Maisin. The annual rainfall ranges between 1800 and 3300 millimetres, increasing as one moves inland towards the mountains. The Maisin speak of distinct "rainy" and "dry" seasons. The rainy season generally runs between November and April, usually marked by short but heavy downpours most days, including dramatic tropical thunderstorms. The rains taper off in the dry season, with afternoons marked by strong winds from the north and east. Temperatures average 24.2C° annually, but may rise to higher than 32.2C° during the wet season. Nights in the dry season can actually feel quite cold. Local climatic patterns have been greatly disrupted since at least the early 1980s by global shifts, especially the El Niño phenomena. Along with the rest of Papua New Guinea, the Maisin have recently suffered through extended periods of drought followed by rainy seasons lasting several years. Their low-lying villages are very vulnerable to threat of global warming, which will not only raise sea levels but also increase the frequency and strength of tropic storms.

The Maisin have always lived close to the land, which furnishes them with food, medicines, and building materials. Yet, as we shall see repeatedly in these pages, the land is far more than a source for resources. It is, for most Maisin, alive with historical memories and ancestral spirits. It is the key to their identity and survival as a people. Maisin say that their ancestors conquered the land; they regard their own custodianship with pride. This sense of pride and identity has strengthened in recent years as a variety of entrepreneurs, including some Maisin living in the towns, have approached villagers with schemes to clear the rainforest and set up commercial plantations. Many Maisin have come to realize, for the first time, that the rainforest which looks so vast from a small boat on Collingwood Bay, could quickly be destroyed. With this awareness has come an understanding that hard choices will need to be made about the future relationship between the people and the environment that sustains them.

THE CULTURAL SETTING

Evidence of human settlement in New Guinea dates back 40,000 years, but there must have been much earlier movements as the ancestors of the Australian Aborigines journeyed through New Guinea from Asia at least 55,000 years ago (Moore 2003). During that long early period, descendants of the early migrants gradually spread to the furthest reaches of New Guinea's vast interior and offshore islands, diversifying into hundreds of distinct cultures and languages, referred to collectively by linguistics as Non-Austronesian or Papuan. As much as 9,000 years ago some groups had learned to cultivate taro as a supplement to foraging and hunting. The last group of Asian migrants were Austronesian-speakers, who settled along the coasts and islands of Papua New Guinea around 4,000 years ago. These formed the jumping off points for further waves of Austronesian migrants pushing eastward. Their descendents crossed vast expanses of open ocean to discover and colonize the far reaches of the southern Pacific, from Vanuatu to Rapa Nui (Easter Island) and from Aotearoa (New Zealand) to Hawai'i (Kirch 2000).

Collingwood Bay appears to have been a cultural and linguistic meeting place in the centuries before the arrival of Europeans (Egloff 1979). The 10,000 or so people who make the bay their home speak five languages, which linguists further break down into several dialects. Korafe and Onjob belong to the older Non-Austronesian group of languages, while Ubir and Miniafia are Austronesian. When Maisin was first studied, it was immediately seen as anomalous, possessing both Non-Austronesian and Austronesian grammatical features (Ray 1911; Strong 1911). The language awaits thorough study, but linguists now consider it to be basically Austronesian with borrowed non-Austronesian elements (Ross 1984) — interesting given that Maisin traditions suggest they originate from around the Musa River, a Papuan area. Prior to the enforcement of colonial control, the various sociolinguistic groups on the bay often fought with each other, resulting in a confusing linguistic situation. The partially Maisin village of Uwe, for instance, is located about 20 kilometres north of Uiaku, separated by Ubir and Miniafia villages. Oral traditions and early observations by visiting Europeans suggest that the various groups on the bay also participated in networks based on trade of valuable items, feasting, and marriage. As we will see in Chapter 2, some trade in locally produced items like clay cooking pots and tapa cloth goes on to this day. Although Maisin prefer to marry within their own language group, nearly everyone can claim relatives across Collingwood Bay and into the Musa because of past marriage alliances.

The 5 million people living in Papua New Guinea today speak at least 700 distinct languages. Confronted by this linguistic diversity, outsiders often wonder how people manage to communicate outside their own groups. In colonial times, government officers, traders, and missionaries encouraged the spread of several simplified trade languages, either based upon a native language, like Hiri Motu, or using mostly European vocabulary with a simplified Melanesian grammar, like Pidgin English, also known as Neo-Melanesian. Today, English, Motu, and Pidgin are the official languages of the country. Many Maisin speak all three, but most adults also speak or at least understand several of the other languages spoken in the Collingwood Bay area. For people like myself who come from largely monolinguistic communities, the multilinguistic abilities of people like the Maisin are at least as impressive as the diverse language situation itself.

The study of a language can reveal a great deal about the history of a people as well as their general cultural orientations. Bronislaw Malinowski (1922), a brilliant linguist and superb ethnographer who worked on the Trobriand Islands to the east of Collingwood Bay from 1914 to 1916, argued that fluency in a native tongue is a precondition of good fieldwork. It is, alas, one of the worse kept secrets that many anthropologists fail to measure up to Malinowski's high standards. In my own case, I diligently studied the Maisin language through my first season of fieldwork, driving my teachers to distraction as I attempted to shape my tongue to the Maisin sound system and stumbled over (to me) complicated verb formations. I developed a good working vocabulary and learned to "hear" spoken Maisin — as long as it wasn't spoken too quickly or by more than a couple of people at a time — but my attempts to speak it did little more than amuse my Maisin friends. This was and remains a limitation to my understanding, although I believe that my struggles with the language have also encouraged me to take a great deal of care in recording and translating with the help of Maisin research assistants. I also take some comfort in knowing that the Maisin's neighbours also consider the language difficult.[7] While many Maisin speak Ubir and Korafe, almost nobody from these language groups learns to speak Maisin. Fortunately for me, a number of Maisin had acquired a good command of English as high school students and from living for a time in the towns. Several worked as research assistants or helped me from time to time with translations. Over time, I carried out most of my research in a mixture of English and Maisin (which I privately think of as "Mais-lish"!).

A BRIEF HISTORY[8]

We will return frequently in this book to the dynamics of continuity and change. At the onset, however, it will be helpful to sketch out an historical chronology of the main changes and challenges the Maisin have faced since the first contact with European outsiders in 1890. We cannot know for certain what Maisin culture was like before this time. The histories related by elders suggest that the Maisin were fairly recent migrants to Collingwood Bay in the late nineteenth century who defeated the local population and were still expanding their territory before checked by the arrival of the colonial government.

In May 1874, when Captain John Moresby first sailed across the northern reaches of Collingwood Bay, he was so impressed by the dramatic scenery that he turned to the figure of the great English naval hero, Horatio Nelson, for suitably grand names for the main features: Cape Nelson, Mount Victory, and the name of the bay itself (Moresby 1876). Later that same year, the Reverend William Lawes of the London Missionary Society became the first European to settle permanently in what would become Papua New Guinea, building his home on the great southern bay Moresby had "discovered" and named after his father the previous year. In 1884, Britain and Germany divided the eastern half of New Guinea and offshore islands (the western half had long been claimed by Holland). Four years later, Dr. William MacGregor took up the post of Administrator of the British possession with the mandate of exploring its reaches, establishing the rudiments of government control, and bringing some semblance of British civilization to the Queen's newest subjects. This was all to be accomplished on the most minimal of budgets. MacGregor was a resourceful innovator who set up the basic structure of the colonial state in what became Papua, after the newly independent Australian government assumed control in 1906 (Joyce 1968).[9] The government took upon itself the task of exploration and pacification of local tribes which, often as not, appeared to be caught up in endemic warfare and raiding. This was accomplished by means of establishing a network of district stations under Resident Magistrates who, with the aid of a native police force, set out on regular patrols first to contact tribes and then to control fighting, enforce ordinances meant to improve village life (at least, as the Europeans perceived it), and eventually integrate villagers into the emerging colonial economy. MacGregor encouraged white entrepreneurs to establish plantations and mines in the colony, creating a system of labour recruitment from villages to provide them with an inexpensive work force. Finally, the Administrator strongly supported the work of Christian missionaries, not only because he was himself staunchly Presbyterian but because missions were able to reach the native peoples in their villages in their own languages and provide, at no cost to the government, basic schooling and medical services.

In late July 1890, on one of his first patrols along the northeastern coast of the Possession, MacGregor steamed into Collingwood Bay on the small government launch, the *Merrie England*. The day before at Cape Vogel he had come across a small island whose steep cliffs could only be scaled with ropes lowered from the top—a refuge from the fierce "Maisina" who, he was told, frequently raided and terrorized their villages. The Maisin themselves were wary of the strange newcomers; no women or children were to be seen, and the men who did venture forth to meet them ran away terrified when one of the landing party lit a match. The men were reluctant to accept gifts of tobacco or iron, obviously unaware of their use. Still, the short visit was friendly. The *Merrie England* returned several times over the next ten years, always to a boisterous reception from the Maisin, who soon developed a hunger for steel axes, knives, cloth, and other trade goods. They continued to raid their neighbours, but it was only a matter of time before their autonomy was brought to an end. In 1900, the government built a district station 40 kilometres to the north at Tufi on Cape Nelson under the control of

C.A.W. Monckton, a brash, often violent New Zealander (Monckton 1922). After receiving news about a number of Maisin raids, including a planned ambush of one his own patrols, Monckton set his police loose on Uiaku where they destroyed several canoes and shot dead three men, wounding an unknown number of others. Following the fracas, a large party of Maisin men travelled to Tufi where they were jailed for a short period. Monckton appointed two of the leading warriors as village constables and, over the next few years, recruited more into his fledgling police force. The Maisin were now "pacified."

MacGregor had been accompanied in 1890 by a young Anglican priest, Albert Maclaren, who was scouting out possible headquarters for a new mission for the northern part of the possession (Synge 1908; Wetherell 1977). He chose Dogura, a high plateau over Bartle Bay, about 80 kilometres to the east of the Maisin. The mission got off to a rocky start. Maclaren died four months after arriving in Dogura, worn out by malaria, a poor diet, and the physical exhaustion of building a station in the hot climate. His partner, the Reverend Copland King, kept the mission going with a tiny staff and meagre support from the Australian parishes. In 1898, on the verge of collapse, the mission received a boost with the appointment of a British clergyman, John Montague Stone-Wigg, as its first bishop. Although frail in health, Stone-Wigg was an effective fundraiser and administrator. Expansion into Collingwood Bay became his first priority. His initial choice for a head station at the Maisin village of Sinapa had to be rejected because it was too swampy. Wanigela, located just north of the Maisin village of Yuayu, instead became the residence of the district missionary in 1898 and, in later years, a district school for advanced students and a small hospital.

In 1902, Percy John Money — an Australian lay missionary then in charge of the Wanigela district — travelled down to Uiaku to supervise the building of an enormous mission station using only native materials, including a school that could accommodate upwards of 210 pupils and a church that could seat 550 (close to the entire population of the village at the time), with a dormitory for boys, a house for teachers, and a lovely two-storey residence for himself (Barker 2005). The Anglicans always intended to place a white missionary in charge of the Maisin, both because of their relatively large population and their perception of them as a "recalcitrant" people who required the "strong hand" of a European. Eventually, a recruit was found, but A.P. Jennings proved too sensitive a soul to abide the dirt, pigs, and incessant drumming for traditional dances that filled the night air. He suffered a nervous breakdown and fled Uiaku in 1920, less than three years after his arrival. Villagers thus learned about Christianity as well as the "three R's" at the feet of Melanesian teacher-evangelists who looked very

29

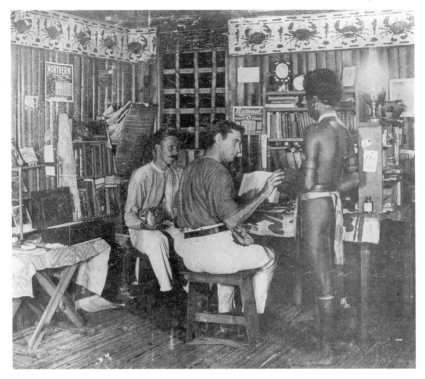

Figure 1.4 Percy John Money in the "den," Uiaku, c. 1905. The names of the two men on either side are not known. Note the tapa cloth covering the tables. (Courtesy of the State Library of New South Wales)

much like themselves.[10] The first generation of teachers was mostly made up of men from the Solomon Islands and New Hebrides (now Vanuatu) recruited by the Anglican mission from the Queensland sugar fields. Recent converts themselves and barely literate, almost all died while labouring in the mission fields of Papua. Their ranks were joined in short order by better-educated Papuan converts, trained by the white missionaries at Dogura. Under the direction of the teachers, with periodic visits from the white missionary at Wanigela, a group of young men and women received baptism in 1911. By the late 1920s, a Christian majority had emerged in Uiaku, made up mostly of the younger people who had attended village schools.

Throughout the colonial period, Collingwood Bay remained an economic backwater, the handful of whites in the area limited to government officers and missionaries with the occasional trader. All the same, the Maisin were steadily integrated into the emerging colonial system. Regular labour recruit-ing began around 1910. By the end of the decade, it had become routine for young unmarried men to spend one or two 18-month stints working on copra[11] or rubber plantations or on the gold fields elsewhere in the territory, and people had come to rely upon the basic commodities purchased and brought back to the villages. The government became more intrusive over time, enforcing a series of decrees meant to improve village health by man-dating the construction of latrines, the creation of cemeteries located away from dwellings, and the rebuilding of houses in parallel lines and in a new form, closer to the ground than the traditional sleeping shelters, and with windows. In 1918, the government imposed a head tax and ordered villagers to set up separate coconut plantations from which they could manufacture copra for sale. The Maisin resented and resisted these changes at first, but by the 1930s they had accommodated to the new regime. Soccer tournaments had become the rage, and Maisin villages regularly won small prizes from the Resident Magistrate in the annual contest for the most attractive village in the Tufi region.

World War II was a watershed moment here as elsewhere in the Pacific. On 22 July 1942, Japanese troops landed in large numbers near the village of Gona to the northwest of Collingwood Bay and began a difficult march along the treacherous Kokoda Track across the central mountains of Papua. They were forced into retreat within sixty kilometres of Port Moresby due to exhaustion, malarial attacks, and stubborn resistance from Australian troops. The subsequent battle around Gona and Buna villages was among the most brutal of the war for both sides (Mayo 1974). Within a month of the invasion, boats arrived in Collingwood Bay, scooping up every available able-bodied man who could be found to serve as a labourer in the war effort. The Maisin were assigned to a large force of Papuans slogging heavy loads of supplies up the northern end of the Kokoda Track and carrying the broken bodies of Australian soldiers on the return trips, as the allied forces of the United States and Australia slowly beat back the Japanese advance. The fighting along the track was followed by a horrific battle against entrenched Japanese forces along the coast which left hundreds of soldiers on both sides dead. Amazingly, only one Maisin labourer was killed during the campaign, shot by a Japanese soldier while investigating what he supposed to be an abandoned tunnel. As bodies piled up and rotted in the coastal swamps, the Maisin carriers saw many horrors.

Forty years later, the old carriers still broke down in tears as they told me of their experiences. The war revealed other more positive truths to the Maisin and other Papua New Guineans. They were surprised by the friendli-ness of the Australian soldiers, their willingness to share food and cigarettes and their frank criticisms of the Papuan colonial regime. Maisin who went to work with American troops at the conclusion of the Buna campaign in 1943 were even more impressed, not only by the comradeship but also by the presence of African-American troops. The war, older Maisin often told me, "changed everything." They had met white soldiers who treated them as equals, and they heard speeches from their own white commanders promising a new era of economic development once the fighting was over.

Following the defeat of Japan in 1945, however, the Australian government proved slow in meeting its promises and, in the eyes of many Papua New Guineans, appeared more interested in restoring the old and now unacceptable colonial system. Local people were not content to wait. So-called "cargo cults" broke out in several areas, particularly parts of the former German colony of New Guinea which had been administered by Australia since 1914.[12] In 1946, a Biniguni man came down from the mountains to Collingwood Bay bearing the message that, with the right rituals, the ancestors would return with abundant European goods and wealth. However, here, as in many long-contacted coastal areas of Papua and New Guinea, the message had limited appeal. The Maisin were more interested in news of an economic experiment carried out at Gona village, the site of some of the worst fighting a few years earlier (Dakeyne 1966). The Reverend James Benson, an Anglican priest who had survived three horrific years of internment in a Japanese prisoner camp on New Britain, had founded a Christian cooperative society in Gona. Benson was influenced by the Christian socialist movement in Australia and hoped that a combination of new types of crops, prayers, and commitment to sharing work and its profits would improve the lives of villagers. The Gona people also saw the possibilities offered by the cooperative model for making money. Soon Christian cooperatives were springing up all over the Northern District.

The Maisin experimented with a series of cooperatives from around 1946 to the mid-1980s (Barker 1996). The cooperatives sought out local commodities that could be sold to traders — such as sea cucumbers, trochus shell, panned gold, copra, coffee, and cocoa — and opened small trade stores offering a selection of commercial goods to locals. Few of these ventures made money, and, when they did, it was soon spent. They faced several obstacles including the distance to markets, the people's unfamiliarity with keeping financial records, and local politics. All the same, the cooperatives profoundly affected the way that the Maisin thought about and organized their community. At the founding meeting for a Christian cooperative held in September 1949, representatives of different Maisin clans publicly broke war clubs, symbolizing an end to internal divisions. Like the church upon which it was modelled, the cooperative sought to unify the entire community. The

Maisin signified the close tie they saw between Christianity, social unity, and economic success with their single most important cooperative project. With the aid of the district priest at Wanigela, who provided them with a bank account and kept financial records, villagers in Uiaku began raising funds through the sale of copra in the mid to late 1950s with the intention of building a permanent church. In 1962, they erected an attractive church with twin towers and an iron roof on the Uiaku mission station. The Anglican Mission responded to this community initiative by providing the Maisin with a Papuan priest, the first priest to reside among them since Father Jennings's unhappy departure in 1920.

Twenty years later when Anne and I arrived to carry out our fieldwork, the Maisin looked back on this event as a golden moment, a crowning achievement against which the apparent failings of the present—the cooperative social store teetering on the edge of collapse, incessant gossip, fears of sorcery, the difficulties of getting people to work together on community projects, and so forth—stood out in sharp contrast (Barker 1993). Other changes occurring through the same period had even more profound implications for the society. Significantly, here again the Mission played a major role. Maisin had attended mission schools since 1902. Most had two or three years at the village school, where they learned the rudiments of "A-B-C" and "1-2-3," as they described the favoured methods of rote learning used by the Melanesian teachers. Only a small number of male students had been able to further their education under white priests at the district station in Wanigela and the small theological college at Dogura, as they trained to become teachers themselves. Following the war, the Anglicans worked to improve the village school system and to expand options for advanced learning. In 1948, they opened the Martyrs Memorial School for boys at Sangara in the central part of the Northern District, named in honour of 11 Anglican missionaries and native teachers assassinated by invading Japanese troops in 1942. Three years later, a massive volcano, Mount Lamington, exploded, destroying the villages on its slopes, including Sangara, and killing more than 3,000 people. Fortunately, students were home on holidays at the time of the disaster, but neither the staff nor the school was spared. The Anglicans rebuilt an expanded school at Agenehambo, a safe distance from the volcano, opening its doors in 1953. Maisin boys began to enroll regularly soon after. In 1956, Holy Name School for girls opened at Dogura, allowing Maisin girls the opportunity for advanced education. Meanwhile, the Mission improved local schools, gradually adding fourth, fifth, and sixth years. Those students successful in completing final exams in the village school could attend the high schools.

The missionaries intended that graduates of the new high schools would go on to staff the expanding mission system of churches, schools, medical centres, and plantations. Many did, but shifts in administration policy also opened other opportunities. During the 1950s, the Administration had intervened in the mission education system to set basic standards, especially the promotion of English, and had tentatively begun to establish its own secular school system. In the early 1960s, stung by a United Nations report criticizing Australia's tardiness at preparing its colonies for eventual independence, the government suddenly stepped up its involvement, investing heavily in education, the civil service, and the economy. New secondary and tertiary schools were opened across the country, including the crown jewel of the system, the University of Papua New Guinea, in 1966. The government's Department of Education now set the standards for the training of teachers and the curriculum in the community schools and assumed responsibility for salaries. The frenetic efforts of the Australians to prepare Papua New Guinea for independence created a boom in relatively well-paying jobs for better educated Papua New Guineans, especially in the burgeoning civil service. Maisin were in an excellent position to take advantage. For a period of about 15 years, from the early 1960s to the late 1970s, most younger Maisin left the villages for high school and higher education, and many landed positions scattered around the country as priests, teachers, nurses, doctors, civil servants, and other professionals.

In 1973, the Mission became the Anglican Church of Papua New Guinea. By 1982, all but one of its parish priests were Papua New Guineans as were two of the five bishops. The country itself became independent in 1975, a scant 13 years after the United Nations report. Most of a generation of Maisin had left the villages to work elsewhere. I was amazed to discover, after completing my census of Uiaku, that people in their 60s greatly outnumbered the combined totals of people in their 20s and 30s. Indeed, the 270 people living in Uiaku proper included only one man in his 30s. This exodus had profound effects upon village life. The drain of younger folk meant that villagers found it difficult to maintain large gardens and to mount traditional life-cycle ceremonies. At the same time, people had become increasingly dependent upon remittances from working relatives. Much of the incoming cash and goods was quickly redistributed through village kin and exchange networks (as well as by means of the hugely popular card game, "Lucky"). Yet even at this early stage, some households were obviously benefiting more than others.

The Maisin's integration into the wider Papua New Guinea society and economy has steadily increased in the years since Independence. While villagers spend much of their days engaged in subsistence activities, particularly gardening, most now supplement local food with store goods, particularly rice and tinned fish, and purchase an ever-increasing range of manufactured goods for daily life, not only clothing but tools, pots and pans, radios, dinghies, and so forth. Villagers also require money to cover transportation costs to visit relatives in town, to pay the priest's stipend and school fees, and for medicines for their families. Finding and keeping sources of money has always been challenging. In the years since Independence, the Maisin have lost much of their educational and employment advantages as ever more high school graduates compete for scarce jobs in the towns. Village populations have swollen as unemployed young people have returned home. During the same time, government services to Collingwood Bay and other rural areas have virtually disappeared. By the late 1990s, the local postal service had almost ceased to operate, the local teachers often went for months without receiving pay, and the local medical aid posts had closed down for lack of supplies. The Maisin now find themselves urgently searching for new ways to support themselves and their children.

The Maisin, no less than the rest of us, live in an increasingly interconnected world. This carries a cost, most noticeably an alarming loss of traditional knowledge. Far fewer Maisin today know and can narrate the histories and stories I recorded in the early 1980s; they have ceased to tattoo the faces of adolescent girls; and no one knows how to construct one of the old chief feast houses. Even the language is not the same as it was, as younger people mix Pidgin and English with Maisin words and more subtly modify the cadences of their speech. Change, of course, has always occurred, but it seems to be accelerating. All the same, were you to visit the Maisin villages in the early years of this new millennium, I suspect you would be struck by the "traditional" appearance of the houses and the rhythms of daily life. The Maisin have little choice but to maintain a traditional lifestyle based upon subsistence activities. They cannot shop for food at the local supermarket or hire carpenters to construct their homes. Yet they are also products of a culture that leads them to perceive the world and organize their social life in particular patterns. Those patterns are apparent even in the mundane activities of making a living. They are among the lines that continue to connect the Maisin to their past in a rapidly changing world.

Notes

1. Betelnut is a mild intoxicant, widely used across South Asia and the western Pacific. When chewed with the leaves of the betel pepper plant (*Piper betle*) and lime, the husked nut of the areca palm releases alkaloids and produces a very bright red saliva that is eventually spat out. It has a very bitter flavour that takes some getting used to, but it is chewed almost incessantly by Maisin, young and old.

2. In the national census of 2000, over 96 per cent of adults in Papua New Guinea declared themselves members of one or another of the more than 200 Christian denominations established in the country (Gibbs 2006). Papua New Guinea now ranks as one of the most thoroughly Christianized nations in the world, matched only by a few Latin American countries like Ecuador.

3. The surprising appearance of white-skinned men bearing immense wealth and powerful weapons caused much speculation among Melanesians everywhere of their origins. Many in the early stages of contact associated white people with ancestral spirits, returned from the dead (Schieffelin and Crittenden 1991). Maisin today refer to Europeans as *bariyawa*, a loan word from further up the coast that means "spirits" in its original language, but have long understood they are as human as themselves.

4. Tobacco was unknown prior to European contact, but like most Melanesians, the Maisin were quick to pick up the habit. During the colonial period, tarry sticks of cured tobacco leaf were used as a kind of currency. In the early 1980s, "black stick" was still the most common form of tobacco used by the Maisin. A smoker would take a knife and shave bits of the tobacco onto a strip of newspaper, producing a thin and foul-smelling type of cigar. Sometime in the late 1980s, black stick disappeared from the market to be replaced by fast-burning cigarettes marketed by global tobacco corporations, a type of tobacco delivery that is far more damaging to health than the older form. Like much of the developing world, Papua New Guinea faces a heavy health burden due to the ready availability and heavy promotion of smoking. These trends were becoming apparent by the early 1980s, and I have not distributed tobacco in subsequent visits although, unfortunately, smoking remains enormously popular.

5. The documentary, *Changing Ground*, aired on the Canadian Broadcasting Corporation (CBC) television network in Canada in early 2001 on *The Nature of Things* science program. In July 2001, seven Maisin paid a return visit to the Stó:lō Nation in British Columbia. This was also the subject of a documentary, *Years from Now*, televised on the CBC in 2002. The Maisin were also one of the subjects of an earlier film, *Anthropology on Trial*, which includes a ten-minute segment focussed on my fieldwork in Uiaku. It appeared in the *NOVA* science series on the PBS network in the United States in 1983. The films are visually arresting and very supportive of the Maisin but unfortunately are not very informative about their culture or history. For a detailed critique, see Barker (2004a).

6. So suggested the pioneer ethnographer, F.E. Williams, who preferred to brave the mosquito-infested interior villages of the Orokaiva than cope with sandflies "whose irritating bite is out of all proportion to their size" (Williams 1930).

7. The difficulties have partly to do with Maisin's complex grammatical features, mentioned above. The language also has an unusually large vocabulary of synonyms, or different words with identical meanings. This has to do with a taboo, discussed in Chapter 3, against mentioning the name — or even a word sounding like the name — of an in-law. As a result, the Maisin have generated two and often three words for many

things, including ordinary items like coconuts (Lynch 1988). Malcolm Ross (personal communication) also suggests that in pre-contact times Maisin warriors may have deliberately created grammatical and vocabulary complexity as a means of obscuring what they were saying from enemies. It appears to have worked!

8. This section summarizes a number of much more detailed studies of Maisin history (Barker 1987, 1996, 2001, 2005). For a good general history of Papua New Guinea through the colonial and early Independence periods, see Waiko 1993.

9. In 1914, Australia seized the German territory, which it ruled separately from Papua during the interwar years. Following World War II, the two administrations were merged into the colony of Papua and New Guinea.

10. Most missionary work in the Pacific region was carried out by islanders under the often loose supervision of a small number of Europeans (Munroe and Thornley 1996). One of my reasons for choosing Uiaku over Wanigela was because I wanted to study a community that had been evangelized mainly by islander converts (Barker 2005).

11. Copra is made from the dried inner flesh of coconuts. The oil is later extracted for use in commercial soap, cosmetics, and in food products. It has been one of the major exports from the South Pacific islands since the mid-nineteenth century.

12. Cargo cults are the most studied and debated of the many forms of religious and political movements arising across Melanesia in the wake of colonial penetration and control (Burridge 1969; Worsley 1968). While there are many variations, the classic form of cargoism rests on a belief that Europeans gained their immense wealth and power due to events that occurred in ancestral times. The rituals engaged in by cultists are meant to undo this condition and result in the return of ancestors bearing copious quantities of manufactured goods and thus restoring dignity to Melanesians. Cargoist doctrines proved to be far more appealing in some parts of the region than others. Generally, the more integrated a people into the colonial economic system, the less likely they were to engage in cargoism. The appeal of cargo teachings, however, may also depend on pre-existing cultural themes and structures.

CHAPTER TWO

Making a Living

In October 1986 I came to Uiaku to spend two months studying tapa cloth and women's facial tattooing. I immediately sought out Mildred Gayave. Mildred had been a great friend of Anne and mine; she was flamboyant, with a wickedly funny sense of humour. Like most adult Maisin, she had no idea of her birth date, but I estimated her to be in her early to mid-40s as her first child was then a young adult. Mildred was a superb tapa maker who had developed a unique style, producing large thick cloths decorated with detailed geometric designs that rather reminded me of Persian carpets. Her cloths sold very well, often fetching higher prices than those of her neighbours. While the designs were wonderful, I was more curious to know how she managed to consistently produce outstanding fabric — thick and near white, with very few holes or blemishes. I thought that I could best learn how to turn raw tree bark into fine cloth by accompanying Mildred to her tapa garden.

At present, to make tapa the Maisin use only one kind of bark from a semi-cultivated, fast-growing tree they call *wuwusi*, which is likely a type of paper mulberry (*Broussonetia papyrifera*), the most common source of bark cloth in the Pacific Islands. Tapa was traditionally made in most of what is today Oro Province. The Maisin, however, declare that *wuwusi* is unique to southern Collingwood Bay and far superior to the types of trees used elsewhere in the province. Indeed, villagers worry from time to time that outsiders might steal cuttings from the local trees, threatening the virtual monopoly they enjoy in sales of tapa in Papua New Guinea. In respect of these concerns, I will use only Maisin vernacular terms for the various plants that provide the bark and dyes used in making tapa.

Mildred and I were accompanied by her adopted son, Clarence, a cheerful 10 year old. I always enjoy visiting the gardens. After leaving the village, you plunge through dank swamplands of mangrove and pandanus trees, emerging into a wide band of secondary bush and garden land. Networks of paths crisscross stretches of jungle and grassland. During the rainy season, the paths become stream beds, and you often have to struggle through ankle-deep mud. The dry season lingered in October, however, and the path was as hard as concrete under a perfectly blue sky. Mildred walked ahead, holding a machete, the strap of a large empty string bag slung over her shoulder, the bag flopping across her back. We crossed a low fence, meant to keep marauding wild pigs out of the gardens, which presented the usual frenzy of life: verdant broad taro leaves, tall banana trees, purple-edged sweet potato creepers, bright flowers, butterflies, and bright white cockatoos calling raucously from the trees at the edge of the clearing.

Much of the land around the Maisin villages is low-lying and swampy, ideal conditions for taro—the main staple crop—but not for *wuwusi*, which requires a fairly dry, sandy loam. All village women make tapa, but those who do not have access to the right kind of land must trade with more fortunate neighbours for *wuwusi*. Mildred had a thick clump of saplings growing at the edge of her garden. The plantation was nearly two years old. The tallest trees had been transplanted from one of Mildred's older gardens—a simple matter of pulling a sapling out of ground with roots attached, lopping off the top with a machete, carrying it to the new garden, and plunking it back into the ground. *Wuwusi* grows very quickly when the soil is right. The tree propagates itself by sending up shoots from the root system. A month after she planted them, a circle of new shoots would have appeared around Mildred's transplanted saplings. She would have kept the area around the new growth clear of weeds for the first month or two. After that, cultivation is a matter of periodically checking the growing trees and snapping off twigs up to around three metres, to prevent the growth of branches, which leave holes in the finished cloth. As the patches of trees spread out, they form thickets of willowy silver-coloured saplings. A thickness of 50 to 100 millimetres is perfect for tapa. Most of the trees attain the proper girth within a couple of years. Older and thicker trees yield a tougher bark that is hard to beat and yields an uneven, dark cloth.

The ideal conditions for harvesting *wuwusi* begin right around the time that productivity declines in the garden, leading to its gradual abandonment. People periodically return to the older gardens for a year or so after they stop planting new crops to harvest longer lasting fruit trees and sweet potato patches and to get cuttings for transplanting to new sites. They continue to cut *wuwusi* during these visits, but gradually the old garden becomes covered by creepers and emerging trees, returning to jungle. It frequently happens that when people return to clear an old garden site a decade or two later, *wuwusi* springs up in the new clearing.

The individual saplings looked pretty much the same to my untrained eyes. Mildred, however, touched one after another, identifying some as *koefi*

Figure 2.1 Mildred holding a *wuwusi* sapling in her garden surrounded by taro and banana plants. (Photo by J. Barker)

—the term for a male's loin cloth—and others as *embobi*, a woman's skirt. The *koefi* trees were slightly narrower in diameter, but I was not able to find out whether it was because of this or some difference in the appearance of the outer bark that Mildred knew these trees would produce the thinner, smooth cloth men wrap around their legs.

As opposed to identifying a good tapa tree, which requires a practiced eye, harvesting is an easy business of lopping off the base and the leafy top of a sapling with a machete, leaving a nicely rounded thick stick, two to three metres in length. Once harvested, the *wuwusi* sticks may be bundled and carried back to the village. If kept in a cool, dark place—usually under a house —they can be left for up to a month before becoming too dried out for making cloth. If a woman plans to make cloth immediately, however, she saves herself the bother of carrying the sticks and strips out the bark on the spot. Mildred demonstrated the process: she cut a strip of bark from an older, tougher *wuwusi* tree and then lashed discarded sticks together into a firm frame to serve as a brace against which she rested a fine straight *wuwusi* sapling. She efficiently scraped off the outer bark with a knife and then made a slit down the length of the stick and carefully pried off the thick, milky-white inner bark. She folded the bark strip over upon itself, with the scraped outer surface exposed, to protect the glistening sticky inner surface from dirt, securing the bundle with another strip of *wuwusi* bark. A half hour later we were on our way back to the village, Mildred's string bag bulging with several bundles of *wuwusi*, vegetables for the evening meal, and a load of firewood.

The bast (inner bark) quickly dries and so needs to be beaten into cloth within a couple of days. Beating is hard, time-consuming work. It is perhaps revealing that while a few men have taken up painting tapa designs in recent years, the hard labour of beating the bast is still left entirely to women. As in most Pacific Island cultures, there is a gendered division of labour that corresponds to the materials used in the production of objects (Teilhet 1983). Women work mostly with pliable "soft" materials to make cloth, mats, and string bags. Men work with wood and shells to make dancing ornaments, drums, canoes, and houses. They are also responsible for making the primary tools for beating tapa. The anvil (*fo*) forms a standard piece of furnishing found on most verandahs, under the taller houses, and in garden shelters. It is a large hardwood log, squared and smoothed by hand, to form a suitable surface for beating out cloth. Traditionally, the men are also responsible for providing two types of mallets, made from the dense, strong, dark wood of the black palm. The smaller, called a *fisiga*, is narrow with two sharpened edges. The larger—like the anvil, it is called a *fo*—resembles a small cricket bat as it is thick with broad, slightly rounded edges. Most mallets are left plain, but a few men of artistic bent carve patterns on the flat sides, which

Figure 2.2 Josephine Arauveve beating tapa cloth with a *fo* mallet. (Photo by A.M. Tietjen)

they bring into relief with white lime powder. Mallets and especially the anvil last a very long time, but there have been some innovations in recent decades. A number of women were the happy recipients a few years back of heavy iron bars with rubber handles manufactured by a male relative working at a foundry in the provincial capital. They found this a very effective replacement for the *fisiga*, especially for beating thicker pieces of bast.

Mildred belonged to the old school and used only wood mallets. Whether using wood or metal, however, the process of beating is the same. One begins by trimming away any dry edges and ends of the bast and then cutting the strip into two or more smaller pieces, depending on the size of tapa desired. Using the sharp edge of the *fisiga* mallet, the maker then systematically pounds the length of the strip on both sides, a process that loosens the fibres and slightly expands the cloth. This takes a lot of energetic beating and much care to make sure that the bast is evenly pounded. Once she is satisfied that the bast has been sufficiently softened, the maker folds the pounded bark tightly several times over itself, lifts up the heavy *fo* mallet with both hands, and wallops the bast with the rounded edge, gradually progressing up its length. Each time she completes a length, she unfolds and refolds the bast to make sure all of the surfaces are evenly beaten. The pounded bark spreads very quickly. Towards the end of the process, the maker will hold up and inspect the cloth. Once satisfied, she folds the cloth one last time and gives it a satisfying slap with the flat side of her mallet.

The bast widens and shortens slightly in the course of beating. The degree of spread varies, depending on the age and thickness of the bast and the desired thickness of the final cloth. Roughly speaking, cloth for male perineal bands double in width, while the thicker bast used for *embobi* skirts may widen by a factor of four or five. At a rough estimate, a skilled woman can produce a large *embobi* from a 260cm to 30cm strip of bark measuring around 260 by 30cm in about two hours, if she is not interrupted. Because the bark comes from younger trees, *koefi* are easier to beat, and the job of creating a male loin cloth usually takes less than an hour.

Freshly beaten tapa is hung up to dry immediately inside or under the house where it will not be exposed to direct sunlight. Sometimes makers miss a bit of outer bark when first scraping the tree, which shows up as a stain on the finished cloth. Stained cloths are gently rinsed in the river and then re-beaten with the *fo*. The cloths are checked carefully and removed from the clotheslines while still a little damp, folded and placed under sleeping mats (made from pandanus strips), and slept upon for a night, which smoothes any surface wrinkles. The larger *embobi* are folded over twice, creating four flat panels between the creases, while the male *koefi* are folded three times, creating eight panels. After the first night, the cloths are hung in direct sunlight and allowed to dry thoroughly to prevent mold from forming. Once dry, they are stored under sleeping mats until it is time to apply designs.

Naturally, I was eager to try my hand at beating bark into cloth. I turned again to experts for help—Lottie Ororogo and Martha Maiyova, who gave me a small strip of bast to practise on. Several things became clear as I pounded away. I discovered that my body was not built for this kind of work. The muscle power required for hefting the heavy mallets was one thing, but what nearly did me in was the sharp impact of the mallet hitting the anvil. After a half hour my arm felt like it would soon separate from my shoulder socket, and my whacks became steadily more feeble and uneven. It was a minor compensation to know that my antics provided harmless entertainment for a rapidly growing crowd of giggling women and children. When Lottie and Martha declared the cloth satisfactory, after about an hour of pounding, I was pleased to see that while by no means a masterful bit of work, it was big and smooth enough for me to apply a design, a far less physically demanding job that I would attempt in a few days. With a quiet sense of accomplishment, I hung my little tapa sheet up to dry under a house and folded it under my mattress for the night.

The experience of beating a tapa, like so many I have had living with the Maisin, helped me to appreciate the degree to which their lives centre around basic physical pursuits—subsistence activities like gardening, fishing, and manufacturing material necessities like canoes, mats, and houses—and the skill and grace with which they undertake such labours. Manufacturing cloth from *wuwusi* bark is one activity of many by which people survive and thrive in their environment and by which they make a living. Such activities are usually glossed as "economic" and seen as providing the foundation for social organization and cultural worldviews. Yet, as we shall see in this chapter, they involve much more than simple survival. The Maisin "make their living" in the fullest sense of the phrase.

SUBSISTENCE ACTIVITIES

The Maisin live in a rich and varied environment. Although they are becoming increasingly dependent upon store-bought goods, they continue to rely primarily upon the resources around them for their basic needs. Steel axes, nylon fishnets, and shotguns have replaced some of the tools used by their ancestors. Still, were an ancestor to return, he or she would find the basic techniques the Maisin use to produce food, to make canoes, or to put up a house to be quite familiar. The same is largely true elsewhere in Papua New Guinea, where at least 70 per cent of the population continue to make a subsistence living off the land and sea.

The Maisin spend most of their waking hours involved in the food quest, working as hunters, fishermen, gatherers, and gardeners. As in other small-scale cultures, they organize work along gender lines. In general, men take on tasks that require relatively brief bursts of energetic activity, such as pig hunting and clearing bush. Women take on more repetitive jobs that require sustained effort, such as carrying produce, weeding gardens, and gathering shellfish. If asked, the Maisin justify this division of labour on the basis of the relative strength of men and women. Still, cultural expectations are clearly at work. Fishing, for instance, calls for less strength than chopping and hauling wood, yet only men may fish and only women chop and carry firewood. Indeed, in some other Melanesian communities, women hold a monopoly on fishing.

Anne and I received a personal lesson on the gendered division of labour soon after we began living in Uiaku. Finding clean water for washing required a daily trip up the muddy river beyond the last village houses and into a side creek, where we filled four buckets with clear water and returned. One day, we had just filled our buckets and begun the trek along the edge of the mission station, each of us lugging two heavy buckets. Normally people were away in the gardens at this time of day, but on this occasion a group of women had remained behind and were chatting some distance ahead of us. They saw us and shrieked. One of them rushed up to relieve me of my buckets, putting one on her head and giving another to a companion. Poor Anne, meanwhile, was left with her burden and a lesson, at least from the Maisin point of view, in the proper duties of a wife. In recent years, some younger people have eased up on the restrictions—you occasionally see a husband helping a wife carry food, for instance—but generally the Maisin continue to follow the old ways. I have often been told that a man lacking a sister or a wife to do the essential garden work would face starvation (although I very much doubt the community would allow it).

Only men hunt. The Maisin greatly relish meat and require it for feasts. A few households keep domesticated pigs, which are always reserved for a major event such as a bride-price payment, but most meat comes from game killed by hunters in the bush and forest. A few villagers own shotguns. In the early 1980s, the Maisin could buy shells in local trade stores, but since then the national government has placed severe restrictions on guns and ammunition in an attempt to counter rising gang violence in the towns. When shells were easy to get, the Maisin used shotguns to shoot birds and bush pigs; now they tend to reserve the guns to kill crocodiles when they get too close to the villages.[1] Maisin hunt mainly for bush pigs, using steel-tipped black palm spears and often accompanied by packs of dogs. Tracking and spearing a pig requires great skill, patience, and bravery, as a cornered pig is extremely dangerous. The best hunters work alone at night, often crouching silently for hours in the swampy areas favoured by pigs, enduring swarms of mosquitoes before making their kill. If he is successful, the hunter guts the pig on the spot, binds its legs, and hoists the heavy carcass across his back to carry it "piggy-back" to the village, usually several kilometres away. The Maisin are opportunistic hunters and will spear wallabies, cassowaries, and other game that cross their paths. In the past, they used a variety of bird and pig traps as well as spears, but knowledge of these has largely been lost.

Fish and shellfish provide important supplements to the diet. While the number of dinghies with outboard motors has been steadily increasing, most people still rely upon outrigger canoes for coastal travel and for fishing. Making a canoe requires great skill. One must find a good "canoe" tree in the forest, chop it down, and then roughly hollow it with an axe or adze, just enough to drag it down to the coast without too much risk of splitting. Once in the village, the hull is shaded from the hot sun. An expert canoe-maker finishes hollowing out the hull with an adze, carefully chipping away at the sides and bottom, to make the craft as light as possible without punching a hole. Once the hull is completed, the canoe-maker lashes together the outrigger superstructure and, in the case of larger canoes, a platform. The task of building canoes, like constructing houses, falls entirely to men. Maisin canoes tend to be rather small, capable of carrying three to five persons. A few men possess the skill to make larger canoes capable of extended trips on the ocean, but the Maisin acquire most of their sea-going canoes from Miniafia villagers on Cape Nelson, who trade them for cash and tapa cloth. Men fish from canoes using spears and nets. They also spear and net fish found in shallows close to shore. While it is generally understood that villages own the fishing areas off their shores, individuals fish wherever they please.

Women do most of the gathering of wild foodstuffs as well as firewood and water. They gather crabs and shellfish from mangrove swamps and reefs near the shore. When they are in season, they also bring home delectable and protein rich okari nuts (*T. kaernbachii*) from the forest. Both men and women gather building materials for houses as well as medicinal plants and tapa dyes. Men and women also work cooperatively in harvesting and preparing sago. Sago is made from the inner pith of a type of semi-cultivated palm tree growing in swamps behind the village. A man—or several men, as a group will often work together on a large tree—cuts down the palm and then cuts off the harder outer bark, revealing the white pith inside. Sitting with their legs resting against the trunk, the men rhythmically pound the pith with adzes, often accompanying this work with boisterous songs. Meanwhile, the women take a length of the bark and set it up near a stream in a framework to produce a kind of funnel with a mesh filter at the lower end. They scoop the pulverized pith, soak it with water, and then squeeze the mash against the filter. The soapy residue is caught in a plastic-lined pool. This is repeated until the pith is used up and the sediment settles to the bottom of

47

the plastic. When the water is drained off, one is left with a pure white starch. The Maisin consider sago a "famine food," to be eaten mostly when regular garden produce is running low. It is, to say the least, an acquired taste. The Maisin prepare sago either by mixing it with water to produce an orange glue-like porridge or by baking it into large white chunks with an interior texture that reminded me of plaster of Paris. Absolutely flavourless, sago is one of only a few foods produced by the Maisin that I have never gotten used to; I dreaded the sight of a visitor coming to the door with a tell-tale leaf-shrouded packet. Sago has the advantage of growing in swampy areas not suitable for gardens and, once prepared, does not spoil quickly. It is the staple crop in several low-lying parts of Papua New Guinea, and most Maisin quite enjoy it.

The Maisin get most of their food from gardens cleared and planted within a zone of secondary bush radiating three to five kilometres from the villages. In their oral traditions, the Maisin speak of clans conquering and owning tracts of land. In practice, however, groups of brothers and closely related patrilateral cousins forming lineages claim specific areas in which they make their gardens and which they pass to their sons. People also frequently make gardens on lands owned by maternal relations and in-laws. They must always ask permission first and should give a gift of produce from the new gardens to the owners. Maternal relatives sometimes will gift a piece of land to one of their sisters' sons, especially if their own numbers are declining, but this is fairly rare. While land should remain within the lineage group, fruiting trees continued to be owned by the people who planted them even when they are planted on another's land. The rules concerning land use and ownership are thus quite straightforward, but in practice they lend themselves to periodic disputes. People mark boundaries mentally, based on the placement, among other things, of trees and rivers. Still, trees die and rivers shift. Sometimes people also have differing recollections of where their ancestors first planted gardens and whether maternal relatives merely gave temporary rights to plant or ceded ownership.

⚹ The Maisin practise swidden horticulture, clearing and using garden sites for two to three years before abandoning them to the bush and moving on. Ideally, a former garden should be left for a period of 10 to 20 years before being re-used, long enough to allow the site to be covered by a lush growth of jungle and trees. Areas gardened too frequently will eventually become grassland and never recover their previous fertility. Most households try to maintain at least three gardens in different areas, including one close to the village where food can be fetched easily. Planting gardens at different times assures a steady supply of food, while dispersing gardens in different areas offers some insurance against flooding, drought, and marauding pigs.

Figure 2.3 A newly cleared garden with logs marking paths between the plots. (Photo by J. Barker)

Horticulture characteristics.
The basic technology of gardening is little changed from pre-European times. The tool kit is simplicity itself. Steel axes and machetes have replaced the stone tools used by the ancestors, greatly easing the work of clearing brush and weeding, but the Maisin continue to use fire-hardened digging sticks for planting. They make no use of composting or irrigation techniques. Villagers replant and extend their gardens throughout the year, but the most intense work of creating new gardens takes place in the dry season. Clearing a garden space is done entirely by men. Once the trees are felled, they lay out trunks and larger branches in lines to mark the boundaries of plots and pathways, piling brush and smaller branches into piles that are allowed to dry and then burned. One of the typical signals of the onset of the dry season is the sight from out on Collingwood Bay of plumes of smoke rising from dozens of new gardens dispersed behind the villages. Once a garden has been cleared, men must turn their attention to two further tasks. The first is the construction of a garden shelter in which household members can stay overnight and store tools and crops. The second task is the construction of a fence to protect the garden from pigs. Bush pigs are a constant worry. Entering gardens under the shelter of darkness, the animals can quickly

49

destroy large areas as they root about for tubers. Some men leave smoulder-
ing fires on the edges of the clearing to scare pigs away, but the only sure
defence is a sturdy fence of small logs roped together to enclose the cultivated
area.

Once the garden is cleared and the plots marked out with fallen logs,
women will fetch taro tops, banana suckers, and other seed plants from older
gardens. Men and women share the work of planting, which generally entails
pushing a digging stick into the soil and shoving in the cuttings. The low
floodland plains of Collingwood Bay support a wide variety of crops of
which taro (sp. *Colocasia*) is the most important. As in other parts of
Melanesia, the Maisin grow a large number of varieties that differ often
quite slightly in the shapes or colouration of the tuber, stalk, leaf, and so
forth. In 1983, I recorded the names of 21 varieties from one master gar-
dener, although most were indistinguishable to my eye. Other staples include
more than 30 varieties of sweet and plantain (cooking) bananas, sweet potatoes, and yams. A Maisin garden also typically contains a wide range of
native and introduced secondary crops such as squashes, manioc, sugar cane,
tomatoes, cucumbers, beans, maize, watermelons, and pineapples. Gardeners
also plant a variety of fruiting trees, most of which come into production
after the garden has been abandoned — papayas, coconuts, areca (betelnut)
palms, and, less often, guava or mangos. People finish off their gardens by
planting fragrant and ornamental bushes and flowers. These add to the
attractiveness of the space and provide materials for dancing costumes.

Once the planting is completed, the bulk of garden work falls to women.
Areas around the new plants have to be weeded two to three times to give the
crops a chance to grow. Women also carry out the regular work of harvesting
and hauling crops and firewood from the gardens back to the villages. In the
late afternoons, one usually sees groups of women trudging back from the
gardens bearing heavy loads of firewood, crops, and sometimes an infant in
large string bags strapped across the forehead and suspended down the back.

The fertility of the thin garden soil rapidly deteriorates once the crops
begin to mature. Gardeners usually can get a second crop, mostly of sweet
potatoes, which demand fewer nutrients than plants like taro, but soon after
the garden must be abandoned. Owners will occasionally return over the
next few years to gather bananas and, once they mature, coconuts and betel-
nuts if they have been planted. Long after a garden has returned to bush,
palms and fruiting trees stand as markers of prior activity.

The Maisin enjoy spending time in their gardens. Often people will live
for days or even weeks away from the village, sleeping in open-sided garden
shelters which, like village houses, are raised on posts to catch cooling
breezes. I also enjoy spending time in the gardens. Although very hot during

the day—the surrounding forests block cooling breezes—the gardens present a lush profusion of shapes and colours. The best moments are early in the morning and late afternoon when it is cool and flocks of small parrots and white and black cockatoos descend to feed on fallen papayas and rotting fruits. The garden shelters provide a lovely place to socialize, to chat about the day's gossip, listen to stories about the exploits of the ancestors, or simply to enjoy the sounds of the jungle.

Most visitors to Maisin and other rural communities in Papua New Guinea get no further than the villages. The villages are attractive and concentrated; it is easy to assume that they form the centre of social life. After a few days in a garden, however, you realize that this is misleading. For the Maisin, gardens are about much more than just growing food.

To begin with, gardens are spiritual centres. In the recent past, well after most of the people had become Christians, one began a new garden by placing a small amount of betelnut and tobacco on a makeshift platform at the centre of the area to be cleared. This sacrifice assured that the ancestors who had previously worked that land would not be upset by the noise and disruption of garden clearing and would reciprocate for the gift by increasing the fertility of the soil. Few Maisin do this today, but several will ask the priest to bless new gardens, and everyone is conscious of the continuing presence of the people who used the land in earlier times. Maisin in their 50s remember being cautioned by their parents not to be too rowdy in the garden lest the noise disturb the ancestors. Still today, Maisin will credit ancestors for a good crop or blame failures due to insect infestations, floods, or drought upon angered ghosts. Recently deceased fathers and mothers often appear in dreams to tell their children where to plant, hunt, or fish. The Maisin regard none of this as extraordinary or spooky. The ancestors are *just there*, as real as the trees or the butterflies.

Gardens are also key locations of moral and social development. As soon as a child receives a name, usually when they are nine months to a year old, her parents will assign her a garden plot and plant and harvest crops in her name. Everyone gardens as soon and for as long as they are able. The good man or woman, in the Maisin's estimation, works hard in the garden and is rewarded by an abundance of good crops, which they should then generously share. Parents will size up a prospective spouse for their son or daughter in terms of their skill as gardeners and their willingness to share labour and food with their kin. Most of the folktales with which the Maisin entertain themselves involve scenes in gardens, the action turning upon the interactions between siblings, spouses, and in-laws working out their relationships through growing, exchanging, and consuming food.[2]

Gardens also lie at the centre of everyday politics, the formation of alliances and vying for influence. When a man clears a garden on his father's and paternal grandfather's land, he demonstrates a continuing claim against others who may also believe they have an ancestral right to part or all of the land. Land thus forms a central element in a person's genealogical identity, in practical terms more important than remembering the names of one's ancestors. At the same time, leaders and would-be leaders build much of their influence through their actions in the gardens. Many senior men encourage clan mates and some in-laws to join together to clear a large area within which each household develops separate garden plots. This strategy eases some of the burden of tasks such as clearing and weeding and also provides participants with welcome opportunities for socializing. It also serves as evidence of a leader's ability to influence and coordinate the labour of others. Managing a large group's garden is usually the first step towards the sponsoring of a major ceremony like the initiation for a first-born child, which requires large quantities of raw food to give away as gifts and cooked food for feasting.

Gardens form the very heart of the local economic system. In the hot and moist conditions of the tropics, garden food begins to rot within a day of harvesting; slow-smoked fish or meat lasts longer, but by the second week begins to turn into an inedible tarry lump. With no steady source of cash income, villagers rely upon a steady flow of food through daily subsistence activities to survive. Most of the food gets consumed by the households that produce it. Yet garden foods also yield the essential ingredients of wider economic and social relationships that bind households together. It is to this system we now turn.

HOUSEHOLDS AND RECIPROCITY

The daily round in Maisin village life centres on food. People spend most days clearing new gardens and cultivating and harvesting crops. As the shadows lengthen in the late afternoon, people make their way back to the village, the women straining under their heavy loads of food and firewood. In the early evening, one's nose is greeted by the aroma of dozens of cooking fires. The basic cooking method is simple but effective. First, the taro is peeled and cut into large chunks that are placed at the bottom of a cooking pot. Depending on what is available, the pot is filled up with layers of yams, cooking bananas, sweet potatoes, squash, and fish or meat. As the women prepare the food, boys and girls in the household scrape coconut meat and then squeeze water through it. The sweetened water is then poured into the pot, which is covered with a lid or, if a clay pot, banana leaves. The pot is then placed on the fire. The denser root crops at the bottom boil while the rest of the food is steamed. Everything comes out with a slightly sweet nutty flavour. Dinner is the one big meal of the day. Breakfast consists of the cold leftovers. During the day, people snack on sweet bananas, sugar cane, or a left-over chunk of taro or sweet potato.

Most productive activities in Maisin society are organized by individual households. A typical Maisin household is made up of a husband, wife, and children, but it is not unusual to find elderly relations, cousins, or adopted children sharing the premises. Usually all of the members share a single building, but sometimes aging parents or a younger sibling may live in a small house near the main one, while men in polygynous marriages usually build separate residences for their different wives and respective children. Members work together on most subsistence activities, donating the food they bring in to the common family pool. Households tend to be nearly self-sufficient. Some tasks, however, require cooperative labour, such as building a new house, making a canoe, or clearing a large garden area. At such times, households belonging to the same clan or related through marriage will band together to form work parties.

A certain amount of sharing of labour as well as food and other products is necessary for survival in any society. Maisin practice, however, goes well beyond basic necessity. Consider this: Maisin households produce exactly the same foods, with some variation in quantity depending on household com-position and the skills of individual gardeners, fishermen, and hunters. Most easily produce enough food for their own needs and for the care of depen-dants—infants and the old and infirm. Most of the time, there is no practical requirement that compels people to share beyond their own household. Yet, each day, villagers give produce, betelnut, tobacco, and other gifts to their kin and neighbours. Most evenings after the evening meal has been cooked, young children can be seen bearing small plates or pots of cooked food from house to house. More often than not, a household receives back from one or more neighbours exactly the same kinds of food as they sent out. During the early stages of my fieldwork, I went to several households every night for two weeks to record a log of their daily activities. I was impressed not only by the sheer amount of giving and taking that was going on but that people remembered even the smallest exchanges. Nobody finds this odd. People instead would be very concerned if they did not send out and receive food regularly.

Anthropologists refer to this kind of arrangement as a "gift economy" (Gregory 1982; Sykes 2005). It is the normal way of doing things in most small-scale subsistence-based cultures, especially those in which money and commodities are scarce. A principle of reciprocity lies at the heart of the sys-tem: Person A gives something to Person B, creating a debt and an obligation to make a return gift. Yet this very simplicity can be deceiving, for in practice the sequence of giving, receiving, and returning permits an extraordinarily broad range of variations. These variations turn on several interrelated factors: the intent of the partners who are exchanging things, the nature of the social relationships between exchange partners, the actual items exchanged, and the time lapse between the reception of a gift and reciprocation.

Let's start with intent. Maisin learn from their earliest years of the necessity of giving (and thus also receiving) gifts by watching older siblings and adults and through repeated encouragement from those around them. They learn reciprocity so well that it becomes a matter of reflex, of common sense. In the course of her research on child socialization among the Maisin, Anne conducted a very revealing experiment. She had invited individual children to meet her at the school to carry out a small exercise. At its conclusion, she gave the child a *toea* (penny) and told her or him that the money was for them to use as they saw fit. They could either keep it to buy a stick of chewing gum from the trade store or place it in a tin at the door of our house for the use of the Mothers Union, a church women's group. The tin was not visible from where Anne was working in the school. At the end of the day we were amazed to find all but one of the coins had been donated to the church group.

The virtue of giving, then, is very deeply engrained in Maisin culture. This is important to grasp because, as we shall see below, reciprocity provides the Maisin with a basic orientation to life, especially to questions of morality. All the same, to say that reciprocity forms a kind of common sense is not to suggest that the Maisin are not aware of what they are doing when they give and receive things but only that they *expect* reciprocity in their dealings with other people. In practice, people pay close attention to exchanges. As I noted above, members of the households who participated in my survey of daily activities were keenly aware of the precise exchanges in which they had engaged during the day. Maisin help each other out through exchanges, but exchanges more fundamentally provide the key means by which people create, assess, manipulate, and sometimes end social relationships. Everyone is involved in social relationships and so everyone exchanges. Like all things, however, exchanging can be done with finesse or gracelessly, with calculation or by reflex. People who want to be respected by others quickly learn to initiate and participate well in exchanges. They become very skilful in "reading" the underlying meanings of the exchanges occurring around them.

Anthropologists have written extensively on reciprocity, especially in Melanesian societies.[3] Prior to our fieldwork, Anne and I had read this literature carefully. Still, reading and experiencing are two very different things. Nothing caused more strains in our early dealings with the Maisin than figuring out how to respond appropriately when people gave us gifts and requested things from us. We had to think about it and, at least at first, were rather slow on the uptake.

I wrote in Chapter 1 of how Anne and I received a huge quantity of food on the day we first arrived in Uiaku. This did not happen again, but most days at least one person would come to our door with some raw taro, bananas, other vegetables, and, occasionally, a fish or raw cut of pig meat. As they waited at the door, we pulled out a small bag of rice or a tobacco stick to give in return. Our most regular supplier was Rufus, a lively middle-aged man who lived with three wives and several children in the village next to the mission station. Rufus and I soon developed a kind of joking relationship, greeting each other with cries of *toma!* ("friend"), whenever we passed each other's place. Still, I soon came to dread and even resent his visits. Many days the offered food was tiny—a few scrawny sweet potatoes or a small fish —and yet we felt obliged to give the rice or tobacco regardless. It felt a bit like extortion and, beyond this, terribly unfair to our other neighbours who only came periodically with more generous gifts of produce yet received the same amount of rice from us.

One day, an old woman from the nearby part of the village came with some food. As usual, I thanked her and asked her to wait while I fetched a bag from our rapidly dwindling store of rice. When I returned, I was surprised and alarmed by her obvious distress. She refused the rice and went off in search of someone who could speak English. She came back with Ilma Joyce, who explained that she had not come to "sell" the food to us: it was a gift, offered in friendship. She had seen that we needed things, that we had no garden, and so had felt sorry for us and wanted to help. The gift was offered in "love" (*marawa-wawe*). The implication was that by giving rice immediately in return, I was actually spurning her offer of friendship and treating her as one would a stranger.

We thus had our first practical lesson in "generalized reciprocity" (Sahlins 1972). Close kin ideally should support each other through a constant give-and-take of gifts, labour, and advice. This is not done in a calculated way, by tracking what each person gives, receives, owes, or is owed. Instead, people demonstrate their mutual trust and support by not insisting on immediate return gifts or a demonstration of balance. The Maisin idealize generalized reciprocity as the prime exemplar of *marawa-wawe*, a key word to which we will return repeatedly in this book. *Mara* refers to the physical sensation in the guts caused by strong emotion. Combined with *wawe*, "giving," the term suggests a state of sharing oneself with another. English-speaking Maisin often gloss it as "love," but, depending on the context, it can also mean "peace" or "social amity." As these glosses suggest, the Maisin see *marawa-wawe* as the ideal outcome of exchanges, the social goal that begins with the simple giving of a gift. Our new friend taught us, in the most practical way, the method of making *marawa-wawe*, by creating a casual ongoing exchange relationship.

I soon applied this lesson to my friend Rufus. I no longer gave rice or tobacco immediately upon receiving his gifts but instead occasionally sent a bag of rice or a couple of sticks of tobacco to his house. To my relief and I expect his, our relationship greatly improved. I was, at last, acting the way the Maisin expect friends to behave.

BEYOND THE HOUSEHOLD

The Maisin often speak about their communities as if they were large, tightly integrated families. The rapid redistribution across villages and beyond of food given out at feasts or second-hand clothing brought in by a relative visiting from town during the Christmas holiday can leave one with the impression that the whole community exists in a kind of communal *marawa-wawe*, a state of generalized exchange. Yet this is not the case. The circle of neighbours and kin in which people typically experience a free give-and-take tends not to extend much further than nearby households, which, as we will see in the next chapter, usually belong to one's own clan. These circles overlap, forming a dense interweaving casual exchange network that expands across the community as a whole but does not form a unitary system.

There is no firm boundary between those people one treats as intimate kin and others, but the shift in expectations and behaviour is quite marked. The more distant people are, both in terms of relatedness and their physical residence, the harder it is to attain an ambience of easy give-and-take. Exchanges occur less frequently and tend to fall into a pattern of "balanced reciprocity" in which the exchanging parties are focussed on the calculus of give-and-take. A gift clearly incurs a debt that must eventually be repaid in full. The larger an activity, the more likely it will involve both socially close and distant relationships and thus generalized and balanced reciprocity. When a man needs to put a new roof on his house, for instance, he can expect help from his own and neighbouring households because that is what close kin do. Usually he will need a large work party to cut sago fronds and to prepare and lay the thatch. The close relatives are treated fairly casually; he can and will help them out in return in a myriad of ways in coming days. At the same time, he will treat more distant kin and neighbours to a small meal including, ideally, generous quantities of the heavily sugared tea favoured by most Maisin. This doesn't finish the debt—a bit of cooked food and tea is not the equivalent of a day of hard labour. The proud owner of the new roof will be in turn asked politely to help repair or replace the roofs of the various men who help him out and who, in their turn, will provide a small meal with tea. And so on.

There are many variations on this pattern, some occurring more frequently than others, but all entailing the expectation of a balanced exchange

Figure 2.4 Women bringing food to a feast. Note the "star" (*damana*) design on the tapa worn by the woman on the left of the photograph. (Photo by A.M. Tietjen)

over a limited period of time. I need to underline the word "expectation" here because, in reality, it is near impossible for a perfectly balanced exchange to be achieved. Take the example of the new roof. The owner of the first house may well meet his obligations by helping those who helped him; but roofs vary in size and pitch; the size of the crew and thus the amount of work involved differs from one job to the next; and not all men can afford to purchase tea and sugar. This is a rather trivial example, however. Things get vastly more complicated when we come to the really big exchanges that mark the major transitions in individuals' lives: birth, marriage, and death.

Marriage forms the lynchpin of a series of life crisis ceremonies that mark one's passage from birth to death. In common with most Melanesians, the Maisin speak of marriage itself as a kind of exchange that begins when one clan gives a woman (including her labour and future children) to another. In accepting the women, the recipients incur a huge debt that literally takes a lifetime to repay. They have a number of options: they may arrange for one of their young women to marry into the other clan; they may give the mother's clan a child for adoption; or they may present a large gift of food, traditional wealth items, and money after a few children are born ("bride-price" or "bride-wealth"). Regardless of what type of repayment they ultimately make, they must also "respect" the wife's people with frequent small gifts of food and labour and with larger prestations (presentations of gifts) when a child is born and to initiate first-born children. Each of these gifts in turn triggers a reciprocal gift from the in-laws. The spiral of gifts and return gifts is ideally finally brought into balance after the death of the spouses, an event also marked by exchanges. The Maisin refer to this idealized state also as *marawa-wawe*, but here it has a different sense than in the case of generalized reciprocity: it refers to a perfect balance between parties that retain their distinct identities.

We will look at marriage and life crisis ceremonies in the next chapter, but enough has been said here to indicate that, although based on reciprocity, the generalized and balanced modes operate with distinctive logic and give rise to different types of social connections. In brief, generalized reciprocity occurs between people who think of themselves as belonging to a group, while balanced reciprocity occurs between and reinforces the identities of social groups as exchanging parties (Wagner 1967). Because the groups retain their identities, these exchanges always involve an element of competition. The man who provides a work crew with an extra treat like sugared tea enjoys a bit of an edge over those who can only serve food from their gardens. Likewise, the clan that gives a notably large quantity of tapa cloth or cash as part of a bride-price prestation may enjoy a sense of accomplishment and superiority over their competitors. The principle is the same (although at a much smaller scale) as that of the famous potlatches in Aboriginal communities on the northwest coast of North America where chiefs gain prestige over time by giving away more than they receive from rivals.

It is important to understand that *social* distance is not the same as *physical* distance. This is clearly illustrated in the case of the kinds of exchanges Marshall Sahlins (1972) calls "negative reciprocity." Normally, such exchanges occur between parties that have little or no social connection and thus no moral obligation to each other. They are strangers or nearly so. People expect their exchange partners to try to take advantage of them and feel little compulsion not to seek advantage themselves, and so both sides watch the transactions very carefully, demanding immediate and direct reciprocity. If one side does gain an advantage or is perceived to have done so, the other will retaliate — a reflex known throughout Melanesia as "payback" (Trompf 1994), *vina* in the Maisin language. Our first transactions with our Maisin neighbours were of this sort: people brought food to us for which they immediately received payment. Because Anne and I didn't feel we could refuse the gifts, we soon began to suspect that we were being taken advantage of. I expect that some of the people coming to the door felt the same. Negative reciprocity is like that: there is little or no trust. We were relieved when the transactions shifted into the more comfortable modes of balanced and generalized reciprocity. Given the densely interwoven ties of kinship and exchange in the villages, negative reciprocity tends to occur on the margins of the community, with outsiders. The exception is sorcery, which will be discussed in Chapter 4. When it comes to explaining serious misfortunes, many Maisin are all too ready to suspect their neighbours of having secretly broken social bonds either to retaliate for some real or imagined wrong or to take unfair advantage.

In sum, we find that in Maisin society there is a correlation between social distance between people and the sorts of exchanges in which they engage. Closely related people engage in a constant give-and-take that confirms and generates a sense of commonality. Further out, exchanges become less frequent, more formal, and larger. Social relationships at this level cannot be taken for granted: they are created, made visible, and validated through a series of formal prestations. As social distance increases, the antagonistic element of the reciprocal scenario becomes ever more prominent, arriving eventually in bartering with, stealing from, and, in the warrior past, killing social outsiders.

The model of generalized, balanced, and negative reciprocity, introduced by Marshall Sahlins (1972) based upon an extensive comparative study of small-scale societies around the world, is very helpful. Yet in the end it is a model: reality is always more innovative than such models might suggest. Given the dense and overlapping exchange and kinship networks in Uiaku and other Maisin villages, people enjoy some flexibility in how they define relationships. The flexibility is not exercised in any overt fashion but rather through how people treat each other in gift exchanges. Consider, for example, an end-of-mourning ceremony I witnessed in 1983 when a widow was brought out of mourning for her husband who had passed away some years earlier. Villagers spoke of two distinct groups of people in a state of balanced reciprocity: the wife and the husband's sides. This seemed neat enough until I discovered that a number of women who had provided and cooked food for the widow's side later received that very same food as members of the husband's side. During the first stage of the exchange, they were acting in terms of generalized reciprocity, moved to help the widow who was a close relation. Yet they had married into her husband's clan, and so when the time came they had to receive their fair share of the food distribution.

The act of reciprocity lies at the heart of the Maisin subsistence economy, but it should be very clear by now that it is neither simple nor limited to the business of moving items between producers and consumers. Reciprocity provides the key means by which the Maisin create and sustain social relationships. In a way, the constant give-and-take of daily exchanges indicates a firm assumption that social relationships can never be taken for granted. They need to be created, affirmed, reproduced, and modified through the obligation and the art of giving and receiving. Beyond the economy and the social order, reciprocity reflects something even more fundamental—the underlying moral precepts that make social life possible and comprehensible. Ask any Maisin, "What are the qualities of a good person?" and they will inevitably reply that the good person is generous, giving freely to others and participating in *marawa-wawe*. They will add that the good person does this with a keen eye on balance: they listen carefully to others, and they don't try to show off as a "big head." Above all else, they meet their obligation to reciprocate for what they receive. The Maisin regard those who resist participating in exchanges with either scorn or fear. A man or woman who fails to meet exchange obligations because of a lack of ability or laziness is "rubbish," a source of annoyance to their neighbours who find they have to make up for the lost production. A person who *chooses* not to exchange is something else, for he or she stands apart from the common rules that make social life predictable and thus threatens it. Outsiders pose one kind of threat, which is why the Maisin view them with suspicion. Yet a greater threat comes from insiders whose selfishness reflects a wilful defiance of the moral rules. Such is the nature of sorcerers. The Maisin believe that sorcerers, operating in secret, cause most major illnesses and accidents and are responsible for the majority of deaths. As we shall see, however, the Maisin also believe that sorcerers tend to attack those people who have themselves breached morality by acting selfishly, non-reciprocally. The hope for social amity reinforces reciprocity in a positive way. The fear of a slow death through sorcery adds a negative sanction against immoral behaviour.

It would be hard to exaggerate the importance of reciprocity to the Maisin. Indeed, the theme runs through most of this book just as it informed most social interactions during the time of my fieldwork. The obligation to make and return gifts is the most basic and most central rule of Maisin life, forming the moral basis of the economy and the social order alike. It is a simple idea that allows enormous flexibility and creativity. It was one that the Maisin practised adroitly upon Anne and me, using gifts of food to change us from strangers to neighbours, to transform us into moral persons.

Yet this is not the whole story. As well as raising their own food or building houses from bush materials, the Maisin have also long lived in a world of cash and commodities, one that operates according to a different moral logic than reciprocity.

CASH, REMITTANCES, AND COMMODITIES: A CHANGING ECONOMY

Visitors to Maisin villages are often impressed that people continue to grow their own food and manufacture much of their own material culture from the resources nature provides them. Subsistence activities and reciprocity provide the foundation for village life, a foundation that was laid long before the arrival of the first Europeans. All the same, the Maisin are no strangers to money and what money can buy. Mass-manufactured commodities first entered Maisin society in the 1890s in the form of steel axes and knives given as trade goods by visiting missionaries and government officers. By the 1920s, villagers were able to purchase their own commodities directly with money earned by young men working on plantations and mines elsewhere in the colony. Following World War II, the Maisin were actively searching for ways of earning money without having to leave their villages. Eventually, most of a generation of young people left the villages to take up paid employment in the towns, sending home gifts of cash and goods to help their rural relations. Over the years, villagers have become increasingly dependent upon purchased commodities ranging from basic necessities, such as clothing and fish hooks, to "luxury" items such as soccer balls and cigarettes. Villagers frequently complain of the problems that money brings in its wake, but no one would suggest that the villages return to a time when people relied solely upon local resources for survival.

The historical introduction and growing dependence upon money has had complex implications for Maisin culture. We will turn to this subject in the next section. First, however, we need to complete our survey of the local economy by examining the place of cash and commodities and the ways the Maisin try to secure them.

Prior to the early 1960s, the Maisin were able to purchase only a limited range of commodities: machetes and knives, bolts of cloth for clothing, black stick tobacco, and so forth. This limitation was partly the consequence of a lack of ready cash but as much due to the difficulties of getting commodities to the villages at a time when very few trade stores existed and infrequent coastal ships provided the only reliable source of transportation in and out of the bay. Since this time, both the range of goods available to the Maisin and their ability to purchase them have increased enormously. When we arrived in the early 1980s, all Maisin wore Western clothing (mostly second-hand, imported from Australia and sold through dealers in the towns) and had become accustomed to a wide array of mass-produced basic goods such as nylon fishing nets, shotguns, hurricane lamps, kerosene, dyes for string bags, rice, and so forth. Most people still cooked with clay pots, purchased or traded for tapa from Wanigela, and ate with their fingers from tin plates or off banana leaves. By the late 1990s, clay pots had been entirely replaced by steel cooking pots for all but ceremonial occasions, and most people in Uiaku, the richest of the villages, had china plates and steel cutlery. Many people now owned pressure lanterns. Those with more resources had replaced the older sea-going canoes with fibreglass boats equipped with outboard motors. While subsistence activities continued to provide most of the food, many households now regularly purchased rice, tinned fish, and other mass-produced foods at local trade stores and from businesses located near the Wanigela airstrip. Radios had become common, although villagers often could not afford the batteries to keep them operating. Upon retiring from his job in town, one man had brought a generator and VCR to the village. In June 2000, two other returning workers introduced electric lights powered by solar panels.

People differ, of course, over what they see as necessary or a luxury. Still, all households have steadily become dependent upon an ever-widening assortment of commodities since the introduction of steel axes in the 1890s. Villagers have also faced the need for ready cash for a variety of community services and programs. Since the late 1970s, the Anglican Church has required local congregations to pay the salary of the parish priest. Villagers are also responsible for the costs of church supplies, such as sacramental wine and wafers (both imported from Australia), as well as the building and maintenance of churches, classrooms, and housing for the priest and teachers. Papua New Guinean politicians reliably promise "free" education with every approaching election, but for much of the post-Independence period parents have had to pay small school fees for students in elementary schools and far higher tuitions for those accepted into the private church or public high schools, along with the transport costs of getting their children to these residential schools and home again for holidays. Various village associations also regularly seek money in the form of government grants and donations from local people. The Mothers' Union, for instance, organizes occasional community meals to raise money for trips to conventions or supplies for the church, while youth groups hire themselves out to build houses or work on gardens to raise money for sports equipment. The Maisin Integrated Development and Conservation organization (MICAD), formed by village leaders in the mid-1990s to fend off industrial logging and foster locally controlled economic development, requires regular funds to purchase medicine on behalf of the community and to cover the travel costs required to bring leaders from the different Maisin villages together for consultations (see Chapter 6).

Opportunities for earning money locally are quite limited. Since the 1920s, villagers have been able to earn small amounts of cash from selling copra—a source of vegetable oil made from the dried meat of coconuts. Through the 1950s and 1960s, villagers planted thousands of coffee and cocoa trees under the guidance of government agricultural officers, but the lack of regular shipping in and out of Collingwood Bay made it difficult to get the produce to market, and the trees were soon abandoned to the jungle. The most reliable local product by far has been tapa cloth. Maisin elders in the 1980s recalled their parents selling small quantities of tapa cloth to European traders in the late 1930s, but a regular market for tapa only came into existence in the late 1960s and early 1970s. Some Maisin travelling in the towns sold quantities of the cloth to shops that, in turn, marketed them as artifacts to the expatriate population looking for souvenirs. Around the same time, Sister Helen Roberts, a missionary nurse based at Wanigela, began to accept tapa as credit towards the high school fees and transportation costs. Sister Helen actively sought out buyers across the country and overseas. The attractive cloths quickly gained a small niche in the artifact market; at the same time, they were sought by Papua New Guinean groups who had ceased to manufacture their own tapas but still needed the cloth for traditional ceremonies.

In the mid-1980s, a skilled tapa maker could earn more than 200 kina per year—a considerable sum in those days—although most women made far less.[4] As the expatriate population in Papua New Guinea dwindled and the tourist trade slowed, however, partly in reaction to the growing theft and violence in the towns, tapa sales slumped. Tapa enjoyed a major boost in the mid-1990s, when the environmental groups working with the Maisin actively promoted it as an environmentally sustainable form of locally controlled development (see Chapter 6). These efforts led to a minor boom, but by 2000 tapa sales were again flagging.

Maisin men often experiment with different ways to make money. In recent years, a few have earned cash by raising crocodiles for their skins or selling vegetables in the Tufi or Alotau markets. Some are looking into insect farming[5] or the newest cash crop craze to hit Collingwood Bay, oil palm. Other entrepreneurs open small trade stores or hire out their motorized boats to other villagers. Most of these enterprises soon go under, but a few men have managed to operate profitable businesses for a number of years. With the exception of those boat drivers lucky enough to be hired by a visiting film crew or environmental group, these businesses do not bring new money into the community but instead redistribute and consume the cash that has arrived through other channels.

Since the early 1970s, the most important and reliable source of income for villagers has come in the form of remittances from working relatives. In the early 1960s, the Australian government, under pressure from the United

Nations, greatly accelerated preparations for Papua New Guinea's independence. The civil service was massively expanded with most of the jobs going to the then small number of graduates from the nascent system of church and state high schools. This worked greatly to the advantage of people from the long-missionized areas of the colony whose children had been the first to enter the high schools. Upon graduation, students were offered opportunities for further specialized training, eventually finding work as teachers, nurses, priests, doctors, agricultural extension workers, and government bureaucrats. Despite its small population, Uiaku produced Papua New Guinea's first doctor (Dr. Wilfred Moi), one of the first dentists (Franklin Seri), and an ambassador to Indonesia (Benson Gegeyo). Once they gained steady employment, the first generation of graduates eased the path of younger siblings and relatives still in the villages by paying their high school fees, providing support for them when they visited the towns looking for work, and recommending them for positions (cf. Carrier 1981). By the early 1980s, as much as a quarter of the population of Uiaku had moved out to towns across the country.

Villagers expect those who find employment to "not forget" the people back in the village. While life in the towns is expensive, most employed Maisin routinely put aside part of their salaries to assist their rural relatives when called upon to help with medicines, a major exchange, or to start up a local business. They accommodate relatives visiting from the village and send them home with parcels of clothing and other goods. The biggest distributions occur when working relatives come home for the Christmas holiday, usually once every two years, bearing large suitcases stuffed with clothing and other gifts for their families. Employed Maisin do this in part because of their upbringing — reinforced by constant reminders from their rural relations — which places the highest value on reciprocity. They also do it because most wish to eventually retire in their natal village. They help those who remain behind who, in turn, care for the land and protect the property rights of absent family members. The pattern of movement to and from the villages has had a profound impact upon Maisin society. Today almost all adult Maisin have lived for a time — and often a long time — in the towns, either employed themselves or as the guest of an employed relative.

Even in the early 1980s, however, it was apparent that the Maisin strategy of exporting labour to the towns could not be sustained. Over the years, as high schools have opened their doors to more communities, coastal people like the Maisin have lost much of their advantage. While high school spaces have expanded, the demand far outstrips their ability to absorb students, and so an increasing number of graduates from the village schools have been blocked from advancing their education, a necessity for securing a well-paying job. Meanwhile, the job market has been steadily shrinking. Papua New

Guinea's economy struggled in the early years and then lurched from crisis to crisis following the outbreak of a ten-year civil war on Bougainville Island and the closure of the country's most profitable gold and copper mine (Dorney 2000). The civil service has been steadily reduced over the years, even as more high school graduates enter the job market, and the private sector has also failed to meet the demand. By 2000, villagers continued to look to remittances as the best source for cash and commodities, but the flow was far less reliable than in the recent past as the pool of employed Maisin shrank. Meanwhile, the village population had been swollen by "school leavers": secondary school graduates who had not found work outside but who had developed a taste for an ever-widening array of imported commodities.

GIFTS AND COMMODITIES

Western visitors to rural communities in the Pacific Islands are often struck by the coexistence of old ways with new — subsistence activities alongside trade stores stocked with tinned fish and rice; kinship and exchange networks mixed with wage employment; sacrifices to family ancestors beside Sunday worship in the church. Today, almost all adult Maisin have lived for extended periods of time in the towns, and most people under 60 speak at least a bit of English, some fluently. Yet people live in thatched houses built by hand from bush materials, take great pride in the oral traditions of their ancestors, and feel intensely suspicious of neighbouring tribal groups. Tapa cloth epitomizes this mix of local and imported elements, for the Maisin use it interchangeably as a type of traditional wealth and ceremonial apparel and as a commodity that can be sold for money used to purchase, among other things, second hand t-shirts, shorts, and skirts imported from overseas.

How do we make sense of this? Many observers, including educated Papua New Guineans, see the presence of Western elements as evidence of a process of "modernization," a movement from a "traditional" past based upon local ties to the land and to kin towards a "modern" society integrated into national and global financial, political, and social systems. They perceive this movement as inevitable, although they may celebrate or regret the changes. At the height of the Maisin's protest against a scheme to log their traditional lands in 1999, for instance, a CNN film crew came to Uiaku to film a short news item on the situation. The segment includes a clip of a lawyer speaking on behalf of the logging company explaining that "progress" was inevitable and generally benefited the people. Most of the segment, however, conveys a sense of loss. The audience is treated to a dramatic scene of Maisin "warriors" dancing in colourful traditional costumes. The feeling one takes away is that another bit of cultural diversity is about to be crushed beneath the juggernaut of "development." The Canadian documentary,

Changing Ground (2001), develops another common variant on the modernization narrative, one that is also prominent in the literature prepared by conservation groups working with the Maisin. Here the presence of traditional activities such as the preparation of sago, manufacture of tapa, and costumed dancing is taken as evidence of resistance to encroaching Western forces, which are represented as rapacious exploiters of the Melanesian environment. The Maisin, we are told, have tasted the fruits of Western society and rejected them in favour of the ways of their own ancestors.

At the very centre of this contest, in theory, lies a conflict between an economic system built upon the direct reciprocal exchange of goods and labour and one in which money purchases both as types of commodities. The shift from gifts to commodities would seem to have severe consequences. In reciprocal economies it is hard for any person to accumulate wealth, and thus traditional Melanesian societies are sometimes described as "egalitarian." It is not that inequality does not exist—certainly men generally dominate women, and some traditional societies had extremely powerful leaders—but such power cannot be sustained on the basis of economic wealth or the creation of classes. Money potentially disrupts the obligation to return a gift in the simplest way possible: it can be stored away out of sight to accumulate, whether under a mattress or in a bank account. At a deeper level, money and markets imply a different type of morality, one focussed upon the individual who through hard work, good luck, or a combination of both succeeds on his or her own, with no help from others. Thus the introduction of money and commodities can be understood as the main engine of a series of transformations—from reciprocity between people to transactions mediated by money and markets; from self-reliance to dependence upon wages paid by employers; from a relatively egalitarian to an economically stratified society; from a moral emphasis upon one's obligations to kin and community to the celebration of the individual (Akin and Robbins 1999; Bloch and Parry 1989).

There are signs of such a transformation in Maisin society. There can be little doubt that many commodities have made life easier and more predictable. No villager today would want to clear a garden using stone tools, even if they still possessed the knowledge to make them. Parents appreciate the medicines that have saved the lives of countless children, and builders praise the superiority of steel nails over bush twine in constructing the framework of houses. Yet a dependence on commodities and money comes at a cost. Few if any Maisin believe that they have enough money for what they need. The more that people become accustomed to things like tinned fish and rice, the more they perceive them as necessities rather than supplements. People thus spend a great deal of time and energy, in the household and in community meetings, discussing how to make more money and diagnosing failed economic initiatives. A second cost is rising divisions within the community. Unlike garden produce, money doesn't rot and can be stored away secretly from the eyes of kin and neighbours. It encourages the independence of households at the expense of wider kinship and exchange networks and thus introduces new inequalities into a society built upon an egalitarian moral ethos. Those people blessed with a large number of employed relatives or with highly skilled tapa makers have a little more of everything than their neighbours.

At every stage, however, Maisin have modified their understanding and use of money and commodities according to their received assumptions about reciprocity and morality. I witnessed an interesting example of this process of localization at work during the second Christmas I spent in Uiaku. A young man arrived from Port Moresby for a two-month holiday with several suitcases bulging with clothes. I was sitting with his family when he arrived and took note of each piece as it was carefully unpacked. By the evening of the next day, I found that most of the clothing had been shared among close kin, but a good number of pieces had been delivered to more distant relatives across the village. The parents told me that while they would have liked to keep more for themselves, people would have considered them selfish had they not been generous with the gifts.

The requirement to reciprocate is a constant refrain in Maisin society, and it shapes the way that villagers approach money and commodities. Parents continually remind children fortunate enough to make it to high school and to find employment of their debt to those who raised them. Employed Maisin often have complained to me of the unrelenting pressure they experience from relatives who request cash for everything from small change to buy cigarettes to starting funds for a trade store. Maisin in towns can expect relatives to drop in on them and live at their expense for months at a time. Those who return to the villages can expect a hostile reception if they fail to bring a generous number of gifts. Often they are criticized in any case. Those who opt out, who fail to support people back in the village, risk breaking ties completely. On a couple of occasions when doing the household census I would learn from one family that they had a cousin working in town who had not been mentioned by the person's own father and mother. Inevitably, when I returned to the person's immediate family to ask why they had failed to mention him, I was told that he did not support his village family with remittances. "My son is dead," declared one father sadly.

The pressure to share extends to villagers who earn income from tapa or copra sales and who have working relatives who send remittances. Many of these people keep much of their funds hidden in savings accounts in distant banks, saving up for school fees and other major expenses. In any case, it does not pay to make too obvious a showing of personal fortune. When we first arrived in Uiaku, we found only a single residence with an iron roof. A Maisin man then working as an agricultural officer at the provincial capital had built it for his elderly father. The father was proud to possess such a fine house, but he used it only for storage, sleeping instead in a tiny bush house beside it. "Were I to live in it," he told me, "people might get jealous; they might talk about me" — a common reference to sorcery. Other families told me that they had refused offers from working relations to pay for iron roofs for the same reason.

Such attitudes may come across to Western readers as calculating and harsh. Still, they are merely the flip side of the positive expressions of sharing, especially the key value of *marawa-wawe*, of "love" within a family and social harmony at large. The pressures and the threats, direct and veiled, are real enough. Yet most people share what they have because it is the normal thing to do. If they have more, they take pleasure and some pride at demonstrating their generosity, their willingness to "care for" others (*kaifi inei*), another key value. While privately complaining about the burden, most Maisin in the towns provide support for their rural relatives. Many express a desire to retire to the quiet and relative safety of village life. By sharing and thus participating in the moral community, they demonstrate their continued membership and the right they and their children enjoy to come home eventually to their ancestral lands.

The money and commodities that come into the villages eventually get consumed; but at the point they are shared, they cease acting as elements of a market economy and instead take on the functions of gifts in an economy based upon reciprocity. This has a number of consequences. The first is that much (but not all) of the inequalities produced by the remittance system get levelled out through village exchange networks. The second consequence has been that, particularly since the 1960s, a great deal of money and goods have entered exchange networks that formerly carried mostly locally produced items. In much of Melanesia, increasing availability of money and commodities led at least initially to an efflorescence of exchange systems, both in everyday reciprocity and formal exchanges, which often increased greatly in scale (Gregory 1982). Maisin probably started using cash and mass-produced commodities for formal exchanges like bride-price in the 1920s. By the 1980s, these had become necessities. Instead of displacing the subsistence economy with its basis in kin and exchange relations, the cash sector of the economy appears to have actually subsidized its continuing existence — a reversal of the modernization model (cf. Carrier and Carrier 1989).

In recent years the Maisin have become more tolerant of inequalities in their communities. One now finds households that are visibly better off than

Figure 2.5 Market day on the Uiaku mission station, June 2000. (Photo by J. Barker)

others. Exchanges do not appear to be as intense and as frequent as in the 1980s. Villagers have also become more accustomed to using money within the village, at a small market where women sell produce to each other, to pay youth to clear gardens, or for admission to events sponsored by church or sports groups. For all that, reciprocity remains central to the Maisin economy and moral system. There is no hunger in Maisin communities; the need to share, to support others, is too compelling. Maisin are keenly aware of the dangers money can bring, of the threat it represents to their ancestral way of life. They need money; there is no turning back. Yet, at least for the time being, the Maisin appear to have been more or less successful in balancing the opposed logic of gift and commodity systems of value. As we shall see in later chapters, however, there has been a price to pay—an often acute shame over their "poverty" and a burning desire to find a road to money that nearly led the people to sell off their ancestral birthright. That the commonsense morality of reciprocity remains so powerful despite the challenges of modernity reflects in no small part the continuing vitality of intimate family relationships in Maisin village society, to which we now turn.

Notes

1. Large crocodiles are often seen in the wide river that divides Uiaku and Ganjiga, usually at night. In 1986, a teenage girl was killed while washing laundry, and in 2000 one of the up-and-coming leaders from Ganjiga was severely mauled in a crocodile attack.

2. See Chapter 3 for an example of such a story.

3. The classic work on reciprocity in Melanesia and other small-scale societies, is Marcel Mauss's *Essay on the Gift*, first published in French in 1925 and still in print (Mauss 1990 [1925]). It would be hard to find any study of a Melanesian society that does not discuss reciprocity, but works from the Trobriand Islands to the east of Collingwood Bay have been especially influential (Malinowski 1922; Weiner 1988). Discussions of gift exchange have also figured centrally in anthropological discussions of the transition to modernity (Godelier 1999; Sykes 2005).

4. At that time, the kina was worth slightly more than a US dollar. Following a series of economic crises in Papua New Guinea in the 1990s, the kina declined to less than $US.25, causing considerable economic hardship as most manufactured items are imported. The kina is currently trading at about one-third of a US dollar. The prices for locally produced items, like tapa, have gone up over the years, but nowhere near the pace of inflation.

5. Papua New Guinea is home to many rare and spectacular insects, including the Queen Alexandra butterfly; with nearly a foot-long wingspan, it is the largest bird-wing butterfly in the world and is found only in the primary rainforests of Oro Province. Since the late 1970s, hundreds of villages across the country have taken up insect farming and collecting for a growing international market in exotic insects. For more details, see the web pages of the Insect Farming and Training Agency of the Papua New Guinea Wildlife Department (http://www.ifta.com.pg/).

CHAPTER THREE

The Social Design

I brought my freshly beaten tapa back to George and Mary Rose Sevaru's house, where I was staying in 1986, and hung it on a shaded clothesline to dry. When night came, I took it down, folded it twice lengthwise, and placed it under my sleeping mat to flatten it. The next day, I hung it on the clothesline behind the house to thoroughly dry in direct sunshine. It was now ready to paint. I was delighted when Martha and Lottie agreed to help me.

I prepared by spending most of an afternoon observing Lottie designing a cloth. Lottie was a widow, probably in her late 50s at the time, who lived with her brother Lambert in a comfortably shaded house with a verandah overlooking the river. Thin but strong, she had recently undertaken her end-of-mourning ceremony, several years after the death of her husband, and proudly displayed the shell necklaces and the bright red shells lining the edge of her ears that had been placed by her in-laws to mark her full return to society. Lottie was among the last links to several diminished and abandoned traditions. As a young woman, she had acquired a V-shaped set of scars across her chest, burned on during the mourning period to honour a close relative. She had also been a participant in an interesting custom that used to take place while the men were absent from the villages during the annual grass hunt. Women who had undergone facial tattooing together—who thus formed a kind of age cohort—would gather in the bush to tattoo each others' thighs and buttocks, areas of their bodies revealed only to lovers and husbands. Lottie had learned much about designing tapa and facial tattoos from her aunt, Nita Keru, whom I had come to know and admire during my earlier fieldwork. It was pleasant to sit this day in the cool of Lambert's verandah, watching as Lottie rapidly sketched out a stunning design.

Prior to designing the cloth, women trim the edges with a knife. Often larger cloths are cut at this point into smaller pieces that tend to sell more easily in the artifact market. One begins designing a cloth by applying an outline with a black dye the Maisin call *mii*. The main ingredients are

71

Figure 3.1 Lottie Ororogo designing her cloth. (Photo by J. Barker)

charcoal, made from the dried husks of coconuts, and the leaves of a creeper called *wayangu*, found in the bush behind the villages, which produces a milky sap that turns pitch black when wet. The recipe involves cutting up a quantity of *wayangu* leaves into a bowl, cup, or coconut shell and then mixing in the charcoal and some water to produce a rather sooty black mash. Some people also add a certain type of clay found behind Sinapa village which they say improves the density of the dye. The *mii* can be used immediately or over a few days by adding water as the mash dries out. As they decompose in the pot, however, the *wayangu* leaves produce an unpleasant odour and attract flies.

Women usually design several pieces of tapa at one sitting. When I arrived at Martha's house in the late afternoon, the favoured time for designing tapa, I found her and Lottie already hard at work on their own cloths. Each of us had our own pot of *mii*. As we set to work, there was little talking. Women usually design their cloths alone. Coming up with a design takes some concentration, particularly for novices, but most women find it a peaceful and relaxing activity.

I was now ready for my lesson. I already knew that there would be little or no verbal instruction. Maisin girls learn to make tapa, along with their other tasks, by watching and imitating their elders. I had seen tapa being designed dozens of times, but as I nervously picked up my brush, I spent a few moments studying my teachers at work. A few women at this time were experimenting with commercial brushes, but I wanted to use traditional instruments — white palm twigs of varying thicknesses, with ends shaven to reveal stiff bristles.

The method of folding an *embobi* skirt results in four panels (the longer *koefi* loin cloth has eight). In Maisin villages to the east of Uiaku, many women draw across the panels so that the entire tapa is covered by a single design. Most Uiaku women, however, prefer to frame the design within the panels, replicating it four times.[1] Following the example of my teachers, I braced my back against a house post and stretched my legs out straight, a flat board across my lap and the dye bowl close to hand. Next, I folded my cloth over, leaving a single panel exposed on the smoother side that had originally formed the inner surface of the bark strip. I took up my brush in the proper position between thumb and forefinger with the pinky extended to guide the hand over the cloth, dipped the end into my pot of *mii*, and placed brush to cloth to make my first bold stroke. What emerged was an indistinct grey smudge. I tried again, this time pushing the tip of my brush well into the black mash. This resulted in a satisfactorily black line but also little piles of soot that smeared my cloth when I tried to brush them off. Moving *mii* from pot to cloth requires a knowledgeable and delicate touch.

The Maisin make only a few standardized designs, usually for ceremonial occasions. Most of these are emblems (known as *kawo* or *evovi*) belonging to specific clans who possess the sole right to make and wear them. These can never be sold or given away. A few gifted tapa designers have also created stylized representations of such things as animals or spirits, often revealed to them in dreams. Nita Keru, for instance, painted beautiful representations of butterflies, one of which now graces my study. Such special designs remain the property of the artist. Most cloths, however, bear abstract paintings. Some tapa makers etch the design on the sand or occasionally on paper prior to drawing the outline. Most just keep it in their heads.[2] Every cloth is unique, but the more prolific tapa makers develop styles that are easily recognized. Designing large cloths requires an especially impressive sense of balance and proportion. The black *mii* must be laid out in narrow parallel lines, allowing space for the red dye (*dun*) to be applied later. Designing cloth efficiently also requires a good visual memory. In Uiaku, the women tend to begin by designing a single panel. Once it is complete, they lay the cloth aside to work on another while it is drying. When they pick up the first cloth again, skilled tapa makers only glance quickly at their previous execution before turning it over to repeat the design on another panel. All four panels of an *embobi* will be completed this way, often with extremely complex designs. In the case of the eight-panelled *koefi*, only the middle six panels receive designs, usually much simpler than those on a typical woman's skirt. The panels always match fairly closely, but there are little variations, the results of tricks of memory or slight differences in the size of the panels.

I had given my design some thought already, making a preliminary sketch in my notebook. A small crowd had gathered as I began gingerly pushing the black *mii*, sooty centimetre by sooty centimetre, across the cloth. As the pattern began to emerge, despite the fits and starts, I started to relax a little. Not bad! Then I noticed that everyone had become very quiet; there was no chatting or giggles. I looked up to see the entire group, including Lottie and Martha, staring at my cloth. They were clearly puzzled. Martha ventured that I was making a mistake—I wasn't drawing the lines in a way that would contain the red dye (*dun*). I traced the edges of the parallel lines with the clean edge of my brush and she reluctantly agreed that they *were* drawn correctly. Yet she and the others continued to worry, certain that I had made a mistake. No matter how "Maisin" it appeared to me, my design clearly offended the local aesthetic sense in some way. The Maisin way of learning and associated vocabulary, however, did not allow for a very exact critique. The Maisin use only a few words to indicate design motifs—"circle," "dot," "line," and so forth. Tapa makers may praise a design or state that it is "wrong," but they cannot easily give instructions in how to make it "right."

Like a young girl, I was learning to design tapa by imitating the experts. Yet I was not a child. Simple as my design was, it was still much more ambitious than the scrawled lines of a five or six year old. Although I have never considered myself much of an artist, I had nonetheless internalized my own cultural aesthetic which, despite my good intentions, must have guided my hand as I designed my cloth.

Once the basic design was completed on all four panels, I began the tedious (at least to me) task of placing little dots of *mii* regularly along the outer edges of the parallel lines. Adding the dots, known as *sufifi*, is always done and is another indication of an underlying aesthetic at work. When I finished, I placed my tapa on the sand to dry in the hot sun, close to the several pieces Lottie and Martha had decorated during my labours. Martha spread a mat under her house and began to bring out some refreshments. Lottie pulled a completed tapa from her string bag and laid it out for me to sit on. It was the beautiful piece I had watched her design a few days earlier. Following Maisin custom, once I sat on the cloth, I owned it.

The design on a tapa cloth bears a number of similarities to that of a society. The circumstance of making a tapa and the form the design take are always somewhat unique. Yet clearly there are social conventions that guide the creation of tapa and aesthetic judgements of the quality of particular designs. These conventions do not exist in written law codes or constitutions. They are passed between the generations and are learned so thoroughly and unconsciously that people do not need to reflect upon them. They form a type of common sense. The main job of a social anthropologist is to discover and explore these underlying rules and conventions. We can rely only partly on what people can explicitly tell us about their social norms and expectations, although this is extremely important. We must also look for patterns in behaviour as well as the ways that typical behaviours sometimes contradict what people think ought to happen. Life even in apparently "simple" societies like those found in rural Papua New Guinea is amazingly complex. All the same, we find certain patterns in the ways that people deal with complexity, certain deeply held values and conventions that provide guidelines for living. The challenges and opportunities of life lead to both the reproduction and transformation of such values over time. Maisin society is not unlike a tapa cloth. It is simultaneously old and new, conventional and innovative, the product of a constant dialogue between ancestral frameworks and shifting experience.

Also like a tapa cloth, a society is composed of basic elements that fit together to produce a whole. In this chapter, I continue my survey of the basic cultural patterns of Maisin society by examining three key facets of contemporary social organization: the socialization of children into gendered adults, the formation of kin-based groups and categories, and the formation of alliances between groups through marriage exchanges and life-crisis ceremonies. While much has changed in Maisin society over the past century, the patterns that we will examine here demonstrate that the conventions of social organization have proven amazingly resilient, providing one of the strongest links to the ancestral past.

MAKING SOCIAL PERSONS

The Maisin love children. As people became more comfortable with Anne and me, they often expressed pity that we were childless. This concern at one point gave rise to a rumour which, as rumours tend to do, swept through the entire village with preternatural speed. I was across the river working in Ganjiga when I heard "Annie's pregnant!" I rushed back home to inform my very surprised wife of the happy news! Of course, people were disappointed by the truth but much relieved upon my return in 1997 to learn that, nine years earlier, we had finally had a child. The Maisin consider it a very bad thing to be alone. Orphans, unmarried adults, and childless couples appear anomalous and vulnerable. Folk tales often centre upon orphans who are forced to leave their villages because they have no parents to feed them. By the same token, the Maisin fret that childless couples will be left with no one to care for them when they become too old and feeble to work in their gardens. Such a calamity never happens in reality. The dense networks of kinship and exchange that link villagers assure that the weak and infirm are cared for. Almost all childless couples and elderly couples are given children to adopt by close relatives. No one is deliberately left alone. Still, the concern is tangible. It is a very bad thing to shun one's kin and neighbours. The Maisin are apt to scorn such individuals as "rubbish" or to fear them, for it is well known that sorcerers prefer their own company.

A moral person, for the Maisin, is one who interacts with others. As we saw in the previous chapter, the Maisin take exchange to be the paradigmatic interaction. Put most simply, the job of turning a child into a social person requires incorporating them into exchange networks and teaching them the values of reciprocity. Caregivers typically scold a child who grabs for food or refuses to share something with others with the phrase, *saa tamatan ka—*"Not human!" Similarly, people speak of adults who act selfishly as being no better than dogs and pigs. To be human in this highly cooperative culture is to engage in exchange.

In that sense, a newly born baby is not yet socially human.[3] Its conception results from the mingling of fluids in the womb, a balanced donation of blood from the mother and semen from the father. Since women are assumed to possess a large quantity of blood, the Maisin say that pregnancy requires several acts of intercourse with the same man to bring the semen into balance. Too much semen, however, will harm the fetus. A newly born child is considered to be very vulnerable to attacks from spirits as its soul is not yet fully attached to its body.[4] Those attending the birth — usually experienced female relatives and, unusual for Melanesia, the father — take precautions. During the birth and for a few days of confinement afterwards, the mother is surrounded by kin both to take care of her and to ward off spiritual attacks, especially at night when sorcerers and spirits are most active. The umbilical cord and placenta are wrapped in tapa and taken to the bush to be buried or placed high in a tree. If these are eaten by animals, the Maisin say the spirit will not attach properly and the child will suffer from madness. The person who takes the package into the bush must return by the same route, acting as a guide to the child's spirit which might otherwise become lost. About a week after the birth, if everything goes well, the mother places her baby comfortably on a pillow in a string bag and carries it to her garden. At each fork or crossroad in the path, she places a token to help the baby's spirit find its way home — crossed sticks representing spears for a boy and grass rings, symbolizing the straps used to carry bundles of firewood, for a girl. After spending some time in the garden, the mother calls out, "Come, we'll go home now!" She'll do this every time she goes to the garden until the baby begins to smile and recognize people, the sign that body and spirit are now firmly united (Tietjen 1985).

A baby remains in this nebulous state of not being firmly human for upwards of a year. If it dies during this period — a not uncommon tragedy in an area of endemic malaria and other tropical diseases — the parents bury the child quietly in the bush. During this time, the baby remains nameless. Its acquisition of a name signals the parents' confidence that it will survive. Anthropologists often learn of basic cultural patterns by making mistakes and being corrected. This is how we found out about the delay in the naming of babies. Our friend Frieda gave birth to a lively baby girl. We asked the baby's older sister, Iris, for her name. She answered, "*Amura.*" For several days, we spoke of Amura, whose vaguely French-sounding name we thought matched her beauty. When Frieda got wind of this, she paid us a visit. "Who told you her name is Amura," she demanded. "*Amura* means 'nothing'! They were telling you the baby doesn't have a name yet." A few weeks later, Frieda and Gideon decided to name their daughter "Ani Baka," after Anne. As we'll see later in this chapter, people who use reciprocal kinship terms are expected to have very close and supportive relationships. The same is true of namesakes.

A mother typically breastfeeds a new child for 18 months to two years. She provides the main source of care during this period, but increasingly over

Figure 3.2 Children playing on a sleeping pig. (Photo by J. Barker)

time other members of the household and extended family pitch in. The Maisin say that an infant possesses little *mon seramon*, the combination of mental and physical ability necessary for survival. The provision of food and guidance is required to shape and strengthen not only a child's *mon seramon* but also his or her physical appearance. Unlike Western culture, the Maisin do not associate physical and personality traits with biological parentage. They refer to an adopted child as someone who is "fed" by their foster parents and thus grows up to resemble them. This nurturing relationship is conceptualized as an exchange. During the time of dependence, a child should respond with "respect" (*muan*) to her caregivers, an attitude that comes more easily as the child develops and her *mon seramon* takes form. The huge debt incurred during childhood is expected to be reciprocated later in the form of labour, food, and other types of support for aging parents and senior relatives. The Maisin never let their grown children forget this debt.

For all that, childhood is a time of great freedom. From the moment they can walk, infants spend much of their days in the company of other children, freely roaming about the village and gardens under the watchful eye of older siblings or cousins. They play games, visit relatives who give them treats, and take long naps when it pleases them. The degree of liberty can be surprising for a Westerner. I have never gotten used to the sight of a three- or four-year-old child strolling through the village, whacking house posts and trees with a large knife — something that bothers the Maisin not at all. Adults do pay attention. They scold children when they interfere with the day's work or make a nuisance of themselves ("Not human!"), lavishly praise them when they join in some activity, take pleasure in their antics, and soothe their wailing when they have a tumble. What they don't do much is instruct them. Young children learn adult tasks primarily by watching, mimicking adult behaviours, and pitching in. As they get older, they are given more responsibilities. By the time they are around eight or nine, for instance, children should be caring for their own garden plots.

When they turn six or seven, children encounter a very different mode of interaction in the community school. There they receive authoritative instruction in the mysteries of letters and numbers from a teacher who does not provide gifts of food and advice in exchange for their obedience. Their time and behaviour while on the school grounds is highly regimented. Those who break the rules, by skipping school or mocking the teacher, are subject to discipline. Rather than an exchange relationship, the school is based upon the singular authority of the teachers and, beyond them, the state. Different as this is, few children seem to have trouble making the transition. Whatever they learn in the classroom, the style of authority and instruction does not appear to carry over into daily life in the villages. By the time they attend school, children have already internalized the main values of their culture.

Making Female and Male Persons: Gender Roles

Young boys and girls spend a great deal of time in each other's company. Sisters and brothers tend to be especially close, an alliance that continues into adulthood. From a very early age, however, children are prodded into gendered roles. Walking through the village, one comes across little girls sweeping up debris around the houses or little boys hurling short spears at fish in the river. Girls are inevitably the first to be put to work, usually helping their mothers by caring for younger infants, cooking, making mats, or any of the myriad other tasks that fall to women. Boys enjoy their freedom longer, but by their mid-teens they will be assisting their fathers on hunting and fishing trips and helping with house repairs and construction.

Many youths today spend a considerable part of their adolescence away from the villages attending distant high schools. The boys and girls who remain behind live largely separate lives. Teenage boys enjoy considerably more freedom of action than girls. One frequently sees or hears them roaming in groups through the villages late at night. In some cases, a group of male friends will build their own house as an independent base of action.[5] In the past, dances provided the main opportunity for romantic liaisons. Young people would don decorations and gather on the beaches for celebrations lasting through the night, especially during full moons. If a couple were attracted to each other they would arrange to meet later. Girls often took the initiative in organizing trysts in the bush or even the girl's house, often using a younger sibling as a go-between. Today there are probably more opportunities for young people to get together — at sports meets and Christian fellowship meetings, for example — but few that are not under the watchful eyes of parents. Most adults disapprove of premarital sex, an attitude almost certainly not held by their ancestors. Still, judging from the gossip and number of babies born to single mothers, it still goes on.[6]

The Maisin used to mark the transition to adulthood with special rites of passage. The most elaborate of these, the *kisevi*, still occasionally takes place to celebrate a couple's first-born child. I'll discuss the *kisevi* later in the context of marriage exchanges. According to several very old informants, clans also used to initiate their younger male members in a ceremony in which elders would decorate them and then share a feast. Girls had their own distinctive rite of passage, which Anne and I were fortunate enough to observe in the early 1980s just before it was abandoned (Barker and Tietjen 1990). Tattooing was a widespread custom across the Pacific Islands, including in Papua New Guinea (Barton 1918; Gell 1993). In Collingwood Bay, girls received elaborate tattoos that covered their entire faces with graceful blue-black swirls and geometric designs. This painful operation, which Anne witnessed, required enormous self-control on the part of the recipient. After tracing a design on the girl's face, the tattooist used a needle to break the skin and push dye underneath, wiping away blood as she proceeded. After allowing scabs to form and fall off and the swelling to subside, the tattooist repeated the operation, upwards of ten times in all, over a period of a month to six weeks. Usually several girls were tattooed together, remaining secluded in the tattooist's house during the operation. Upon completion, the girls were richly decorated in traditional finery, their faces anointed with coconut oil to enhance the sheen of their skin and better bring out the lines of the tattoo. As they proudly displayed their new faces around the village over the next two weeks, the Maisin would say that they were now ready for marriage and adulthood.

Puberty ceremonies serve a variety of purposes. The long-abandoned male initiations were organized by leaders in the name of their clans. They served to tie boys to their clans while reinforcing a sense of allegiance among the adult members. The tattooing custom was different. It was organized independently by households for their daughters and was not accompanied by public celebrations, feasting, or ceremonial exchanges. Its overt purpose was to make the girls attractive by replacing their "blank faces" with ones designed by the tattooist.[7] The tattoo also symbolized the strength and endurance required of female adulthood. The custom lapsed, I was told, because during the 1970s and 1980s so many girls left the villages to attend high school and to marry.[8] All the same, Maisin women still take a lot of pride in their distinctive facial designs. I have been told, but have never checked it out, that there is a woman in a non-Maisin village to the east whose face is only half tattooed. Maisin women tell of how she was able to endure the pain only so far before fleeing. She was not strong, they say. Not like them!

It is certainly true that adult women need to be tough. They work extremely hard compared to most men. Around 1905, the Anglican lay missionary, Percy John Money, took a photograph he labelled "Man the Protector — Woman the Porter." It depicts a man with a spear flung over his shoulder walking ahead of a woman whose shoulders are sagging under the weight of a loaded string bag, with a child riding on top. This was Money's best known photograph, reproduced in several books and a popular regional trade magazine, the *Pacific Islands Monthly*. Hardly a day passed during my visits to Uiaku where I have not witnessed an identical scene. Walk to the beach at dusk and you are sure to see women, singly or in small groups, returning from a hard day's work in the gardens and straining under heavy loads of food and firewood as they head home to make the evening meal.

When not tending gardens, bearing loads, or cooking, the women are engaged in a long list of other tasks: repairing mats, beating tapa, mending clothes, making string bags, and so forth. Unlike men, who spend pleasant evenings and sometimes days visiting friends, women have few opportunities for socializing. Socializing in any case usually entails more work. Public ceremonies like bride-price exchanges or church festivals provide women with the best opportunities to mingle with kin and friends but always in the context of preparing and cooking food. Men seem to have it pretty good. Consider another archetypical scene: the village meeting. The seating arrangement speaks volumes. Senior men arrange themselves comfortably on the raised floor of a covered shelter, where they are cooled by passing breezes. Younger men lounge nearby, under the shade of trees. Women and children sit further out on the ground, finding whatever shade they can, straining to hear the talk on the shelter. Usually, the men on the shelter do all of the talking. When the meeting ends, after several hours of conversation, young women bring refreshments. Climbing up to the platform at the end furthest from the men, they carry platters of tea and cups and crawl on their knees across the rough surface with eyes downcast, showing respect for the seniority of the males.

The evidence of inequality and exploitation appears so obvious that it might seem perverse to suggest that things might not be quite what they seem. Yet this is exactly what most modern anthropologists do suggest. While women were not entirely ignored in the early years of research in Melanesia, their status only became a specific focus after the 1960s, spurred in large part by the rise of feminism in Western countries and an increasing number of female anthropologists working in the region. The ethnographic literature on gender relations both in traditional and changing Melanesian communities is now extensive (e.g., Errington and Gewertz 1987; Lepowsky 1993; Strathern 1987). It is enlivened by passionate debates over the nature of the inequalities that seem to mark sex roles and whether the lot of women has improved or deteriorated in the aftermath of the many changes that have arrived in the wake of the colonial takeover. Still, there is consensus that women's experiences need to be grasped as far as possible from their own point of view in terms of the ways in which women perceive and act on the circumstances of their lives—the ways they exercise *agency*.

Maisin women are perfectly aware that they do the bulk of work. They often complain about men's "laziness." They usually do this in a teasing manner, but when the work loads become too oppressive the joking turns quickly to open complaint. Constrained as they are by the conventional sexual division of labour and by male domination of public political talk, Maisin women are not without power. Indeed, compared to women in some other Papua New Guinea societies, they enjoy a fairly high level of security and influence. In part, this is because there has been much intermarriage within Maisin villages. While women normally move to their husband's area upon marriage, they usually have kin living nearby who watch out for them and their children and to whom they can return if the marriage turns abusive.[9] Women also bring very tangible assets into a marriage. Although they cannot pass property to their own children, they do retain use rights to their fathers' lands, which greatly increases the pool of garden land available to a household. In addition, women bring in money by selling tapa cloth and by receiving remittances from relatives in town. A woman who is pushed too hard can refuse to work in her husband's garden, shame him by scolding him in public, and ultimately return to her father's place. Maisin men often talk about "belting" their wives when angered, but I have seen very few instances of physical abuse (it is almost impossible to keep such things quiet in the intimate environment of the villages, although the gardens are another story). Men who are known for ordering their wives around are often belittled by others (including other men) as "rubbish." Ideally and normally, as far as I'm aware, wives and husbands confer over shared labour like garden expansion, their children's progress in school, and household finances. Most also talk in the privacy of their homes and garden shelters about village affairs. While women are expected to remain silent during village meetings, most arrive with some knowledge and often strong opinions about the issues under discussion.

Women and men in Maisin society adhere to a set of behavioural expectations. Still, they are not robots. Personalities differ, often considerably. The cultural system tends to favour meek women and assertive men, but the opposite is sometimes true and, within limits, not considered improper. Many of my best informants on matters of politics, history, and religion have been women who, usually in the semi-public space of their house verandahs, speak freely and openly, whether in the presence of their husbands or alone. Generally as they get older, women have more latitude to speak out. The Maisin are especially respectful of elderly women, who are valued for the depth of their knowledge of traditions. Yet even younger women can be assertive, especially when they feel that their husbands are not providing sufficient support for themselves and their children. Take the example of "Alice" (a pseudonym), the youngest of three wives in one of the five polygynous families living in Uiaku in the early 1980s. Spunky and funny, Alice was not afraid to bend gender rules on occasion. One day I heard women shrieking. I ran to the riverbank, thinking that someone had drowned or been attacked by a crocodile. Instead, I stood witness with a crowd of very upset women as Alice waded ashore with her co-wives, each bearing a string of small fish for their supper. The rule is that only men can fish. The women shouting abuse were ashamed and furious at Alice. She calmly and defiantly faced down their fury. Her husband had been away in town for more than a month, she declared, and few of his clan brothers had helped out with providing meat to his large family, so the women had done it for themselves. This was an enormously gutsy act in a culture where people feel public shaming keenly and fear retaliation from sorcerers for individualistic acts. Still, Alice had made her point. Her husband's brothers should have been helping out more. They did so now, and the incident was not repeated.

Not surprisingly, Maisin men almost universally support the gender status quo. Yet so do most women. Middle-aged and senior women are able to exercise a considerable amount of authority over their daughters and even more over daughters-in-law. They are quick to criticize (usually loudly) any sign of laziness or immodesty on the part of younger women under their command. If you ask villagers why they should treat men and women so differently, you will certainly get their universal answer for this type of question: "It's our tradition. It came from the ancestors." Probe a little further, however, and you uncover a more complex set of assumptions about the complementarity of the sexes.

Complementarity is implied in conception beliefs, the idea that a child comes about through the equal mixing of a women's blood and a man's semen — male and female are understood as essentially different but required to complete each other. This assumption underlies a series of other popular beliefs. Thus, the Maisin tend to associate females with soft perishable materials and men with hard and more durable products, that is, tapa cloth and mats as opposed to shell money and drums, each made by the opposite sex. As in many Melanesian societies, the Maisin consider male and female essences to be dangerous to one another in certain circumstances. Thus, a man should not step over his pregnant wife nor a woman ever step over her husband for fear of causing sickness. Women face a few more restrictions then men. They should not bathe upstream from men, and it is thought that they will destroy the usefulness of hunting or fishing spears if they step over them. Compared to many Melanesian societies, however, the restrictions surrounding interactions between the sexes are quite relaxed. Indeed, the expectation that husbands assist in their children's births is extraordinary in a cultural region noted for male fears of female blood. By the same token, women do not go into seclusion when menstruating, although I am told their husbands or lovers tend to avoid sex during their periods.

The Maisin tend to speak of gender complementarity in practical terms. Men and women need each other to survive. Beyond that, they need each other to be human. During the evenings, elders convey this lesson in the popular folk stories. Here is an example:

The man cleared an area. He left the rubbish to dry and then set fire to it. He worked very hard indeed. He cleared a very large garden and soon it began producing food. But the man grew tired of this work and took to hanging around the village. His wife would go to the garden to harvest the taro. With nowhere to plant them, she had to leave the taro tops, which soon began to rot. She complained, "Husband, I cut off the taro tops but now they are rotting." Yet husband paid no attention. He merely slept the nights through and spent the days visiting friends in the village. Eventually the wife finished the taro. She told her husband, but he paid no mind and kept hanging around the village day after day. Soon they were out of food.

One day, the wife called her children. "This afternoon, we will go to where some people have cut down sago palms. We will collect the ends of the logs and use whatever pith remains to make sago. Once we have eaten, we will feel awake and strong again. Then we can sleep well." So off they went. They spied the remains of a sago log that had been beaten for its pith. The mother said to her children, "Wait. I will look for a yaau" (a stick used to pry off the hard outer bark of the sago palm). As soon as she broke through the bush to the cut sago, she transformed herself into a grunting pig. The children also became pigs. Their mother called to them and they followed her into the bush. (Related by Frederick Bogara, 1 January 1982)

This story centres upon a key difference between humans and pigs. Both take food from gardens, but only humans have the ability to make new gardens from old. The reproduction of gardens, however, depends upon the cooperation of men and women performing their complementary tasks. This story portrays the husband and wife working completely separately. The husband makes the garden; his wife harvests it. Yet the garden cannot be reproduced without the aid of the man's digging stick to replant taro tops. The household soon consumes the entire taro crop and, with no means of reproducing it, faces starvation. The woman and her children are reduced to scrounging food from the debris left from making sago which, not incidentally, also attracts bush pigs. Hence, they become pigs themselves. The breakdown of the cooperative, procreative relationship between woman and man is thus equated in the story to the diminishing of the distinction between human and animal.

The larger lesson here is that, for the Maisin, personhood is not given by nature; it is made in the context of social relationships. Men and women do different sorts of things that together make society possible. Yet, as persons, they also share common moral ideals. Good persons respect and follow the advice of their elders and, when they themselves become elders, care for those who are younger by providing the necessities of life and sound advice. Good persons also treat others of their own generation generously, sharing and receiving to bring themselves into the state of social amity and equivalence that the Maisin call *marawa-wawe*. People learn these values in the context of their families. So it is to this next level of social organization we must now turn.

ALL IN THE FAMILY: KINSHIP AND DESCENT

When visiting Uiaku in July 2000, our son Jake was delighted to learn that he had scores of "fathers," "mothers," "sisters," and "brothers" living in the community. Maisin families resemble those found in Western countries in many respects. With few exceptions, people spend most of their lives as part of a nuclear family consisting of a mother, father, and their children sharing a common household. Yet, as in the case of most small-scale societies, the Maisin have a much more extended understanding and experience of family relations than Jake was used to. In part, this is the outcome of generations of intermarriage within and between Maisin villages. Everyone is related to everyone else, often in myriad ways. However, it is also a reflection of the culturally specific ways in which the Maisin think of family. Most people in

Western countries distinguish between close family members and extended kin. The Maisin make no such distinction. In fact, they have no word that corresponds to the English "family." The kinship terminology we use also differentiates between one's nuclear family and more distant relatives.[10] English-speakers distinguish siblings from cousins and parents from aunts and uncles. As opposed to this "descriptive" kinship terminology system, the Maisin employ a "classificatory" scheme that groups categories of relatives along generational lines. Thus, by virtue of our adoption by some Maisin families, Jake happily discovered that he had many "parents" and many "siblings."

As an undergraduate student, I found the study of kinship both fascinating and daunting. All humans have families, but there exists a wide range of cultural variation. Anthropologists have developed a very sophisticated set of techniques for classifying and diagramming kinship systems. Yet understanding another people's ideas about families as they play out in real life presents a special challenge, I suspect, because to do so we must come to grips with some of our most deeply held assumptions about human nature. If you have spent your life assuming that families are biological units, as most Westerners do, it takes a bit of a leap to appreciate a system that applies only secondary importance to blood relationships. In dealing with a community in which kinship terms do not distinguish between close and distant relatives, you have to remind yourself that the Maisin word for, say, "mother" conveys a rather different sense than its closest English equivalent.

This does not present a problem, of course, for a child who grows up knowing nothing but the local kinship system. The Maisin employ a variation of the "Iroquois-Dravidian" kinship terminology, the most common type in the world. This kind of system makes distinctions on the basis of generation, seniority, and sex. Put most simply, you refer to members of generations relative to your own by separate sets of kin terms. Within those sets, you make further distinctions on the basis of relative age and sex. Thus, as a Maisin male, I would refer to my biological father, his brothers, and all of the men he calls "brother" by the term, *yabi*.[11] I would refer to my mother, her sisters, and every woman she calls "sister" by the term *yo*. However, I would refer to the opposite sex siblings of my father *or* mother by the term, *yaya* (that is to say, my father's sister or mother's brother). Turning to the generation after me, my male children as well as the children of my brothers and those men I call "brother" are referred to as *teiti* (son) or *morobi* (daughter). I would refer to my sister's children, however, as *yaya*—that is, by the same term that they use for me. Relationships marked by the use of reciprocal terms tend to be especially warm and supportive. Grandparents, for instance, share a common term—*abu*—with their children's children. Those who call each other *abu*, or more often by the familiar "*bu-bu*," greatly enjoy each other's company.

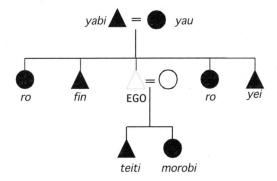

a) Maisin kinship reference terminology
in the immediate (nuclear) family

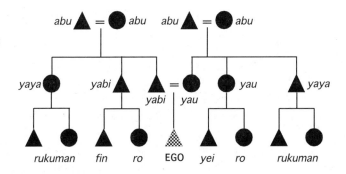

b) Maisin kinship terminology in the extended family,
indicating parallel and cross-cousins

Figure 3.3 Maisin kinship terminology.

Maisin kinship terms vary somewhat depending on whether one is referring to someone else or addressing them directly. The diagrams above set out reference terms. In standard anthropological kinship diagrams, the triangles represent males, the circles indicate females, and the equal sign stands for a marriage. Each level represents a generation, moving from oldest at the top to youngest at the bottom. Younger siblings are positioned to the left, older to the right. Maisin also have special terms for in-laws. Husbands and wives, for instance, are known as *fafi* and *sauki*.

Kinship terms are relative, dependent upon who is speaking. These diagrams assume that "Ego" is a male. If "Ego" were female, she would refer to her male siblings and parallel cousins as *ro* and her female siblings and parallel cousins as *fin* or *yei*.

Things get most interesting on one's own generational level. Again, assume that I am a Maisin male. I refer to my sister as *ro*. This is another reciprocal term: she also calls me *ro*. The relationship between brothers and sisters in Maisin culture is generally very supportive. In contrast, I refer to my brothers by two different terms depending on their age relative to my own: as *yei* (older) or *fin* (younger). The term I use for siblings thus depends upon, first, their gender relative to my own and, second, their relative age if they are of the same sex as myself. Thus, if you are female, you refer to your brother as *ro* and older and younger sisters as *yei* and *fin* respectively. Things become slightly more complex when the categories get extended beyond immediate family to the people who, in English, we call cousins. The children of your father's brothers or mother's sisters are technically known as "parallel-cousins" while the children of your parent's opposite-sex siblings — that is, the children of those people you call *yaya* — are "cross-cousins." Cross-cousins share a reciprocal term, *rukaman*. Boys and girls often count *rukaman* among their closest friends. The relationship involves a great deal of joking and sexual banter during adolescence and beyond. In contrast, you address parallel-cousins using sibling terms, with one significant twist. The seniority of same-gender parallel-cousins is determined by the relation of their parent to your own, not by the actual age of the cousin. Thus, as a male, I refer to all of the male children of my father's older brother as *yei* and to all of the male children of his younger brother as *fin*, regardless of their actual ages. A cousin I call my *yei* might be younger — considerably younger — than me and vice versa.[12]

In Western culture, people often assume that kin terms correspond to biological descent, the main exception being cases of adoption. The broadest category used is "cousin," a term that potentially includes a vast array of people. Yet unless there is some evidence of shared ancestry, we do not regard the people Westerners typically interact with as relatives. The Maisin system is both more embracing and flexible. Most Maisin are able to trace descent only back to their grandparents and occasionally great-grandparents' generation. One refers to all of the living descendents of one's grandparents as *taa besse* — literally, "blood-same." These people form a kind of "security circle" for individuals, a group of relatives you can count on to come to your defence if you are attacked and to help you out with food and labour when needed.[13] The *taa besse* also marks the boundary for the incest taboo, the point at which sexual activities become permissible. Once they move to relatives beyond the *taa besse*, people usually cannot account for the kin terms they use with reference to actual shared ancestry; they instead take their cue from others. Thus if a man I call "father" (*yabi*) refers to another man as his "older brother" (*yei*), I know that I should also call that man *yabi* and refer to *his* male children as my "older brothers." Given the dense network of kin and marriage ties and the flexibility of the system, people often can come up with two or more possible kin terms for a particular person. Depending on circumstances, two distantly related women of the same age might thus refer to each other as older or younger sisters, as mother and daughter, or as cross-cousins. This is not a case of anything goes: the terms need to be plausible and both parties need to agree to them. The system, however, permits for a degree of negotiation unknown in European terminology systems.

It is a simple matter to incorporate newcomers into the system. Soon after Anne and I arrived in Uiaku, some of the older folk began to call us "daughter" and "son." We soon reciprocated. From there it was an easy matter to figure out what to call other people, mostly by following the lead of our fictive kin. In theory, the system has no limits. In their more enthusiastic moments, the Maisin talk about how conversion to Christianity made them *roisesinamme*, "brothers and sisters," to the entire world — a conceit that, given the expansive nature of the kinship system, is something more than a metaphor. Still, the fact that the Maisin can and often do address each other by kin terms does not mean that they form one big family.[14] Individuals are perfectly aware of the differences between near and distant kin and act accordingly. The encompassing levels of kin generally correspond with the sorts of reciprocal relationships we examined in Chapter 2. *Taa besse* generally operate within the zone of generalized reciprocity, characterized by freely given mutual support between close kin. The further out one goes, the fewer the interactions, the greater the insistence upon balanced reciprocity, and the less a sense of moral connection.

Descent Groups

The circle of kin that radiates outward from every individual is unique to themselves. This is because one's "kindred" — all those relatives traced through one's parents — are relative to a person's position in a family network. Siblings within a nuclear family come closest to sharing a common kindred, but even here there are slight differences in the terms they use depending upon their relative seniority and gender. Kinship terminology diagrams thus always specify an "*ego*" as a point of reference. All individuals draw upon their extended kin networks for various kinds of assistance, albeit to differing degrees. However, as in most small-scale societies, the Maisin also use principles of descent to organize themselves into more stable and well-defined social groups. Specifically, they follow a unilineal rule of patrilineal descent, in which ancestry is traced through a series of male links. This is the most common pattern found in Papua New Guinea, although many of the societies to the east of the Maisin have matrilineal systems in which descent is traced through female links. One also finds several examples of cognatic descent systems, in which groups trace their descent from either male or female ancestors.

The Maisin refer to descent groups as *iyon*, a word that they usually translate as "clan" and sometimes as "tribe." Such glosses, however, are misleading if we think of a clan or tribe as a distinct bounded group. *Iyon* is better translated as "division." The Maisin are born into a hierarchy of such divisions. Depending on the circumstances, when a person speaks of his or her *iyon*, they may be referring to a group of households headed by brothers, to members of a village hamlet, or to one of several larger groups whose membership spans across the Maisin villages and beyond. It is usually clear from the context what level of grouping they are referring to. Each level of the hierarchy derives from a more distant founding ancestor and thus includes an ever-broadening range of lower-level descent groups.

It is useful here to make a distinction between a descent *group* and descent *category* (Keesing 1975: 29). A descent group is a going concern in which members know and associate with each other and hold common property and rights. Members of a descent category, on the other hand, tend to live apart and rarely if ever come together as a group. They possess less common property, and their association is mostly important as a political point of reference. For the Maisin, the line between group and category is fuzzy and shifting, but for all practical purposes every villager identifies with a hierarchy of two or more lower-level groups and at least one higher-level category. The closer the shared ancestor, the smaller and more tightly knit the descent group.

The basic principles of Maisin descent groups are pretty straightforward. One can discern three levels in which groups or categories get defined in distinct ways and take on different functions. The smaller and more cohesive type of descent group is made up of all the male descendents, and their female progeny (although not the children born to the females), of a direct male ancestor, usually a grandfather. Technically, such a group whose members can trace their genealogical links reliably to an apical ancestor is known as a "lineage." Almost all males build their houses as close as possible to their father's upon marriage—a rule known as post-marital patrilocal residence.[15] A man's wife remains a member of her own father's lineage, but once bride-price is paid, her children become members of the husband's group. Larger hamlets in Maisin villages are typically made up of clusters of houses belonging to lineage members who usually cooperate closely, making gardens together, pitching in when a house needs to be built or repaired, helping out when one of their brother's households is short of food, and so forth. Those lineage members who have migrated to town also form part of this tightly knit group; migrants in paid employment are expected to send gifts of money and commodities to those people they have grown up knowing as "fathers" and "brothers" within the lineage. As generations succeed each other, most tangible property passes down through the lineage. Fathers bequeath garden lands to their sons or, if they have no sons or the sons leave for the city, to the sons of their brothers. A man's fruiting trees, hunting spears, drums, magic, and other practical items usually pass down in the same lines.

Important as they are, lineages are not named, perhaps because they are impermanent. As generations succeed each other — as what was for one generation a fondly remembered grandfather becomes a great-grandfather, the memory of whose name gradually fades — older lineages break apart and new ones form. In contrast, "clans," which comprise the second level of descent group in Maisin society, do bear names and are thought of as permanent. They are conceived as all of the descendents of the first ancestors to emerge from an underground cave at the dawn of time, after whom they are named. Maisin clans include at least two lineages, but usually several more and no doubt many others that have become extinct and are forgotten. While a handful of elders may possess genealogical knowledge linking all present members back to the founding ancestor, for the most part people simply accept the fact they belong to their father's clan.[16] Most clans form co-resident groups which occupy their own areas within villages and, in a couple of cases, entire villages. A few of the large clans have branches in two or more communities. Many clans are further broken down into sections descended from the sons of the founder and ranked accordingly from junior to senior.

People often told me that land is held and passed down at the clan level, but a close study of actual patterns of inheritance showed that this is not true. Except in small clans (which operate much like lineages), clan-mates tend to cooperate only on special occasions that involve feasting and formal exchanges with other clans. Clans do possess important property which they pass down through time, but it is more symbolic than tangible. Clans find their main legitimacy in oral traditions concerning their origins. Along with a number of other cultures in Oro Province, the Maisin believe that their ancestors originally lived underground at a site near the Musa River to the west of Collingwood Bay. According to the histories related by elders, the ancestors emerged in possession of a number of emblems and ritual prerogatives, the most distinctive of which are clan tapa designs known as *evovi*. A clan's estate may also include certain designs carved in wood or stone; names; special types of spatulas (used to spoon lime into one's mouth to chew with betelnut); forms of magic, songs, and ritual actions; and certain birds or plants to which the group shows "respect" by refusing to use or eat them.[17]

Figure 3.4 Nigel Bairan and Priscilla Gaure wearing *kawo*, Ganjiga village, 1986. Note the *evovi* tapa design, the positioning of the large cowry shells, and the rooster plumes held in the teeth. These are all *kawo* emblems belonging to a specific branch of the Rerebin clan. (Photo by J. Barker)

Collectively, such items and actions are known as *kawo*—a much used and complex concept which in this context means something like "emblem." Some of these *kawo* may strike outsiders as rather esoteric. For instance, one clan claims the exclusive right to hold torches in both hands. I learned to be very careful around members of the Wofun clan after inadvertently acquiring a lovely tapa by praising its design; it turned out that one of their *kawo* obliges them to give away any object that is openly admired. In theory, the *kawo* belonging to each clan are distinctive. The emblems provide clan members with an eternal identity associated with a primordial past. In practice, there is actually a lot of overlapping that in turn gives rise to the occasional dispute over ownership. Still, the principle is clear: clan members share a common essence, which is confirmed in their histories and in the tangible presence of *kawo*. This common identity is further affirmed in the belief that sexual relations within a clan—even when the partners are not closely related—forms a type of incest. Clans are defined in no small part as the largest exogamous descent groups, that is, groups whose members must seek marriage partners from outside, from other clans.

Lineages and clans form descent *groups*. The highest and broadest level of association recognized by the Maisin, on the other hand, forms a *category*, as members at this level never come together as a whole. The most significant of these associations are not descendents of a common ancestor but early confederacies of clans. After clans emerged from underground, according to the common accounts, they settled for a period along different stretches of the Musa River. Those who settled along the upper (*wo*) reaches are known as *Wo ari Kawo*. They eventually made their way as a group across land to Collingwood Bay. Clans settling along the middle (*me*) section of the Musa became known as *Mera ari Kawo*. They broke into two groups, one going down the Musa and then around Cape Nelson and the other crossing behind Mount Victory and then coming south along the coast to the bay. Some Maisin also speak of a third group, *Yun Fofo* ("water that is dirty"), that settled near the mouth of the river and also came into Collingwood Bay by sea. Others, however, group these clans with *Mera ari Kawo*.

In the old days according to Maisin elders, *Wo ari Kawo* and *Mera ari Kawo* engaged in competitive food exchanges with each other. They were "food enemies" (*ruan rawa*) whose leaders garnered prestige in competitive feasts marked by days of dancing and feasting, culminating in a massive gift of raw food. The aim of the organizers was to create a spectacle and to give away more food than the opposing side could possibly match when their turn came about, a principle that also informs potlatching among the Aboriginal nations on the northwest coast of North America. Leaders of the confederacies also sponsored even more spectacular inter-tribal feasts with non-Maisin villages in the region, sometimes to create alliances and sometimes to make peace after a period of hostilities.

These functions have long lapsed, but the oral traditions concerning Maisin origins and the grand old days of warfare and feasting continue to provide the basis for a key political and ritual distinction between two types of clans within the confederacies, known respectively as *Kawo* and *Sabu*.[18] By tradition, *Kawo* clans have the right to host feasts and ceremonial dances in their hamlet plazas. In the old days, they commanded the labour and dancing skills of their associated *Sabu* for food competitions and inter-tribal feasts. Members of the *Kawo* clans hold a number of emblems and prerogatives, which, like those for individual clans, are known as *kawo*. These include the right to wear rooster plumes in one's headdress when dancing, to speak first during public gatherings, to trim the edges of house thatch, and to erect a special ceremonial house during feasts. Because feasts provided the means by which the Maisin forged alliances and made peace, *Kawo* clans are also referred to as either "peace-makers" (*Sinan ari Kawo*) or as owners of the drum (*Ira ari Kawo*). *Sabu* clans lack special emblems but were considered to be leaders in warfare. They are thus also known as *Ganan ari Kawo*, holders of the fighting spear. The Maisin today often refer to the leading men of *Kawo* clans as "chiefs." Such men are respected and have influence; however, they are not chiefs in the usual sense of the term as they do not inherit an office and their effective authority is quite limited.

Strictly speaking, the two large divisions of Maisin society are not descent constructs as they are not based on descent from a single ancestor. All the same, people treat them as if they formed descent categories. The identity of a clan as *Kawo* or *Sabu* is inherited just as much as the design that adorns its tapa. Members of *Kawo* clans guard their privileges zealously. I thus heard of a major ruckus that occurred when an ambitious *Sabu* leader trimmed the edge of the thatch over his verandah, in effect declaring his clan to be *Kawo*. The next day, he awoke to the sight of *Kawo* elders from both the Wo and *Mera* divisions sitting silently in front of his house. They remained there until he tore down the offending roof. The descent model shows up in another important way. Wo and *Mera* are alternatively known by the names of their two leading *Kawo* clans, as Gafi-Simboro and Ume-Rerebin respectively. These paired clans are in turn thought of as older and younger brothers. Similarly, people speak of *Kawo* and *Sabu* clans as brothers. Like younger brothers, *Sabu* are said to be impetuous, easy to anger. Their associated *Kawo* act as older brothers by "taking care" of them, tempering their anger with calming advice to which the *Sabu* should listen respectfully.

In sum, then, every Maisin is a member of a lineage, a clan, and one of two (possibly three) clan confederacies. Each successive level encompasses a larger number of people and takes on distinct functions. Men inherit tangible property primarily from their fathers and fathers' brothers within lineages; they locate their houses in areas of the villages belonging to named clans from which they derive their strongest sense of identity; and as members of clans, they identify with historic confederacies, taking on the rank of either *Kawo* or *Sabu*.

Variations on the Theme of Descent

The descent system, as I've described it so far, appears fairly ordered and logical. Indeed, at first this is the way things appeared to me. Less than a month after arriving in Uiaku, I sent one of my research supervisors a lengthy letter setting out the system. I was quite proud that I had been able to work it out so quickly on the basis of a map I had drawn up locating the different clan areas in the village and from what a handful of people had told me about the proper duties of fathers, clan histories, and traditional leadership. People insisted that each clan possessed a separate history as well as distinct symbols and urged me to record these along with the genealogies that would trace their roots back to their founders. These oral histories, I was told, had not been previously recorded as only clan members could tell them to each other, and they were carefully guarded lest members of other clans "steal" them. Since I wasn't myself a member of a clan, I could be a neutral, honest scribe. As I prepared for this great task, I imagined that as I compiled the clan histories and genealogies a massive epic would emerge, a sort of Maisin *Lord of the Rings*.

Alas, things didn't quite work out that way. A handful of elders related long clan histories, and I collected a great deal of information about such things as clan tapa designs and the duties of *Sabu* and *Kawo* leaders. However, most people actually knew only the barest outlines of the histories and even less of genealogy; many of the clan emblems, I was told, had been long forgotten. Even so, I found that the histories and claims to various *kawo* emblems and rights overlapped and that even within clans different people often made contradictory claims. Everyone who spoke with me was adamant that they were giving me the unvarnished truth and warned me not to listen to members of other clans who would surely lie to me. It gradually dawned on me that the main reason people had been eager for me to record the histories and genealogies in the first place was their hope that I would somehow certify their version as the true one. The on-the-ground reality turned out to be far more complicated, disputed, and fluid than I had imagined.

I don't mean to suggest that people were actually lying to me, although doubtless some individuals inflated the claims of their own groups. What I had failed to grasp at first with my neat analysis is that any living social system is constantly in motion. Knowledge of one's immediate relatives, the identity of a clan ancestor, well-known clan emblems, or fragments of a history—all of these things combine to form a kind of "charter" that works to legitimate groups by providing them with a common sense of identity and purpose.[19] However, the *actual* makeup of any descent group or category at any one time will be equally affected by the composition of its living members and by the play of politics as different individuals vie for influence. My first village census revealed that the clans varied greatly in size. One of the major *Kawo* clans had only a single male member in the village, while another had more than 30 (counting the children), occupying three hamlets in different parts of Uiaku. Even in the short time I have worked in Uiaku, the population of one formerly tiny clan has exploded, while another, made up of four households in the early 1980s, has disappeared entirely. Over the course of generations, some clans have divided due to disputes or simply to search for better gardening lands, resulting in the present mix of concentrated and dispersed clans. The growing and shrinking of clans and the movement of members has no doubt gone on since time immemorial even if this reality is not acknowledged in oral traditions, which tend to refer to clans as if they were equal in size and formed coherent bodies.

To make matters even more complicated, most of the larger clans and even some small ones have internal divisions. Several clans are referred to alternately by their "big name" and by the names of paired sub-clans, ranked as older and younger, who are said to be the direct descendents of two ancestral brothers. Thus, one can speak of the Wofun clan alternately as "Wondi-Joba." In some cases, sub-clans may possess different insignia, and in at least one case a single clan possesses both *Sabu* and *Kawo* branches. The more details I learned, the more I appreciated that the singular term "clan" was a matter of convenience—for me, not the Maisin, who referred to any and all social groups from lineages to entire countries as *iyon*. Usually one can fairly easily identify exogamous descent groups that correspond to "clan" in the anthropological sense. Yet consider the case of "Rerebin." This name is claimed by groups in almost all of the Maisin villages. In Uiaku proper, it designates a descent group, but elsewhere it is a descent category. Rerebin in the village of Ganjiga is made up of three large descent groups each with its own distinct set of clan emblems and ancestral name. Most significantly (at least for an anthropologist), while the component groups are exogamous, there are no restrictions on marriages between them. This would seem to place Ganjiga Rerebin at a more general level than clan. However, members became very upset with me when I referred to the component groups by name. Not only was Rerebin their "real name," they told me, but those folks across the river in Uiaku had no right to use it. At the other extreme, the three surviving members of the Simboro clan all claimed to represent independent branches with their own emblems that had been introduced generations ago by non-Maisin women who had married into the society and brought their fathers' *kawo* with them.[20]

As the complexities, contradictions, and disputed recollections and claims piled up, I was tempted to think that there is no system at all, that the Maisin had been making up these descent groups on the fly, no doubt to torment me as I struggled to make sense of it. The Maisin themselves sometimes get frustrated, especially when a row breaks out over who owns a particular privilege or which group arrived first in Collingwood Bay (implying that they are the real owners of the land). They complain that people are forgetting their ancestral rights and identities and that, as they do so, the boundaries that were once so clear have become muddled. There is probably some truth in this. In the past, before the arrival of the colonial government and missions, most social life was organized through kin groups whose identities were likely more rigidly defined than today. All the same, one can detect more than a little nostalgia in such statements. The genealogical and historical charters for Maisin descent groups provide a general framework, but they also permit negotiations, political manoeuverings, and change. This is nothing new. The current descent system is one of many examples of culture providing for both continuity and change in the simultaneous process of replicating an ancestral pattern while adapting to the conditions and potentialities of the present.

Marriage and the Making of Alliances
A Maisin child is born into a household that connects outwards through a hierarchy of descent groups and a radiating network of kin. Together these provide security and a framework for action. A person's success in life depends on his or her ability to meet both responsibilities to close kin and to create and maintain bonds with more distant relatives and strangers. The most important of these bonds is marriage. As in many cultures, the Maisin regard marriage not merely as a union between two individuals but as an alliance between households, extended families, and clans. This is not to say that love and affection are not involved. The rich oral traditions related by elders over the evening fires include many romantic stories of courtship. While the emotional bond between husband and wife varies as much here as in most places, I've been impressed by the stability of Maisin marriages once children appear and even more so by the evident affection most spouses show for each other. Yet, if you ask villagers why people marry, you inevitably receive very pragmatic answers: people need children to care for them in their old age and to replace them when they are gone, assuring the survival of their households and lineages; clans rely on marriages to recruit

new members who learn the histories and take possession of the *kawo* emblems and thus allow the clan to reproduce itself through time; and the often complex exchanges triggered by marriage provide aspiring clan leaders with their best opportunity to show off their managerial abilities.

Clans are exogamous units: their members must seek mates from outside. The Maisin often speak of marriages as if they were between two clans. Normally, however, the first moves are made by individuals and their immediate families. Old people insist that this was not always the case. As late as the 1950s, elders often tried to arrange marriages through a practice known as "sister exchange" in which two clans agreed to provide each other with a wife. Such arrangements were made while the children were still very young. As they grew up, the matched couples were called "husband" and "wife," although they continued to live with their own people. By the time they became teenagers, they would spend increasing amounts of time working in the gardens of their prospective in-laws, a practice anthropologists refer to as "bride" or "groom service." Clan leaders liked these kinds of arrangements because they automatically brought the contracting groups into a balanced relationship: a wife for a wife, a husband for a husband. Even in the "good old days," however, the betrothed children often had their own ideas. If just one of the four betrothed persons died, refused to settle down with their assigned partner, or eloped with someone else, all of the careful diplomacy was for naught. Elopements sometimes triggered violence, especially when one clan had already done its duty by providing a wife for the initial marriage. The eloping couple usually had to flee for their lives, leaving their clanmates to face the spears and war clubs of the aggrieved party.

While individual young people have a greater say than in the past, their parents and clan elders continue to try to influence their choices. They nudge their sons and daughters towards potential partners who have shown themselves hard workers in the gardens and other subsistence activities and who are deferential to their elders. They strongly encourage their children (particularly their daughters) to marry within their own villages, to assure that they will remain nearby to take care of their aging parents. The survey of households that I conducted in 1982 revealed a very high level of village endogamy; almost 75 per cent of marriages in Uiaku had occurred within the bounds of the village. Yet even at that time, an increasing number of Maisin were looking further afield to partners in other Maisin villages and, for the large number who had moved to the town, to non-Maisin mates. Ultimately, so long as the preferred spouse is not a member of the clan or a close blood relative, young people enjoy a considerable amount of freedom. Most people live for brief periods with a series of partners before settling down. Once a couple has children, however, they rarely divorce. The main exception is when a man is physically violent or when he takes a second or third wife.[21] Many women return to their brothers rather than tolerate an unhappy situation. A few adjust, and others, whose natal families live far away, become unhappily trapped.

The first indication most villagers get that a couple has decided to marry comes when they appear sitting and eating breakfast together on the verandah or underneath the young man's residence. From this point on, they are called "husband" and "wife" so long as they remain together. Often there is no further ceremony. On other occasions, for reasons of family pride or because they hope to make the union stick, parents and clan elders take matters in hand, temporarily separating the couple while they arrange for a wedding ceremony. A few devout families will approach the priest to arrange for a church wedding, but this is fairly rare. Because of the very strong strictures against divorce in the Anglican Church, most couples prefer to live without Church approval until they are certain that the relationship will last, usually after the birth of several children.[22] At that point, they seek and receive a blessing from the priest and have their children baptized. Most village wedding ceremonies skip any involvement with the church.

While fairly uncommon, wedding ceremonies reveal much about Maisin assumptions concerning marriage. They usually take place a few weeks after the couple has been separated. In the morning, the bride is richly adorned in traditional dress and decorations and then brought to her husband's place accompanied by a boisterous crowd of kinfolk from both sides of her family. After the crowd settles down, she is led by two clan brothers gripping either arm towards her husband and male in-laws, who sit passively on a house verandah. As she draws near, three or four middle-aged women belonging to the groom's side get down on their hands and knees in a line in front of the ladder leading up to the porch. The bride walks across their backs and then steps onto a large clay cooking pot, which she smashes with her foot before climbing up to join her husband, symbolizing her break with her old family. Sometimes her kin will then present a gift of raw garden vegetables, tapa, cooking pots, mats, shell money, and cash. Clan elders from the groom's side then loudly proclaim that they will soon provide the wife's people with large quantities of three types of item, such as bananas, taro, or tapa, to be delivered as separate gifts in the near future. Speeches, feasting, and much merriment follow before the crowd disperses. The next morning, the bride brings the ceremony to a conclusion. Still decorated and surrounded by a crowd of jovial female in-laws who urge her on, she sweeps litter from the grounds of her husband's hamlet from one end to the other.

The sweeping ritual signifies the new responsibilities that come with marriage. As in so many areas of Maisin life, these weigh especially heavily upon women. The new bride not only takes on the heaviest burden of work but moves from her family to live among comparative strangers. Some young brides find the prospect so frightening that for a time they are accompanied by a younger sister or cousin who stays with them until they become accustomed to their new home. The young husband is by no means left off the hook. Both his own people and his in-laws will watch his actions intently to see whether he treats his wife well and willingly takes on the duties of creating a new household, separate from his father's. Still, he usually doesn't have to live among his in-laws. In the early stages of a marriage in particular, a couple comes under the authority of their in-laws who can be very critical if they fall short. They are expected to make themselves available to work in their in-laws' gardens, to help with the full range of household tasks, and to provide them with regular supplies of food, tobacco, and betelnut. They should do this with the greatest deference, never complaining and certainly never criticizing their in-laws. Over time, as people get used to each other, the stress of the relationship eases. Yet even with the most sympathetic and caring of in-laws, most people find the initial stage of marriage very trying, which may account in part for why so many relationships quickly break down.

I have personally experienced some of this. When they heard that Anne and I had married only a few months prior to leaving for Papua New Guinea, several of our Maisin friends came up with the idea of staging a traditional wedding in our honour. We were duly assigned fathers and mothers and "adopted" into different clans. The wedding never came off, but I quickly found out that my new "in-laws" meant to treat the arrangement as something more than fun and games. Every time I passed Anne's "father's" house, he called me over to sit with him and share any tobacco, rice, or betelnut I might be carrying. He was a lovely person, and I enjoyed our time together, but it wasn't long before I found myself avoiding his part of the village in order to preserve my dwindling supplies and to get on with my work. The arrangement complicated my research in an additional way. The Maisin show respect towards in-laws by never uttering their names. This taboo added some difficulties in compiling a village census and doing genealogies as there were certain names I couldn't say (the same, of course, was true for my informants). Although they take the business of dealing respectfully with in-laws very seriously, the Maisin also see humour in the situation. Young men are fond of a game in which they corner a new husband, spouting off insults about his father-in-law. If their victim so much as cracks a smile, his "insult" is immediately reported, forcing him to offer a gift to his aggrieved in-law to set matters right. One elder summed up the relationship with in-laws as follows: "You can sit with them, tell stories, and make fun. But we respect them. We can't make fun of any in-law.... They can demand that you work for them. You should do this before they say too much. If you live in another place, they will send a message for you to help — say, to make a new garden.... You married their daughter so you must respect them. They must respect you because you are their daughter's husband."

The respect relationship between in-laws derives from a conception of marriage as an exchange between clans. When one of their sons marries, a clan incurs a significant debt to the wife's people who have gifted her labour and children to them. Balancing this gift literally takes a lifetime. From the perspective of the clans, however, this is the aim: to convert an inherently unequal relationship to one marked by equivalence and thus social amity. In former times, sister exchange provided an ideal solution by matching the gift of a woman with another woman. Formerly and today, adoption provides another appealing strategy. If a new household is blessed with a large number of children, the couple often will foster one to a family on the in-laws' side, either a couple with few or no children or to an older couple whose children have grown up. The wife-takers are still expected to present the wife's people with periodic gifts of food and labour, but the gift of a child removes the need for a large bride-price payment.

Most people, however, put together a bride-price gift. A bride's family will usually encourage her husband to give the bride-price quickly, but more often than not a man waits until several children are born. The longer he waits, the greater the pressure. If his wife leaves him before bride-price is presented, she has the right to take her children back to her natal clan. Further, a man's own reputation suffers, and he runs the risk of annoying his in-laws. They may just grumble, but if things go on too long they may decide to stage a *waafoti*, a shaming ceremony. One morning, the husband will wake up to find his in-laws sitting solemnly in front of his house. They will not leave until the man and his embarrassed clan-mates pool their resources and pay a diminished bride-price on the spot. As a further inducement, the Maisin believe that angered in-laws are quite capable of hiring a sorcerer to retaliate against a "selfish" son-in-law who fails to meet his obligations.

The Maisin call the ceremonial presentation of bride-price, *wii jobi* ("vagina payment"). It's a big event. A husband will organize his own *wii jobi* with the aid of more experienced senior kinsmen, his clan brothers, his wife, and more distant kin. In the past, the essential component in a *wii jobi* payment was *kerefun*, strings of polished white shell discs about a fathom long,[23] imported from communities to the east. These are still given, although in smaller amounts than formerly. A typical bride-price presentation also includes an abundance of tapa cloth, mats, clay pots, shell ornaments, garden produce, cooked pork, different types of store goods, and cash.[24] The organizer will assemble these things in his own village and then, accompanied by clan siblings, carry them to his in-laws' house to present them. The in-laws usually know well in advance that the *wii jobi* is coming and will offer cooked food for their guests and later, after this is eaten, sit down with them to chew betelnut and smoke.[25]

The giving of a child in adoption or the payment of bride-price changes the relationship between the groups linked by a marriage. Up to this point, the husband's clan risks losing any children produced by the marriage should it break up, since they will return with their mother to her own people. They are now *bona fide* members of their father's clan regardless of the fate of the marriage. It may appear from this that the father's people have purchased the wife and her children, but this doesn't reflect Maisin assumptions. These exchanges, they say, should bring the two groups into a balanced state, marked by amicable relations. In actuality, the presentation of a generous bride-price in the context of a boisterous celebration marked by feasting and dancing to which both sides contribute does act to build confidence and a strong alliance. The important point, however, is that this is an alliance in which the *perception* of balance remains important. Perceptions are subjective. Even the closest of marital alliances experience flare-ups in which one side or the other feels that things are out of balance, that the other side is not meeting its obligations, that they are being taken advantage of. As we shall see in the next chapter, unhappy relationships in general not only make life unpleasant, they threaten life by tempting the wronged side to resort to sorcery in retaliation. The Maisin thus have both positive and negative inducements to cultivate good relations with their in-laws well after the two groups have, in principle, achieved a state of balance.

FIRST AND LAST THINGS: RITES OF PASSAGE AS SOCIAL THEATRE

So far in this chapter, I've been describing kinship, descent, and marriage as sets of rules that guide social behaviour. This is necessary but also a bit misleading. The Maisin are not given a rulebook or script early in life for how to live. Assumptions and expectations about kin and in-laws certainly guide behaviour but do not determine it. People adjust their actions according to the circumstances of the moment and strategize as to what is in their best interests. This does not mean anything goes, for people also continually evaluate others' actions largely in terms of the frameworks we've examined in this chapter and will only tolerate a certain amount of licence. The rules, then, are constantly being adapted, stretched, and reinforced in the course of everyday life. Further, it is important to understand that the Maisin do not generally experience relationships with kin, clans, or in-laws as discrete domains. In order to reveal the underlying patterns of a society, anthropologists have to abstract presumed rules and frameworks from far more complex lived realities. The Maisin often find themselves in circumstances in which they must balance the expectations of all three sets of relationships at once.

A number of anthropologists, most prominently Victor Turner (1974; see also Schieffelin 1976), suggest that we think about social life less as a set of normative rules than as a kind of improvisational theatre. In this social theatre, people shift between acting on the stage and observing from the audience. There are no set scripts, but instead there are generally accepted rules and scenarios. The theatrical analogy is especially compelling as a way of approaching large public ceremonials. In Uiaku, these typically involve large formal exchanges that mark major life transitions: rites of passage. To bring this chapter to a conclusion, I want briefly to examine two moments in which ceremonial exchanges result in a kind of social theatre both for the Maisin and for the anthropologist. These involve respectively first and last things: the initiation of first-born children and the end-of-mourning ceremony following a death.

First-born children (*membu*) enjoy a special status in Maisin society. The arrival of the *membu* marks the start of a new generation for the father's clan. As the first in a new sibling set, the *membu* is expected to take on more responsibilities and to defer many of the freedoms and pleasures of adolescence until they undergo a special ceremony, the *kisevi*. By the same token, the *membu*'s younger siblings are expected to treat him or her with respect and deference. In *Kawo* clans, a male *membu* belonging to a senior lineage is often groomed to take leadership positions. The *membu* thus exemplifies the principle of seniority that underlies the structure of descent groups. At the same time, the appearance of the *membu* raises the stakes of the marriage contract, for until the bride-price is presented the status of all of the couple's children is uncertain. The birth of the *membu* thus increases pressure on the father's clan to meet their exchange obligations to the mother's people. At the same time, it triggers a parallel set of exchanges around the person of the *membu*. These begin with gifts of raw food quietly delivered to the mother's people around the time of the birth and for several years thereafter. It should climax with the *kisevi* in which the mother's brothers play a crucial role.

I say "should climax" because the *kisevi* rarely happens any more, in part because the *membu* is often away attending high school during the critical period and in part because the ceremony is very expensive to mount, requiring a large accumulation of garden produce, tapa cloth, shell money, cash, and other valuables as well as the coordination of many stake-holders. I haven't seen one myself, but I have extensive descriptions from participants, including *membu* themselves. The Maisin typically describe the ceremony as being organized by the two clans allied in marriage. The father's side invites the mother's relatives to initiate the first-born on a certain day. After an evening of feasting and dancing, the *membu*'s maternal uncles bathe and decorate the *membu* in traditional finery. The *membu* now sits silently on a mat covered with tapa with a maternal cousin on either side. Sometimes making short speeches, the uncles step forward to swing a shell necklace or tapa over the head of the *membu* and they then lay it over the initiate's neck or legs. These gifts typically include the prized *kawo* emblems of the mother's clans, giving the *membu* the right to use them in future, although not to pass on to their own children. At this point, the *membu*'s mother swings a small clay pot over his or her head and then smashes it to the ground. The paternal kin now come forward, swinging their gifts of tapa, money, shell necklaces, and so forth over the head of the *membu* and placing them in a pile for later distribution to the mother's people.

By all accounts, the *kisevi* is very exciting. Hundreds of people attend, including non-Maisin guests from across Collingwood Bay. People get very excited as the piles of gifts mount on top of and beside the *membu* and will often rush back into their houses or to their canoes to find additional things to give away—so much so that the old people say, "After this *kisevi* they will cry for there is nothing left in their houses." The ceremony involves an impressive amount of management, especially on the part of the *membu*'s paternal family. The public performance is ostensibly between two clans, but no single clan possesses the resources to mount a *kisevi*. Organizers have to call upon their extended kin to make donations of food and gifts, to build shelters for guests, and to help with cooking and ceremonial dances. Thus, Veronica Kaivasi proudly told me how she and her husband, Simeon Wea, spent years pulling together the *kisevi* for their daughter Damaris through extensive negotiations, fed by smaller exchanges, not only with Simeon's kin but with Veronica's family. As it turned out, many of the mother's people made significant contributions to the gifts that they later received from the father's clan. I found a similar backstage flexibility on the part of the mother's clan. Because a presentation strictly limited to the clan wouldn't be nearly impressive enough, the maternal uncles called upon many of their own classificatory "brothers" to place gifts upon Damaris even though they actually belonged to different clans. One couple related to both Veronica and Simeon decided to split the difference—the wife sat with Simeon's people while the husband stayed with the uncles.

Any large exchange involves similar backstage adjustments and compromises in which the organizers draw upon kinship links and exchange obligations to produce a certain public appearance. The formal purpose of a *kisevi* is to publicly demonstrate that the parties to a marriage have achieved a state of balance, as exemplified in the public exchange of gifts over the body of the *membu* to which they have a common claim. Because they are both actors and audience, the participants in a *kisevi* are fully aware of the social complexities even if they have differing perspectives on the details. The talk of *clans* conducting an exchange thus forms a kind of shorthand for what is in fact a much more entangled set of social interactions. Participants judge the success of a *kisevi* by the degree to which the organizers have successfully created the *appearance* of clans achieving a balance and the affirmation of the status of the first-born. By this measure, Damaris's *kisevi* was a great success, raising the public stature of Simeon's clan.

In modern times, the *kisevi* has become optional. Most parents say they wish to arrange one for their first-born child, but unlike the payment of bride-price, there are no major consequences for failing to do so. The *roi babasi* or "face cleaning" ceremony that ends a person's mourning for a close relative is a different matter (Barker 1985). When a person dies, his or her surviving spouse and parents are expected to go into mourning. Other close relatives may also choose to formally mourn the deceased by wearing dark clothes, allowing their hair and beards to grow, and by avoiding a certain food or activity. A spouse faces especially stringent requirements. At the moment of death, they are considered to become like infants, incapable of caring for themselves. They become the responsibility of their in-laws, that is, the family of the deceased. The spouse initially goes into seclusion. Over succeeding days and weeks, the in-laws formally reintroduce the mourner into the world of the living one step at a time: they take them to the bush, thus giving them permission to relieve themselves; they feed them with taro, sweet potatoes, bananas, and other foods, thus giving them permission to feed themselves; they take them to the garden area, thus giving them permission to resume work on their own gardens; and so forth. The in-laws usually lift restrictions within a few weeks. Usually, the bereaved then returns to his or her own people to remain in a state of semi-formal mourning for a period of months lasting into years during which they wear only dark clothes and allow their hair to grow out and become matted and, if male, beards to grow out. The period of mourning is brought to a final conclusion with a public ceremony in which the mourners are "cleaned up" by the family of the deceased.

The *roi babasi* resembles a *kisevi*, although typically on a much smaller scale. This is especially the case for widows and widowers. Like the *membu*, the bereaved spouse is bathed, clothed, and decorated by his or her in-laws before being presented with gifts, usually articles of clothing and sometimes tapa cloth. Also like the *kisevi*, the *roi babasi* creates a new status for its subject. Once the ceremony is concluded, the surviving spouse no longer has obligations to the in-laws. They are free to remarry if they wish. There are

Figure 3.5 A *roi babasi* (face cleaning) ceremony, 1998. (Photo by J. Barker)

also important differences. While some families with the time and resources mount large ceremonies marked by feasting and sometimes dancing, most are small affairs bringing together the immediate kin. The ceremony normally lasts just a few hours. There are no large presentations of gifts, and the ceremony is brought to an end with a small dinner for the guests.

Over the years, I have participated in many *roi babasi* ceremonies and investigated many more. All follow the general pattern outlined above. And all have been different, often significantly so. The pioneering anthropologist, Bronislaw Malinowski (1954), argued that death tore apart the social fabric in small-scale societies, and so the function of mortuary ceremonies is to calm people's grief and fears by reasserting social connections. Most Maisin, I think, would be comfortable with that explanation: the *roi babasi* is meant to resolve the relationships between people connected through the deceased. The differences in the ceremonies often enough have to do with making adjustments to achieve that end. Yet, there is a big difference between what ought to be and what people do. Most Maisin in my experience do not look at the *roi babasi* only as an obligation but also as an index of the state of relationships between the people connected by the deceased. Hence, any particular *roi babasi* is open to several readings. If a person remains in mourning for a long time, for instance, people will often wonder whether the in-laws are holding up the ceremony because they are angry, perhaps feeling that the survivor had not cared as much as they should have for the deceased. If the in-laws are really angry, however, they are much more likely to rush the *roi babasi*. In one case, a widower was made to undergo the ceremony only three days after his young wife's death. His in-laws claimed that they felt, as Christians, that they should not allow the husband to suffer the privations of mourning, but few bought this argument and the husband was deeply shamed. By the same token, the details of the ceremonies — who shows up, what they contribute, what they say before and after — provide fodder for gossip.

As social theatre, then, the *roi babasi* operates at two levels of performance: it formally acts out the ending not only of a life but of a series of relationships built around that life, particularly between in-laws; and it dramatically underscores the current state of relationships between various factions within the community. It speaks to the continuing vitality of ancestral ways in the context of the present.

CONCLUSION

All societies recognize forms of kinship, descent, and marriage. However, these loom very large in small-scale cultures like that of the Maisin, where people spend their lives in close proximity to a small circle of kin and neighbours with whom they are bound by frequent reciprocal exchanges. Kinship terminologies, the system of descent groups, and expectations concerning relationships between in-laws provide the Maisin with general frameworks for social action. It is important to recognize these as frameworks, not as recipes. They provide individual Maisin with direction as to what they need to do and, at the same time, provide a standard against which activities get evaluated. What actually happens is always far more variable and complex than the rules taken in isolation would suggest. One can assume that a kind of feedback occurs over time as behaviour and evaluations of activities reinforce standard assumptions or challenge them. Change tends to be gradual and more or less under the radar, as most people try to balance the expectation that they will conform to the accepted rules with the circumstances and challenges that life throws up while keeping an eye open to improve their stature within the community.

Uiaku is a small, intimate place. Along with basic subsistence, relationships with kin, members of one's descent groups, and in-laws inform much of social life. Yet not all. The Maisin must also contend with spiritual forces that both reinforce and disrupt the best laid plans and hopes. They must also contend with the challenges of living together as a community in the context of regional and national institutions and political structures that pay no attention to kinship. In the next two chapters, then, we need to enlarge our picture of Maisin society by considering the wider realms of the spiritual world and the community.

Notes

1. In the 1980s, most *embobi* were composed of four panels. As tapa has become more commercially successful, however, there has been a tendency to make smaller pieces, cut to one or two panels, which are easier to sell.

2. In recent years several men have taken up designing cloths (not beating them!) to profit from the expanding market. Anna-Karina Hermkens (2005: 72) found that the men employed a different cognitive technique, working out the design as they drew it.

3. This is not to suggest that Maisin parents do not love or care for newborns. Clearly they do, and the death of a baby is experienced quietly as a tragedy. Full *social* humanness, however, is recognized as a potential that emerges out of the child's developing social interactions; it is not a biological given.

4. Pregnancy and childbirth also involve a range of other customary practices, including a number of food taboos and preferences meant to assure the health of the mother and child. Many of these were already lapsing in the early 1980s in response to better medical care from the local church-run clinic in Wanigela. For a fuller account, see Tietjen (1985).

5. In many other parts of Melanesia, boys underwent initiations at the onset of puberty and then lived entirely apart from their mothers and sisters in special male cult houses (Godelier 1986; Herdt 1981; Tuzin 1980). In comparison, the relationship between adolescent girls and boys among the Maisin is quite relaxed, although according to elders this was less true in the now distant past when adolescent boys were expected to live together in special "clan houses" (*iyon va*).

6. If missionary records and the recollections of old people are to be believed, adult Maisin had a more relaxed attitude towards premarital sex in the past, perhaps because of the belief that a boy and girl had to have sex repeatedly for pregnancy to occur (Barker 1986). Even today, a girl who has a baby prior to marriage is usually not harshly criticized. The baby is welcomed by her family and remains with them when she later marries.

7. To our eyes at least, tattoo designs strongly resembled those found on tapa. Not surprisingly, the few master tattooists were also superb tapa artists. We were surprised, however, that the Maisin could or would not see the resemblances that

seemed so apparent to us. They insisted that tattoos and tapa were utterly different.

8. Anna-Karina Hermkens (personal communication), who studied tapa making in the Maisin village of Airara, was more recently told that at least some younger women did not find the tattoos attractive and weren't prepared to take on the pain of the operation. It is impossible to know whether this marks a shift in attitude over the past 20 years or the true but suppressed views of the young people when the custom was still practised. Many Maisin have told me that they would like to revive tattooing, and I understand that one girl was tattooed recently.

9. The same cannot be said of non-Maisin women who have married into the community. Lacking nearby relatives, they are much more vulnerable to bullying on the part of their in-laws, both male and female.

10. Technically, English kinship terminology is an example of an "Eskimo" (or Inuit) system.

11. To add to the complexity—for the outsider, not the Maisin—some terms differ depending on whether they are used to *refer* to someone or *address* them directly. Thus, if I was talking to someone about my mother I would say, *au yo* ("my mother"). If I wanted her attention, on the other hand, I would call out, *Yau*!

12. This sketch includes only immediate family terms. Maisin kinship terminology also includes affinal (In-law) terms, plural forms, and honorific variants meant to convey one's respect towards the addressed relative.

13. The concept of "security circle" was introduced by one of the great pioneers of Melanesian anthropology, Peter Lawrence (1984), based on his work among the Garia of Madang Province.

14. This was not immediately apparent to the earliest students of non-Western kinship systems. Lewis Henry Morgan (1877), who introduced the distinction between "classificatory" and "descriptive" kinship systems, jumped to the bizarre conclusion that terminologies that grouped together fathers and mothers with their siblings were relics of an earlier period of "primitive promiscuity" in which children were ignorant of the true identity of their biological parents.

15. This pattern has become complicated with the large scale out-migration of younger Maisin to the urban areas since the 1960s. Still, when men retire from their jobs and return to the village, they establish themselves in their fathers' areas. In a few cases, however, a man may live for a time or permanently with his wife's people, usually as a result of an argument in the family.

16. Fostered children become members of their adoptive father's clan, although they may retain informal privileges in their birth father's clan as well.

17. The Maisin system of emblems bears some similarities to forms of totemism found elsewhere, most notably in Aboriginal Australia where social groups are associated with particular natural species or objects.

18. I capitalize the types of clans to distinguish this use of *Kawo* from the more general sense of emblem (*kawo*).

19. The powerful idea that origin histories ("mythologies") may form a type of social charter amongst those who tell them was first suggested by Bronislaw Malinowski (1954), based upon his study of the Trobriand Islanders between 1914 and 1916.

20. There are further complexities, including the presence of a number of clans that claim to have foreign origins. Most are associated with different Maisin clans to whom their ancestors attached themselves in the past, either during the migrations into Collingwood Bay or later as migrants and refugees. One, however, is a fully fledged *Kawo* ally in the *Wo ari Kawo* confederacy. Sometimes I was told that the members of these clans were "not really Maisin," although their members have lived for generations in Uiaku and differ only in terms of distant ancestral origins.

21. In the early 1980s, five men living in Uiaku had two or three wives. By the late 1990s, only two of these unions had survived, although some men still made the attempt to take on a second wife. Most Maisin frown on polygyny in part because it contradicts Christian teachings but mostly because of the fights that often erupt between co-wives. Genealogies reveal a much higher level of polygyny in the past when leading men took on additional wives as a mark of prestige and to acquire additional labour for their extensive gardens.

22. Some couples inevitably do split up after their marriages have received the priest's blessing. If they remarry, they are subject to church discipline: they are not allowed to receive sacramental wine and bread, denoting the body and blood of Christ, in communion services, and their children must await adulthood before they can be baptized. In the past, Anglican bishops sometimes took the extreme step of excommunicating divorced individuals who remarried, symbolically condemning their souls to eternal damnation. The practice of blessing established marriages marks a historic face-saving compromise that allows the church to continue to proclaim marriage a sacrament while quietly allowing for a degree of divorce, particularly in the early years of a marriage.

23. This is a traditional measure, from outstretched arm to outstretched arm. For the Maisin, a fathom is about 1.6 metres.

24. Many parts of Papua New Guinea have experienced a massive inflation in bride-price with the introduction of money. In places where people are known to have access to money, either through their own jobs or via relatives, the bride's people may demand exorbitant bride-price payments, or, just as often, the husband's people use the occasion of the exchange as a public display of their wealth and influence. Bride-prices running in the tens of thousands of kina are not unusual. The money component of Maisin bride-price is comparatively small, generally a few hundred kina. Still, this represents a large sum for most rural Maisin, and those with few working relatives to call upon often find they have to delay bride-price payments to avoid a shamefully small prestation.

25. The hosts of feasts never eat with their guests. They keep some cooked food back to enjoy after their guests have left or retired for the night.

CHAPTER FOUR

The Spiritual Realm

I looked forward to finishing my cloth. Unlike the beating and designing stages, which individual women usually carry out alone, applying the red dye known as *dun* is a social event. I had often passed groups of women chatting happily in the cool area under a house or tree, while they applied *dun* to their tapas from a shared pot. This looked like fun. I also assumed that applying the dye would not tax my meagre technical skills nearly as much as the hard labour of beating the bark or the frustrations of coaxing the sooty black *mii* into neat parallel lines.

First, we had to make the dye. Lottie and I gathered the materials. We walked along the beach until we came to a moderately tall tree the Maisin call *saman*. Lottie wielded the long knife she had brought to slice off a long strip of bark, which she then bundled into her string bag. We then strolled behind the village to gather leaves from a second tree known as *dun*. Unlike the *wayangu* creeper used in making the black dye, which Maisin consider to grow wild, *saman* and *dun* trees are owned. One must seek permission to harvest them if they do not grow on one's own land.

We now returned to the village and crossed the river to Martha's house. In the comfortable shade underneath, she and Lottie prepared the *dun*. Lottie used her knife to shred the inner bark from the *saman* bark. She then layered pieces of bark and leaves in a small pot. Once it was nearly full, she added water to the brim and placed the pot over a fire. We settled back to enjoy a small snack and conversation while the pot boiled away for the next 90 minutes or so, with Lottie occasionally adding water. As the water heated up, the vegetation released a pinkish dye. The leaves and bark gradually combined into a mash, while the thickening soup gradually took on a satisfactorily thick blood-red hue. Martha brought out a collection of dried pandanus fruits whose tips had been crushed to expose the fibers. The *imongiti*, as these are known, come in a variety of sizes and make handy brushes. Martha now dipped one into the bubbling pot of *dun* and applied it to a scrap of tapa. She found the consistency and colour satisfactory and declared that we were ready to begin.

As in all social events, there is a certain etiquette to sharing a *dun* pot. Once she has arranged herself and her tapa around the pot, the owner is often joined by women from neighbouring houses and relatives visiting from other parts of the village, each bearing a bundle of her own unfinished cloth. When they arrive, each woman should take up one of the host's tapas to work on. When the host feels that she has received sufficient help, she gives the others permission to turn to their own cloths. Usually a pot of *dun* is used up in an afternoon in this pleasant activity.

We were joined by a few women, but only one brought her own cloths. Clearly I was to provide the entertainment for the day! I immediately broke with custom by taking up my own cloth, unwilling to risk messing up Lottie or Martha's creations, and tentatively dipped my pandanus brush into the dye. I found to my relief that applying the *dun* was much easier than working with the black *mii*, but it still required concentration and a steady hand. My first tentative strokes resulted in a blotchy pink stain. I was surprised by how quickly the cloth absorbed the dye. When one splotch seeped across the black line, I jerked my hand up. Bad idea! Spatters of red now festooned what was supposed to be a white area. So I stopped and paid closer attention to Martha and Lottie's technique. They dipped their brushes into the hot liquid, flicked off the excess, and then applied it to a line, using a light hand and rapid forward brush stroke.

After a while, I got the hang of it, and my lines took on a satisfactory consistency, even if the colour was not as boldly red as my companions'. I was surprised by how quickly the work went. The *dun* dries rapidly. You don't need to wait long upon completing one panel before turning the cloth to work on the next. We hung each piece on a clothesline as soon as it was finished. The painted surface is exposed to bake in the sun for a short time before flipping the cloth inside out. When the women were satisfied that the cloths were thoroughly dry, they took them off the line. Much like a little kid bringing home his first shop project, I proudly took my tapa back to show to Mary Rose and George. I don't know if they really liked it, but they were very kind.

The vibrant red of the *dun* quickly fades in the bright Papua New Guinea sunshine, and the cloth itself is easily damaged by moisture, so tapa makers carefully store their creations in a dark corner of their house, usually inside a suitcase. Most tapa doesn't stay packed for long. While a few women regularly make cloth, most take up the demanding chore only when an opportunity arises to sell it or it is required for an exchange or dancing. Even so, George told me that it is best to hold a few well-designed large *embobi* back in the house for special occasions. When an important visitor arrives, for

Figure 4.1 Recently completed tapa drying on a clothesline. (Photo by J. Barker)

instance, one should show respect by spreading out a handsome tapa to sit upon (which then becomes the property of the guest). George and Mary Rose welcomed their children returning home from high school in this way. I was reminded of how I was greeted when first arriving in Maisin villages and also of how Lottie had honoured me with her beautiful tapa earlier when I had been designing my own.

Tapa has many facets for the Maisin. In the past, it was primarily a utilitarian object. This is no longer the case, but even in earlier times tapa was much more than simply clothing. It was and still is a form of wealth. A villager would not even begin to think of sponsoring or participating in a major exchange without a good supply of cloth. Along with other types of wealth — cash, food, shell necklaces, and so forth — the public giving of tapa serves to demonstrate the giver's social status while affirming or creating social relationships upon which that status relies. One gives and receives tapa because one must. Not to do so would be a denial of community, to act as if one were "not human." Tapa is also a commodity, something that can be converted into cash to be used to purchase goods from the trade store, pay school fees, or buy airplane fares to Port Moresby. The Maisin have long used tapa as both gift and commodity, but as we saw in Chapter 2, there are tensions between these two economic modes.

At a more subtle level, tapa also speaks to religious and cosmological assumptions. It took me some time to understand this. Early in my research, I read an article claiming that Maisin derived tapa designs from mythological stories (Schwimmer 1979).[1] Only in a few cases is this true. The Jorega clan, for instance, associates a fern-like design known as *sividi* with a marvellous tale set in the Musa swamp area during the origin times. There are a few instances of clan designs associated with specific events in the migration histories. Most, however, are simply emblems. A couple of my favourite tapa makers, Natalie Kitore and Nita Keru, drew wonderful stylized images of animals, insects, spirits, and people. This was very unusual, however, and in any case there was nothing particularly spiritual about them. As far as I could see, the Maisin regarded tapa as something entirely free of religious associations.

My comfortable assumption that Maisin regard tapa as a purely secular object unravelled in a curious way. On the day before I was to leave Uiaku in November 1986, at the very end of two months of research focussed upon tapa making and tattooing, I visited Agnes Sanangi and her sister Natalie Kitore to tie up a few loose ends. We were just running through the etiquette Maisin observe when sharing a pot of *dun* when Agnes added some new and surprising information. "In the old days," she said, a woman would announce to the household that she was about to apply the red dye. The night before, she and her husband refrained from sexual activity. The following morning, her husband and children left the house while she prepared the *dun* inside. She explained that if men were present or children were running around and making noise, the *dun* would dry out. Once the *dun* was ready, the tapa maker invited other women to join her in the privacy of the house. The *dun*, Agnes added, was "very strong," unlike the black *mii* dye, and thus had to be handled carefully and only by women. While listening, I thought of how when a newly tattooed girl first emerges from the tattooist's house she wears a special tapa known as *wamatuvi* that is dyed entirely red except for an unpainted fringe at the base. The Maisin thus seemed to associate the red dye with women, perhaps more specifically with women's blood. This association was recently confirmed by a Dutch anthropologist working in Airara village, Anna-Karina Hermkens (2005). Several of her elderly informants told her that the red dye was called *tambuta* (an extremely bright or "ripe" blood red) during the time it was in the house.

These observations, so casually revealed, opened up a whole new dimension of tapa to me. They suggested that in the past the Maisin associated aspects of the making of tapa with the essence of femininity. Making tapa, especially the final stages, thus connected up to a complex of practices and rituals involving food taboos, birthing, and infant care practices and gender etiquette (Tietjen 1985). Many of these practices have spiritual sanctions.

Were a man to break the taboo on entering the house while the *dun* was present, he would surely become ill. Agnes told me that Maisin women stopped secluding themselves while using *dun* sometime around the end of World War II, although she was unable to tell me why. It would be naïve to think, however, that villagers do not continue to make subtle connections between the making of tapa, gender, and spiritual forces.

Of course I asked Agnes and Natalie why they had not told me about this fascinating custom during our many sessions together. I already knew the answer: "You didn't ask." I have no reason to doubt their explanation. There was nothing secret about the older way of handling *dun*. Elderly men spoke as easily about it as did the women once I knew to ask them about it. The problem really lay with me. My job was to make sense of Maisin life, especially in its religious dimensions. So I asked questions, sought explanations. Many of my informants were very happy to speak about aspects of spirituality. Indeed, they told me that my questions were quite stimulating. However, the Maisin experience the spiritual world much more than they rationalize it. They feel no need to pull together the often contradictory bits of ritual practices, observances of taboos, or encounters with spiritual forces into a big picture. Much of an individual's knowledge of the spiritual rests upon tacit, unarticulated assumptions. Thus, if the inherent incompatibility of red *dun* and men is something that everyone just knows, there is no reason to expect that anyone would think to volunteer the information to an anthropologist unless asked.

There is no subject so fascinating or challenging for an anthropologist to study as the religious dimensions of a culture. The contemporary religion of the Maisin is rather like one of their finished tapas. One sees, at first, the bold patterns of red bounded by black, the equivalent of the widely shared religious beliefs and practices we shall examine in this chapter: church services, ideas about the nature of spirits, sorcery and healing practices, and rituals to deal with the passage between life and death. The basic elements of a tapa design are quite limited. Yet, as you develop a greater knowledge and appreciation, you become aware that every tapa design combines those elements into a unique expression. In this chapter, I shall focus mostly on the general, shared aspects of Maisin religious experience. However, as we shall see, the Maisin's approach to the spiritual realm is marvellously innovative and creative. This, more than anything else, explains why 80 years after most people became Christians, their religious lives retain a strong indigenous signature.

CHRISTIANITY

St. Thomas Church is the largest building in Uiaku, although it is easily overlooked by visitors. It sits at the very back of the mission station, behind wide grassy sports fields edged by neat croton-lined paths that run past the teachers' *church and disciple* (handwritten margin note)

houses and classrooms. The church itself looks from a distance like a long shed, its roof a patchwork of corrugated iron sheets in various shades of rust. Closer in, one notices a space between the sloping roof and sago-rib walls to allow light and cooling breezes into the building. You enter at the far end from the altar, making your way between two sets of small logs that form the pews. The altar sits on a raised platform of sand and gravel that takes up the front quarter of the church. The back wall and the altar itself are richly adorned with tapa cloth, but apart from this there are few decorations. The simple interior, however, is clean and attractive. Prior to each service, a few women from the Mothers Union sweep the floor, rake the gravel, and place a few clay flower pots along the "altar rail"—the edge of the raised platform.

On a typical Sunday, perhaps one-third of the adults from Uiaku and Ganjiga show up for the 8 a.m. service. As people quietly shuffle in, they divide, the women moving to the left pews and men to the right, with school children of both sexes occupying the front rows on the right, under the watchful eye of one of the deacons. The number of adolescents and unmarried young adults attending ebbs and flows. Most weeks there are few, but the ranks swell on occasions like sports meets or youth fellowship gatherings that bring visitors to the village. Sometimes, a number of young people bring guitars and a battery-powered electronic keyboard, filling the air with lively contemporary gospel songs instead of the usual Victorian-era hymns.

Apart from the squirming children, people sit silently in the pews waiting for the service to begin, their heads slightly bowed, some reading their Bibles. The services follow a standardized format in simple English, based upon the Anglican *Book of Common Prayer*. Bible readings and prayers are also in English, as is the sermon when a Maisin-speaking priest or deacon is not available. Prior to the mid-1980s, Church authorities discouraged clergy from working in their own tribal groups. Neither of the two priests serving Uiaku during my first fieldwork could speak Maisin, and they delivered their sermons in simple and, to my ears at least, fractured English with a Maisin deacon or church council member providing translation. The rest of the service is not translated for the benefit of those who cannot understand English (a solid majority in the early 1980s). Indeed, the liturgy allows for very limited participation from the congregation or spontaneity on the part of the clergy. The congregation sits passively through the readings and sermons, ritualistically responding to the prayers and coming forward to receive communion in a never-changing rhythm that echoes Anglican services around the world. The sermon allows for more variation, but only lay readers, deacons, and priests licensed by the bishop are allowed to preach.[2] Most of them stick to a simple formula of reiterating the Bible lessons and urging their flocks to obey God and love their neighbours. They very rarely refer to events or concerns in the local community and then only in the most general terms.

I had come to Uiaku specifically to study the impact of Christianity on the Maisin and so became one of the most faithful and regular members of the small band of congregants attending church in 1981-83. I had plenty of time, perched on my hard pew, to speculate on what Christianity meant to villagers. My early impression was: not very much. To be sure, there was a small minority that faithfully attended church, studied the Bible, and prefaced each meal with a grace. Still, most people did not bother, and there seemed to be few if any consequences for missing services or for failing to contribute money to help pay the priest's salary. People also got away with flouting key Church teachings, most notably about marriage. It seemed that their adherence to Christianity was quite superficial.

I was mistaken, however. Christianity has a profound presence in Maisin life. All but one adult in the village have been baptized, and all received instructions in the religion as children; community meetings commonly opened and closed with prayers, and speakers often urged their listeners to adhere to Christian teachings; and church festivals, particularly the patron saint's day, were major social events, involving nearly all villagers in the preparations and celebrations. As of 2000, Uiaku had produced at least eight priests, two of whom rose to prominent positions in the national Church. People from across the community took great pride in their identity as Christians, insisting that the appearance of missionaries on the Uiaku beach in 1890 had transformed life for the better by bringing warfare and raiding to an end and ushering in peace. People told me more intimate stories as well, about how they had recovered from life-threatening illnesses after experiencing visions or dreams of Jesus, Mary, and other biblical figures or of how their faith in God had preserved them from a terrifying sorcery attack.

Even taking such attitudes into account, many observers would probably still insist that the Maisin have not "really" become Christians or that their adherence is shallow, pointing to such things as spotty attendance at church services and the continuing belief in magic, spirits, and sorcery. Indeed, a small but growing minority of Maisin feel this way and have left the Anglican Church to join denominations like the Pentecostals and the Seventh-Day Adventists that insist upon a radical break with many traditional customs as a condition of being a Christian. Yet it does not follow that Maisin Anglicans are not "really Christians." From a non-sectarian point of view, it is clear that Christianity has assumed a bewildering variety of guises during its 2,000-year history and expansion across the globe. Ethnographers are not called upon to judge which if any of these versions is legitimate. As part of a holistic study of their culture and history our job is to investigate what people mean when they claim to be Christians.

It is important to bear in mind that Christianity is not new for the Maisin. The village church was established long before the birth of the oldest living villager today.[3] To the present generation, Christianity is not a foreign religion but is as much part of their shared history as the origin stories of the clans. Yet the way Maisin understand Christianity, while drawing upon the same biblical and ecclesiastical sources, differs significantly from the types of beliefs found among congregations in Western countries. It is largely the product of a local evolution, formed out of a "long conversation" between external church authorities, mostly Anglican, and local cultural assumptions about the nature of spiritual powers.[4] This conversation has progressed on two overlapping registers. The first and most overt has to do with the official teachings and requirements of the church. The Anglican Church of Papua New Guinea is a very hierarchical organization, with authority flowing down from the bishop, through licensed priests, deacons, and lay-evangelists, to ordinary congregants. The Church exercises considerable control over the performance of services and teachings. Historically, there has been little space for local innovation, although this is now beginning to change with the encouragement of youth fellowship rallies and other largely lay-run initiatives. While conservative regarding its own practices and doctrines, the Church has historically been very tolerant of local customs and beliefs. Unlike many Protestant missions operating in Papua during the colonial period, the Anglicans did not insist that converts separate themselves from their pagan neighbours and called for reform rather than abandonment of most Indigenous customs such as death rites and dancing (Wetherell 1977). If the congregants of St. Thomas Church don't insist on taking a larger role in church services, then, this is not because they are disinterested but rather because they accept a version of Christianity that accords the leading liturgical role to the clergy. If the Church has failed to reshape social practices to fit its doctrines, this is because its officials for the most part have seen little reason to do so.

This doesn't mean that there hasn't been dialogue, compromise, and innovations. The practice of blessing couples after a child or two has been born, discussed in the last chapter, represents such a compromise in which the Church recognizes marriage as a sacrament while allowing the Maisin a flexible means of dealing with the strict rules against divorce. At the same time, Church authorities have demonstrated a willingness to allow a limited presence for local culture in church services. This is especially marked during festivals like patron saints days or Easter, celebrated in Anglican villages with feasting and traditional dancing. During the 1980s, Deacon Russell Maikin took this a step further by translating the liturgy into Maisin and setting it to traditional drummed chants performed by a troop of decorated men during the Church high days.

Figure 4.2 Celebrating Easter in St. Thomas Church, Uiaku, 1982. On high church days, a chorus of men in traditional dress sometimes chants the liturgy in Maisin accompanied by drums. (Photo by A.M. Tietjen)

Still, the general picture at the level of official Anglican practices and doctrines is one of balanced separation: acceptance of the authority of the clergy in their own sphere of action on the part of villagers and tolerance of villagers' beliefs and actions in their daily life on the part of the clergy. This is not the end of the story, however, because the long conversation has also been carried on at a second level, in the course of individuals' life experiences. Drawing upon the thought of Max Weber, a great pioneer in the sociology of religion, Clifford Geertz (1973: 100) has argued that, at its core, religion is a response to intractable crises of meaning that radically challenge our sense that the world is comprehensible, endurable, and ethical. When faced by a calamity (or opportunity, for that matter), most Maisin do not stop to sort out Christian doctrines from Indigenous beliefs. Instead, they draw on the full compass of things they know or suspect, seeking confirmation from kin, neighbours, and clergy as they do so. The result is an ever-evolving popular religion made up of both local and imported ideas and practices.

The remainder of this chapter focusses mainly upon this second register: the religious beliefs and practices of everyday life in Uiaku. Our concern is to understand the ways that the Maisin think about and experience spirituality, whatever the source of their ideas. That understanding, in turn, is dependent upon a conception of the nature of the cosmos and their place in it. And so we must turn now to cosmology.

COSMOLOGY

Even by Maisin standards, it was an extraordinary story, and I wondered if I understood what John Wesley Vaso and Weston Nonisa were telling me. Two weeks earlier, John Wesley's father, John Hunt Vaso, had vanished for several days after heading out to the bush to hunt. A search party was sent out. Early in the morning of the second day, Weston had come upon John Hunt stumbling up a garden path. He was accompanied by three figures that vanished into thin air within seconds of Weston's arrival. A few days later, I got the full story from John Hunt himself. The hunt had been promising at first. His dogs scared up a large pig, but every time he came close enough to throw his spear, the pig escaped deeper into the bush. Eventually, he found himself in the deep forest, well beyond the garden zone. It was getting dark. The pig suddenly turned into a large old man with dirty hair and a twisted beard. John Hunt realized at once that he had been lured by a *yawu kosaro*, an extremely dangerous type of bush spirit. The spirit grabbed him and in the ensuing struggle through the night and part of the next day attempted to kill him by dragging him across sharp sago thorns and then trying to drown him. John Hunt had the presence of mind to call to the ghost of his dead younger brother for aid. He felt a tap on his shoulder. The *yawu kosaro* vanished to be replaced by his brother and two of his deceased aunts. His brother asked, "Why are you worried? If he wanted to kill you, he would have done it." Exhausted, John Hunt slept under the protection of the ghosts. The next morning, they woke him up and led him back to the garden path where the group encountered Weston.

Fantastic as the story sounded, no one I spoke with doubted that the event had occurred exactly as John Hunt described it. Every adult could tell me similar if usually less dramatic tales of encounters with ghosts, spirits, and other supernatural beings. Such encounters were infrequent, initiated by the spirits themselves. I also heard of sorcerers who could conjure up spirits to harm people. On one rather freaky occasion, I found myself struggling to answer challenging questions posed by spirits who were channelled by a healer I had come to interview.[5]

Like many tribal peoples, the Maisin assume that they share the physical world with a host of invisible spiritual entities and forces. They are not, however, particularly superstitious in the sense of being credulous. Stories of encounters with the supernatural get weighed and assessed according to what people know of these forces; they question and sometimes reject claims that strike them as unrealistic. Nor do the Maisin live in a kind of communion with the spiritual world. Some people pray to the Christian god, and many more allow the priest to pray on their behalf, but only sorcerers and healers regularly appeal directly to spirits for help. People know that they are there but usually don't pay much attention to spirits except when they intervene directly in their lives, as when the *yawu kosaro* attacked John Hunt.

If the Maisin understanding of the nature of the spiritual strikes many of us as strange, it is because we work with different assumptions about the way the universe works — with a different cosmology. Many Westerners assume that the supernatural realm exists at some remove from the mundane affairs of everyday life. If they believe in God at all, they conceive of Him as residing far away, concerned and caring, but nonetheless leaving us to deal with our day-to-day affairs as best we can. Most leave the business of explaining spirituality to specialists like theologians, religious ministers, or clairvoyants. It is possible in the West to get by without concerning oneself at all with spiritual matters, and many people do. People share a general set of cosmological assumptions which makes it possible to define themselves as "very religious" or "not religious" at all. Such claims would make no sense to the Maisin because they work from cosmological assumptions that place living humans and supernatural forces within the same physical environment. The Maisin simply *know* that there are spiritual forces that periodically intrude directly in people's lives in the same way that we know that germs cause sickness. For most people most of the time, these are common sense assumptions that require no further explanation.

Maisin notions of the supernatural tend to be rather fluid and flexible. Some people, particularly healers, claim to know a lot about specific spirits, and there is a general pool of shared knowledge, which I'll outline below. However, apart from the clergy, who speak only about Christian entities, there are no Indigenous theologians or authorities to ensure orthodoxy. Aside from responding to inquisitive anthropologists, people talk about the supernatural mostly in response to events that are believed to have supernatural causes. They draw upon oral traditions, general assumptions about the nature of the spiritual, and the state of social relations at the time to come up with plausible explanations. The more significant the event, the wider the range of speculation as to the spiritual causes.

Here is an example. In January 1983, the Vayova River overflowed its banks after weeks of heavy rains in the mountains. A large portion of Ganjiga was flooded. While no houses collapsed, several were seriously undermined. Nobody doubted that the disaster had a spiritual cause. Many people in Ganjiga suspected that sorcerers from the Uiaku side of the river had called on spirit familiars to cause the flood in retaliation for a long-standing feud. The Uiaku people, however, raised other possibilities: some Ganjiga people had annoyed other villagers by making gardens on disputed land, thus prompting a sorcery attack, or perhaps God had sent the flood to punish Ganjiga people for lax church attendance. During a long contentious meeting to discuss the disaster, several people noted how one of the clans on the Uiaku side had traditionally possessed magic to cause flooding and so surely were involved. This was vigorously denied by the senior members of the clan, who protested that their ancestors had given up the magic when they became Christians. Nothing in the end was resolved, but no one had any doubt that the flood had a supernatural cause.

The Maisin recognize that spirits and spiritual forces are both powerful and for the most part invisible to living humans. Explanations cannot help but be variable because so much rests upon surmise. All the same, an examination of many explanations clearly reveals common underlying assumptions. These concern the nature of spiritual power, the types of entities that embody that power, and the relationship between living humans and the divine.

Spiritual entities share the common trait of "strength" or "power," *anno wenna*. When applied to humans, the term describes physical strength: an adult may evince *anno wenna* but an infant does not. When applied to supernatural entities, the concept resembles the eastern Melanesian and Polynesian idea of *mana*. *Anno wenna* is not a substance; it is an attribute of entities that effect transformations (Keesing 1984). This potency is at once dangerous and creative. Humans must prepare themselves through certain rituals to build up their own "strength" before approaching spiritual entities if they wish to survive the encounter. Approached correctly, spiritual force effects the positive transformations necessary for survival: success in subsistence activities, for instance, and the maturation of children. Yet spiritual forces may also be manipulated to cause misfortunes as in the case of sorcery attacks or disasters like the Ganjiga flood. Humans have no choice but to try to manipulate spiritual forces, to draw upon and direct their transformative power. Humans ultimately cannot control the divine world. With the somewhat ambiguous exception of the Christian god, spiritual entities are ultimately amoral. They can aid, harm, or ignore the living as they please.

The Maisin encounter a range of entities that manifest spiritual *anno wenna*. Some places, like gardens for instance, hold spiritual potency because of their association with ancestors. The most common form, however, is magic. Individual Maisin possess magic they use for a wide variety of applications: for gardening, hunting, fishing, healing fevers, sexually attracting a mate, preventing pregnancy, and so forth. People are very secretive about the magic they possess, but the forms I've seen or heard about all involve special leaves, barks, or odd-shaped rocks over which a simple incantation is chanted. Before using their magic, owners need to prepare themselves, usually by avoiding sexual intercourse and eating foods deemed to be "hot." Those who fail to prepare themselves or use the magic improperly may be harmed and even killed by it. Whenever people come into contact with spiritual forces, they take on the quality of *anno wenna* themselves and pose a risk for others. Hence, magicians avoid others when practising their art. They refuse to share food with them and keep their magic out of sight.

The Maisin's environment is inhabited by a variety of spiritual entities. The most commonly encountered are spirits of the recent or distant dead. As Christians, the Maisin state that when a person dies, his or her spirit (*yawu* = "breath") goes to Heaven. All the same, people generally expect spirits of the dead to remain in the vicinity of their homes for some time after their deaths. One never sees them directly. They appear in dreams and visions, usually to close relatives or as reflections on the surface of water, visible only to healers. The recently deceased retain their names and identities. They are known as *kaniniwa*, a word also used to denote "soul," "reflection," "shadow," and "picture." When a young person dies suddenly and unexpectedly, his or her ghost may hover around the village for days or even weeks. People do not venture into the gardens at such times. Women and children, whose "strength" is not as great as men's, are believed to be especially vulnerable to attack from the ghost, who may be angry over an untimely death or merely lonely. The Maisin often attribute the deaths of babies to ghost attack. All the same, the ghosts of the recent dead can also be very helpful. They often appear in the dreams of their close relatives, helping them out by showing places to make gardens, to hunt, or to fish.[6] Some also act as spirit familiars for sorcerers and for healers, as we shall see later in this chapter.

For the most part, however, the spirits that the Maisin believe inhabit the bush and garden areas are anonymous. They are generally known as *waa*. *Waa* were once human, but their specific identities have been lost. Maisin know of them mainly through folktales. Ghosts in these stories sometimes appear as old people, ravenous for human flesh; in others, they trick the living by donning skins that make them appear as sexy young men and women. The stories are often gruesome, but in general the Maisin don't worry much about *waa* as they are not imagined to be very interested in the living and thus not likely to attack.

At a further remove from the villages, in the deep forest and in rivers flowing down from the heights of the mountain wall, dwell certain spirits that may never have been among the living. Very few hunters venture this far and thus rarely encounter these spirits. John Hunt's *yawu kosaro* belonged to this class of spirit. A few elders I worked with claimed to know the names of some of them. For instance, I purchased a striking tapa cloth whose design featured a monstrous form, with spades in the place of its legs and arms. The woman who designed the cloth, herself a healer, came from the Aisore clan, which traditionally had the magic to call this spirit from its home in the mountains to cause flooding. The Maisin more often encounter another form of bush spirit that inhabits the bodies of river eels. These eels, called *yun tamati*, "water men," attack women by invisibly entering their bodies through their vaginas and causing severe sickness marked by cold chills.

Prior to the arrival of the missionaries, the Maisin do not seem to have recognized any gods. However, this was many years ago, and everyone today knows of God, Jesus, and other Christian figures through church services and the Bible. In general, people treat all biblical figures as divine entities. They assume that they live at the greatest distance from ordinary life in Heaven. Lesser beings, like angels or figures such as Jacob from the Old Testament or the Virgin Mary, sometimes visit people in dreams, usually when they are seriously ill. Some people told me that they had been visited by Jesus himself, although they were only able to look upon his feet, not his face. In general, people consider such interventions as benign if rare; they seem only to occur during moments of personal crisis. They thus form an exception to the assumption that spirits are amoral. Yet there is some ambiguity on this point, especially in Maisin thinking about God. The Maisin accept church teaching that God is an omnipresent being. They credit Him with the creation of everything and, as we'll see below, hold that faith in God and Jesus provides protection against lesser spirits and sorcerers. Yet not everyone sees God as always benign or helpful. Like a lesser spirit, He can be capricious or moved to anger by a small slight. They also assume that God's interventions in the world must be on a scale with His greatness and power. Thus, people tend to attribute major natural disasters to God's anger. Older people who remembered the Mount Lamington volcanic explosion of 1951, which killed around 4,000 people in the central part of Oro Province, told me that it was God's revenge against the Orokaiva people of the area who had angered Him by failing to keep their churches neat and clean.[7] Most people saw the typhoon of 1974, which levelled Tufi, as another instance of God's revenge against local failings, and similar rumours circulated after Ganjiga was flooded.

God, bush spirits, ancestors, and ghosts as the Maisin conceive them are autonomous spirits. Human beings can only try to influence them; they can't control them. All the same, it is obviously the case that spiritual entities and forces react to the actions taken by humans. In the Maisin conception of the cosmos, the invisible world of spiritual forces and beings exists in intimate relation with the visible world of human action. This intimacy is nowhere more pronounced than at the moments and situations in which living humans engage directly with the divine. As we have already seen in the case of magic, when people interact with spiritual forces, they take on some of its characteristics, gaining their own potency and propensity to act autonomously. Sorcerers and healers go one stage further, simultaneously operating in both dimensions. By connecting the world of the living with the amoral dimension of spiritual power, their activities — real and imagined — serve to throw the current moral condition of society into sharp relief. Because they cannot ultimately control amoral spirits, the Maisin are most urgently concerned with what spirit encounters and attacks reveal about their moral condition, that is, the aspects of their lives they actually *can* control. This becomes especially clear in the case of sorcery and healing, discussed below.

This brings us back to the incident that opened this section. John Hunt and everyone else I talked to about his encounter with the bush spirit was convinced that a sorcerer had set him up. As a student of Maisin religion, I was interested in learning about the spiritual world. John Hunt, however, talked mostly about the possible reasons someone wished him dead. Unless he could deal with what he considered the real causes, he might well be attacked again. Any discussion of the local religion thus turns on an understanding of morality and its limits, a location occupied in the Maisin imagination by the mysterious and terrifying figure of the sorcerer.

THE MEANING OF SORCERY

Over the course of a week or so in October 1982, I overheard a growing chorus of concern about Mona. Mona was a middle-aged widow who had suffered from a debilitating illness for over a year. Her alarmed family had turned to every medical resource available to them: the government-sponsored village medical aid post, various traditional medicines, and a prayer service on her behalf led by the priest.[8] When the nurses at the small hospital in Wanigela failed to cure Mona, her working relatives put up the funds to transport her to hospitals in the city of Lae and then Popondetta to be examined and treated by doctors. The doctors decided they could do nothing for her and sent her home. This was the clearest evidence, as far as villagers were concerned, that Mona was suffering from "village sickness." Powerful as they were, it was well understood that Western medicines were impotent against sorcery.

Soon after, under a gloriously bright full moon, I canoed across the river to Ganjiga where Mona was staying in the care of a clan brother. She was emaciated, nearly a skeleton, lying on a thin mattress on the verandah where the occasional breeze cooled her feverish body. A group of men sat on the ground nearby, speaking in low tones. They were keeping *gumema*, a vigil meant to protect her from further attacks by spirits or sorcerers, who are believed to take advantage of the weak. One elderly man was applying bush medicine to her legs, which were paralyzed. A few nights later, a larger group gathered for a spirit séance, led by Adeva, an elderly blind woman who was well-regarded for her healing abilities. Accompanied by a chorus of young girls, Adeva chanted spirit songs through the night, occasionally pausing to spray red betelnut spittle over Mona's body. Adeva later told me that during her trance her spirit had left her body in search of Mona's soul, which had been stolen and hidden by a sorcerer. Adeva had been successful in returning Mona's soul to her body, but she could not guarantee that the sorcerer might not just steal it back again.

As Mona continued to decline, I heard increasing talk about how the sorcerers were getting out of control. People reflected upon several recent deaths. If Mona were to die, perhaps her angered relatives would themselves resort to sorcery to retaliate against those they felt were responsible. Where would it all end? The whole village seemed under siege. The village councillor decided that it was time to call a meeting. It was heavily attended, drawing nearly all adults from Uiaku, Ganjiga, and the nearby village of Yuayu. In the course of the meeting, participants reviewed all of the reasons someone might have wanted to hurt Mona or Mona's family. The most likely reason, most people agreed, was that a Yuayu man who was rumoured to have attempted an affair with her had employed sorcery after being rejected. He and his relatives denied this vigorously. As people reviewed past tensions and spats, the elders reminded everyone that the purpose of the meeting was not to accuse or punish the sorcerer but to bring the community together, to find an answer to the social tensions that led, in the words of one elder, to "all of the ladies dying." Over and over again, they stated, "We have not gathered here to blame anyone." The underlying message seemed to be that healing the poor woman's body depended upon healing the social breaches in the society. Deacon Russell confirmed this at the end of the meeting. He first asked everyone to join him in a prayer for Mona's recovery. He then prompted the entire assembly to shout as one: "She will be well!"

After the third such meeting, Mona quietly passed away. The reaction to her illness was not typical. Early death is common in the area. People suffer from a wide range of serious diseases like malaria, dengue fever, dysentery, and tuberculosis. Accidents from machetes, wild boars, or falling trees are not unusual. Western medical facilities are sparse at best. During the 1980s, the village aid post offered only a small range of medicines, often running out; it closed down entirely in the late 1990s after years of intermittent government funding. Still, most deaths occur among the very young and the very old. Close relatives will often attribute these deaths to sorcery, but for the most part people accept them stoically. It is different when an adult, in the full vigour of life, suffers a serious accident or a life-threatening illness, and it is especially frightening when they die. Not only are such deaths tragic, they are dangerous to the living for they may touch off a sorcery feud that will threaten the survival of the community as a whole. This is the dark side of reciprocity: an eye for an eye. Payback. Coming in the wake of several deaths of mostly middle-aged women, Mona's sickness thus triggered panic. People needed to know the reasons behind the attacks before they spun out of control. Fortunately, no one else fell sick after Mona's death, and talk of sorcery gradually faded away.

Sorcery and witchcraft beliefs are very common, and anthropologists have devoted much attention to them. Variations can be found across Melanesia and, indeed, much of the world. In centuries past in Europe and the American colonies, church and government officials, abetted by terrified mobs, put hundreds of mostly poor women to death on charges of witchcraft and accused many more of secretly practising the black arts. For all of this, most contemporary Westerners find sorcery as understood by people like the Maisin to be perplexing. The Maisin know about germs, happily use Western medicine when available, and understand that carelessness leads to accidents. Further, nobody admits to actually practising sorcery or seeing it practised, although some people — mainly healers — claim to know a great deal about how it is done. People know about alternative explanations for misfortune, and they possess no direct evidence that sorcerers even exist. They also know that the church officially frowns upon sorcery and traditional healing and that Westerners are sceptical of sorcery's very existence. It is possible, even likely, that some Maisin really do resort occasionally to actually trying sorcery.[9] However, from an empirical standpoint, sorcery exists as a *post facto* explanation rather than an actual practice: as an explanation after the fact. The Maisin don't require proof of the existence of sorcery any more than most of us do of germs; they know it exists in large part because it provides a satisfactory explanation of why misfortunes like serious illnesses happen.

As we shall see in the last part of this chapter, the Maisin have long wanted to rid themselves of sorcery, and many are impressed that Westerners seem to have done so. However, from their perspective it defies common sense to deny its reality. No one ever questions whether sorcery happens, although people do question specific interpretations and accusations. In the case of serious mishaps, people reflexively wonder, "Why did this happen?" They may think awhile about the identity or methods employed by the sorcerer, but inevitably they focus upon the state of social relationships. This is because sorcerers are assumed to be most often motivated by moral breaches or to be hired by people who are retaliating for some wrong. Talk of sorcery, then, serves two immediate functions: it makes sense of unfortunate events, and it sheds light on the state of moral relationships.

The figure of the sorcerer provides the pivot for these two functions. The power of the sorcerer, as imagined by the Maisin, derives from his position with one foot in the world of the living and one foot in the spiritual realm. Sorcerers are thought to make themselves "hot" by shunning "cooling" foods, avoiding sex, and refusing to share their food and possessions with others. They take on the traits of spirits. People imagine them as solitary, living at the margins of the community, avoiding contact. Like spirits, sorcerers are thought to be amoral. They are prone to jealousy, they hoard their possessions and refuse to share food with their neighbours, and they are easily angered. They are greatly feared for this. Yet there is also a trace of tragedy in the way the Maisin think of sorcerers, for they are the victims as much as victors of their powers. The Maisin describe sorcerers as *dagari*, a complex concept that combines the characteristic of greediness with being physically crippled. Sorcerers exemplify individualism for the Maisin, which in this reciprocal society is generally not a desirable trait. Indeed, the sorcerer in many ways represents the antithesis of moral being for the Maisin: he is a figure of evil. Shrouded in secrecy, powerful and feared, he is at the same time lonely and vulnerable. Sorcerers must always be on guard against retaliation from others with similar or greater powers. Even if they are successful for a time, their engagement with spiritual forces slowly erodes their health and eventually kills them. Thus, the Maisin often picture the sorcerer as physically bent and twisted, a man both suffering and causing pain.

Healers are known and operate mostly in the open, but they share key traits with sorcerers.[10] Because they also deal directly with spiritual forces, they too must prepare their bodies to make themselves "hot" and be cautious in their interactions with others. They tend to be elderly men and women. People are cautious around healers. They turn to them at moments of desperation, as a last resort against what appears to be certain sorcery attack, as in the case of Mona. Still, they are keenly aware that healers have the capability of launching spiritual attacks on others; they aren't entirely to be trusted. So people tend to avoid their houses and watch what they say in their presence.

It is important to bear in mind that people's knowledge of sorcerers is based upon lore, hearsay, and general notions of the power and perils of dealing with spiritual forces. Unless a young person suddenly drops dead — a dire situation that the Maisin call "raw death" — the idea that a sorcerer has been at work usually begins as a suspicion, carried in worried whispers by loved ones, gradually growing in volume, spreading and intensifying if the usual medical resorts fail to work. In terms of their own belief system, the Maisin are far from credulous; they watch carefully, probing the possibilities before coming to a conclusion. As suspicions harden into certainty, people engaged by the victim's plight begin to speculate on why he or she was attacked. The closest kin may insist that the sorcerer operated from mere malice. This is always a possibility, but not one that most people entertain for long. For the most part, sorcery attacks are thought to be motivated by some action of the victim or their close relatives. The supposed actions triggering the attack, in turn, divide roughly into two types: those that directly provoked the sorcerer and those that provoked people who hired a sorcerer.

Most explanations put forward for sorcery attack fall within the first category. When a person suffers a serious illness or accident, they and their closest relatives will rack their memories for things they might have done that provoked retaliation. In the close confines of village society, the list of slights and petty jealousies are endless. A sorcerer may attack because the victim or the victim's kin stole some food from a garden or failed to share a smoke, or he may act out of jealousy because the victim possessed more valued things than others or because they were particularly successful as gardeners or lovers. The Maisin refer to such provocations as *daa*, a word English-speakers translate as "mistake." A "mistake" is not wrong in any absolute sense. All the same, "mistakes" share a common feature: they deny reciprocal balance in some way. This facet is more obvious in the case of theft or adultery, but it is in play as well in cases where the sorcerer reacts in jealousy against someone who has a better garden, valuable shell ornaments, or merely more friends than the average. Success as much as deliberate misdeed can upset the fine balance of reciprocal relationships and trigger retaliation from a sorcerer. It was for this reason, you will recall from Chapter 2, that a villager decided to turn the iron-roofed dwelling built for him by his son into a shed rather than risk provoking jealousy by moving in.

A tragic illness or accident, particularly in the case of young to middle-aged adults, triggers a process of recollection and reflection that spreads if the victim fails to respond to treatment. A remedy depends upon healing the social breach that provoked the attack. Yet, of course, there is no certain way to know. After identifying possible "mistakes," the family of the victim may quietly send a gift of food to the suspected sorcerer or his kin in an effort to ease his anger. This is risky, however, as the gift — particularly if it is made public — can appear as an accusation, a "mistake" that in itself might provoke an attack. Healers help people deal with sorcery attacks not only through their direct ministrations but by divining possible causes. The community meeting, in which people are enjoined to air any and all relevant tensions, provides the final resort. The cure at all of these levels remains the same: restoring social amity by overcoming a breached relationship. People do not seek to punish the sorcerer or the people who may have hired him, at least while the victim lives. This was the thrust of Deacon Russell's attempt at the end of the first meeting addressing Mona's illness to get everyone to shout in unison, "She will be well!" The health of the sorcery victim was tied intrinsically to the health of social relations within the community.

Anthropologists have long been fascinated by sorcery and witchcraft and have over the years developed a range of explanations for such beliefs. Sorcery in places like Uiaku can be seen as functioning to reinforce the social order. Many Maisin are comfortable with that type of explanation. While they don't like sorcerers much, they credit them with keeping people in line. Children grow up not only knowing that sharing things is good but also that those who fail to reciprocate get attacked and killed. They also learn of the dangers of standing out too much from the crowd, either by owning too many things or by showing off their accomplishments. Sorcery thus acts as a kind of social levelling mechanism. The functionalist explanation, however, is not sufficient in itself, for sorcery is just as capable of disrupting social life as reinforcing it. Many anthropologists see sorcery as a form of symbolic violence, a projection of the struggles and tensions between social factions. At any one time, sorcery accusations provide a fairly good gauge of the points and levels of tension. It is not surprising, given the nature of the marriage contract, that in-laws are often suspected of resorting to sorcery against each other. Finally, and not least, sorcery beliefs provide people with a framework for understanding why tragedies happen and how they should respond to them. In the words of one of the most famous students of the phenomenon, "witchcraft [and sorcery] helps explain unfortunate events" (Evans-Pritchard 1937).

All of these explanations help us to understand the workings and logic of sorcery beliefs among the Maisin. Yet they leave out, I think, a deeper dimension. A consideration of sorcery leads us back to the way the Maisin conceive of the cosmos and the human place within it. The trigger for a sorcery attack in almost all cases is a breach of morality, a denial of reciprocal balance. This is easy for us to grasp. The notion of sharing fairly is by no means a foreign concept for Westerners. What I have found foreign and to this day extremely difficult to comprehend is that the Maisin do not rank the wrongs that provoke attacks. The reasons given for sorcery attacks leading to death have often struck me as amazingly trivial and petty. One man I got to know quite well, for instance, was widely believed to have employed sorcery to murder his own sister because she had not shared a cigarette with him. That sorcerers kill just as readily for trivial as serious reasons reflects the assumption that they, like other spiritual forces, are amoral and capricious. Yet, it is clear that the Maisin nearly always reserve some if not most of the blame for the victim. It is they, after all, who provoked the attack in the first place, they who made the "mistake" and thus brought the wrath of the sorcery upon themselves. Individuals who are kind, generous, and caring are just as likely to be the target of sorcery attacks as those who neglect their families and laze about the village rather than work hard in the gardens. Maisin understandings of sorcery thus reveal a rather bleak assessment of the human condition. To live a good and long life, a person needs to meet his and her reciprocal obligations to kin completely and without fail. Yet, it is virtually impossible to do so. No wonder, then, that the Maisin look upon old people with respect verging on awe. Anyone who has reached old age, it can be assumed, has successfully navigated the difficult shoals of social relationships and the perils posed by spiritual forces. No wonder that from the time of the arrival of the first Anglican missionaries, the Maisin have sought to rid themselves of sorcerers.

SORCERY AND GHOSTS, THE PAST AND THE PRESENT

The Maisin's beliefs concerning spirits, magic, and sorcery would seem to have little to do with Christianity. Indeed, there is a striking discord between the message of universal love delivered in Sunday sermons and the moral assumptions underlying local understandings of sorcery. All the same, nobody seems to worry much about the contradictions. I have yet to hear a preacher so much as mention sorcery from the pulpit, let alone condemn it. They usually pitch their appeals to Christian morality at a very abstract level, with little direct reference to actual village life. Nor have I heard any Maisin suggest that the *belief* in magic, spirits, or sorcerers might be, in itself, unchristian or incompatible with faith in God. An anthropologist examining a similar situation in the Anglican village of Wamira about 80 kilometres to the east of Uiaku once described the people there as "Sunday Christians, Monday Sorcerers," concluding that the Wamiran acceptance of missionary teachings has been highly selective: they are, at heart, still traditionalists (Kahn 1983).

The Maisin, however, don't consider their beliefs about spirits and sorcerers as being opposed to Christianity or particularly traditionalist. In part this is because they take a pragmatic view of such entities rather than thinking of them in more abstract terms as making up a "traditional" religion in opposition to Christianity. As far as they are concerned, spirits, sorcerers, Jesus, and God are equally real, if not equal in power. Such spiritual entities are not as tangible as trees or crops, but they are no less real in that humans come to know them mostly through their manifestations in the physical world. Like most Pacific Islanders, the Maisin accepted, rejected, and resisted various

Figure 4.3 Elders in public mourning following a death. For three days following a death, people sit quietly near the house of the deceased to show their sorrow and respect. (Photo by A.M. Tietjen)

missionary initiatives to change, abandon, or replace various customs and social practices, but they largely took missionary teachings about God at face value. Initially, this is likely because they associated the idea of a powerful non-local god with the evident power and wealth of the European colonialists. It also helped that in the expanded view of the cosmos introduced by the missionaries, God's occupation of a distant heaven didn't require the removal of the spirits, ghosts, magical forces, and sorcerers already inhabiting the neighbourhood. The Maisin understand their ancestors' acceptance of Christianity not as a displacement of one religion with another but as a process of enlightenment. As Frank Davis Dodi, a thoughtful church elder explained to me, "God always existed in this place, but our ancestors were ignorant men. When the missionaries came, everyone knew the truth."

The term "traditionalists" is misleading in another key respect. The Maisin think of spiritual forces and figures, including those in the Bible, as existing in real time. Just like humans, they are affected by the circumstances in which they operate. As far as the Maisin are concerned, there is nothing particularly "traditional" or customary about sorcerers or ghosts. They are every bit as much a part of today's world as Christian church services. Indeed, if anything, they have been more responsive to historical changes than the (rather conservative) Anglican Church. The Maisin say that sorcery and the behaviour of the dead dramatically changed over the past century. They credit much of the change to the people's growing awareness of God's power.

More than a century ago, the Maisin grasped quickly that the presence of powerful foreign missionaries might provide a way of ridding themselves of the scourge of sorcery. Within a few months of the opening of the mission and church at Uiaku in late 1902, at a time when the missionary and teachers could speak only a few words of the language, a group of Maisin presented them with a large collection of charms, clearly hoping that they would take and destroy them (which they did, in a bonfire). It is likely that the villagers thought of the newcomers as holding a level of spiritual power that trumped that of local sorcerers and spirits — perhaps they were spirits themselves? — and thus might have the ability to purge the community of sorcery. It didn't work, of course, but the Maisin over the years have kept trying, long after they learned of the Christian God and accepted baptism. In the early 1930s, an Uiaku man called Maikin claimed to have visited Heaven where he met angels and sat at the feet of Jesus. He returned to earth with the ability to sense the presence of sorcery materials. He and his followers forced suspected sorcerers from villages across the region to surrender their magical objects and bundles, which they then destroyed (Barker 1990). As recently as 1997, members of the Melanesian Brotherhood, an Anglican religious order that originated in the Solomon Islands, entered the Maisin villages and, with the assistance of some of the locals, detected the presence of "bad things" in various houses, the old objects and bundles of charms that villagers feared were used to ensorcel others. As the crowd built up, most of the owners (although not all) reluctantly surrendered the condemned objects to the Brothers. Declaring that God's power would protect them, the Brothers took away the objects and threw them into the sea.

Judging from the 1997 incident, such purges are very disruptive and most (probably all) of the objects destroyed were never actually employed for evil purposes (Barker 2001). Certainly, those Maisin forced to surrender cherished old carved lime spatulas inherited from their fathers or special rocks used to promote taro objected vociferously that they were being made into scapegoats. Still, most surrendered the objects. Elderly Maisin who remembered the earlier purges believed that they have been effective. Prior to the early purges, I was told, certain men were openly acknowledged as sorcerers. They practised a deadly type of sorcery known as *wea* or "poison" which had come to them from the origin times, when the clans had first emerged from underground. While exact techniques varied, they all involved the

133

sorcerer surreptitiously collecting something from the victim—such as some hair, a piece of clothing, or sand from a footprint—and heating this up, mixed with magical potions, in a bamboo tube over a fire. This was a type of "sympathetic magic," operating according to a similar principle as voodoo dolls: as the tube got hot, the victim broke into a fever. The *wea* sorcerers acted as enforcers for their clans. In those days, people say, clans formed their own hamlets off the main village path. People did not venture into other clan's hamlets without permission and did not wander about at night for fear of sorcery attack. The purges caused the sorcerers to abandon their powers and offices; in turn, the village took its present form, with the main path meandering through the clan hamlets, which are open to all.

This might have brought sorcery to an end, the elders say, but instead it was driven underground. Some men continued to use the old forms of *wea*, but most sorcerers took up a new form involving the cultivation of spirit familiars that are sent out to capture and hide the souls of the victims. Attempts were also made to stamp this out, but sorcery has proven to be very adaptable, especially in the aftermath of the establishment of colonial rule, which made it easier for people to travel. New forms have entered the region. I am told, for instance, that one can purchase at the Tufi market a charmed flashlight that ensorcels its victims by capturing them in its beam. In addition, as the Maisin have mixed and married with outsiders, they have exposed themselves to new dangers. Today, the Maisin especially fear the "flying witches" of the coastal villages of Milne Bay Province to the east. At night, these *yafuni*, as the Maisin call them, leave the bodies of their living hosts (mostly women) and make their way up the coast in spirit powerboats, planes, and cars. They are imagined as extremely violent. If a person suddenly dies, *yafuni* are usually suspected, particularly if a member of the family has visited Milne Bay or married a woman from that area.

While sorcery has deep ancestral roots, then, it is not simply a creaky survival of the past but very much an active and innovative presence in the present. Still, the history I've outlined might suggest that sorcery and Christianity stand in clear opposition, that the Maisin assume an essential incompatibility between them, and that it is only a matter of time before Christianity defeats its age-old enemy. Some Maisin do speak in this way. Yet, I have found consistently in conversation that people hold far more varied and nuanced views of the relationship between Christianity and sorcery. Many people begin with the premise that since God "created everything," He must have placed the sorcerer on Earth for a purpose. Some people are content to stop with this observation. For them, God is like any other spirit: autonomous, mysterious, and capricious, rather like a sorcerer Himself, only operating at a vastly larger scale. Why would God create sorcerers? When asked this question, villagers come up with a range of opinions. Some view the sorcerer, and by extension God, as a kind of moral policeman. By punishing those who breach moral expectations, the sorcerer maintains peace and good order within the community. This is, however, a minority view in my experience. The Maisin generally regard sorcerers as evil. This leads some to reason that as the sorcerer is a living human being, he is best regarded as a sinner who risks his own salvation by practising the black art. The victim may also have committed an immoral act, but the sorcerer makes a bigger mistake by taking the power of God upon himself to act as judge, jury, and executioner. Still another and apparently growing body of opinion views God as a benign deity who acts to protect those with sufficient faith in His presence. That people profess a belief in God but still succumb to sorcery attacks is best understood, in this view, as a failure of faith.

One finds a similar range and mix of opinion concerning the nature of ghosts of the recent dead. In the old days, according to elderly Maisin, a death required elaborate and quite violent rituals meant to demonstrate sorrow and to determine the identity of the sorcerer responsible for the killing. Mourning women, for instance, shuffled around the house of the deceased for hours on end, singing a dirge while lacerating their breasts with sharp obsidian. After the burial, relatives of the deceased crept into the graveyard, braving the dangers posed by the angry ghost, to conduct divination rituals. These and related practices were vigorously opposed by the missionaries and yet continued into the 1950s, long after most villagers had been baptized. There are remnants today. After the period of public mourning, marked by hours of eerie wails and dirges from the gathered women, a senior man appears at the doorway of the house in which the corpse lies. In the sudden silence that greets his appearance, he calls out to the ghost, "See! We have cried for you. Now leave this place. Do not be angry. Do not bother the women and children." People remain quiet in the village for the next few days, especially if the death was sudden and the person young, for fear that the lingering spirit might be annoyed and attack. Relatives hang the deceased's favourite clothes, some tapa, and other objects on the grave itself in an effort to keep the ghost happy in its new status.

All the same, apart from moments of panic, such as Mona's sickness and death, people say that ghosts are far less dangerous than they used to be. They credit the change to the adoption of Christianity. Since the people who die today are baptized Christians, I was told, they have heard the teachings of the Church and thus are far less likely to want to hurt the living. The days immediately following death are the most dangerous, because the newly dead often feel angry or lonely and thus are most likely to attack, but Christians leave the vicinity for the distant abode of Heaven from which they only occasionally return to this world. People are far less frightened of ghosts than they used to be. As far as my informants were concerned, the fact that ghosts are now Christians, rather than opposition from missionaries, accounted for the abandonment of the old rituals.

I have a strong impression from my more recent visits that people are less concerned about the doings of sorcerers than when I first arrived in Uiaku. The purge of 1997 occurred as do occasional community meetings prompted by a serious illness, but most people seem less prone to speculate about the causes of misfortunes than in the early 1980s. This is not the result of any conscious decision, as the Maisin themselves seem unaware that anything has changed. No one I know thinks that sorcerers have gone away. Nor have most people changed their opinions about them, except for a few families who have joined a Pentecostal sect that views sorcerers, bush spirits, ghosts, and the like as emissaries of Satan. It would seem, for most people, that sorcerers are just not as relevant to their lives today. There could be many factors at work, but I suspect a key one is a shift in popular conceptions of morality, particularly a weakening of the ethic of reciprocity in favour of a more individualistic orientation.

While this change affects all aspects of Maisin life, it is centred primarily at the level of the community. At this point, then, we need to shift our focus from the life-worlds of individuals, households, and kin groups to the village as a whole, a sphere in which the the church and the state have played their most direct role in shaping Maisin society.

Notes

1. Schwimmer's information on Maisin tapa appears to have been based on a one-day visit in the mid-1970s. While it includes some useful information, it is perhaps more interesting for what it reveals about the ways that the Maisin presented themselves at the time to the occasional European visitor. In this case, it appears a large reception was arranged during which 40 or more women, in traditional dress, demonstrated the making of tapa. Schwimmer, entirely reliant on translators, assumed that Maisin women continued to favour tapa cloth as regular clothing and that the "25 clans" she was told were present in the village each had origin myths depicted in tapa designs.

2. Women are thus effectively barred from preaching in church services. During meetings of the Mothers Union and youth fellowship group, however, some women will offer special prayers or short homilies.

3. Until recently, the Maisin did not keep track of their birth dates, making it very difficult to estimate precise ages. In 1982, I discovered that one of my oldest informants, Guy Kamanu, had been among the first Maisin baptized in 1911. Baptismal

records held in the Anglican Archives at the University of Papua New Guinea indi-cated that Guy was a young adult at the time, so it is possible that he was born just before first contact with Europeans. While a font of information about the older cul-ture, however, Guy had no personal recollection of Maisin life prior to the imposition of colonial rule.

4. Jean and John Comaroff (1991, 1997) use the phrase "the long conversation" in a magisterial study of the impact of Protestant missionaries on Tswana peoples in southern Africa during the nineteenth century. For other anthropological interpreta-tions of Christian conversion, see the essays in Hefner (1993).

5. The two healers I came to know the best, Marcella Adeva and Stonewigg Kotena, relied upon deceased relatives as spirit familiars who sought out and attempted to recover souls stolen by sorcerers. When I first attempted to interview Adeva, a wizened blind woman with an other-earthly way of staring through you, she abruptly cut off the questions and engaged in an animated argument with, as far as I could see, herself. My interpreter told me that her "daughters" were demanding to know who I was and why I was so interested in their mother. Adeva relayed several sharp questions and then disappeared into the house. We heard a weird voice telling me to go away. A few days later, I received a message that the daughters had decided that their mother should share her experiences with me, and I returned to complete the interview. I consistently found healers to be among the most engaging people I dealt with, intensely interested in spiritual matters and very open about them. All of them volunteered that their powers were a gift of God and thus entirely compatible with their Christian beliefs, despite earlier oppositions from some missionaries.

6. Dreams convey a critical source of truth and revelation in Melanesian cultures. For a collection of excellent studies on the subject, see Lohmann (2003).

7. Erik Schwimmer (1969) recorded similar explanations in the Orokaiva area 15 years after the disaster.

8. Limited Western health care has been available to the people of Collingwood Bay since around 1912, when a missionary nurse set up a base in Wanigela. In the 1950s, the government established village-based aid posts run by medical orderlies with basic training in first aid and a limited range of supplies. Like most Melanesians, the Maisin make use of a wide range of medical resorts, including Indigenous cures, when they are sick or they have an accident (Frankel and Lewis 1989).

9. The secrecy surrounding sorcery in Maisin culture is typical in Melanesia. However, there are a few places where traditionally sorcerers were well-known, such as Mekeo in the Central Province of Papua New Guinea (Stephen 1995). Indeed, as we shall see, this may have been true of the Maisin in the past.

10. The Maisin insist in general that only men are "strong" enough to practise sorcery. All the same, villagers are cautious around female healers and I have occa-sionally heard rumours that they have resorted to sorcery.

CHAPTER FIVE

Community

Having completed my little tapa cloth, I packed it away and have rarely looked at it since. It was time to move on to the major thrust of my research: conducting a rounded, holistic analysis of tapa. I was interested in everything: cultural heritage, local uses, and the implications of a growing market for the cloth as a form of "ethnic art." I had hoped to work with my favourite research assistant from 1981-83 — MacSherry Gegeyo — but he had since moved to Port Moresby. George met with other community leaders to discuss my project and nominated Roland Wawe, a handsome 25-year-old bachelor who they felt had great leadership potential and would benefit from the experience. It was an inspired choice. I have had mixed success with my research assistants. Many find the work of conducting surveys, helping with translations, and other tasks boring after a while and stop coming. Roland, like MacSherry, had a keen curiosity about his culture. While at high school, he had started writing short plays depicting traditional activities and events. Towards the end of my stay, I joined an enthusiastic audience to watch the youth group perform one of Roland's works: a play about the elopement of two lovers and the subsequent battle between their enraged clans. Roland and I established a good working rapport right from the start. As the research progressed, Roland would often suggest topics that needed further attention and correct some of my more egregious mistakes.

Roland and I proceeded to conduct a systematic survey of households in Uiaku and Ganjiga focussed upon tapa. I worked from a questionnaire of 12 standard questions. I asked women whether they grew any *wuwusi* trees in their gardens, who taught them how to make tapa, whether they worked with others when beating or dyeing the cloth, to whom they had recently given cloth, and whether they had sold any cloth recently. The survey progressed slowly, as time had to allowed for chit-chat, chewing betelnut, and sharing tea and often food. Very often, the survey triggered more general conversations not only about tapa but about past lives and current concerns.

One day, part way through the survey, Roland and I sat down to work out

Figure 5.1 Roland Wawe, wearing a headdress he designed himself, with possum fur and bird of paradise plumes. (Photo by J. Barker)

a list of the various ways tapa got used in the past and in the present. Up until the early 1960s, tapa had been the standard day-to-day clothing for most people, only gradually being replaced first by calico cloth and later by second-hand clothing marketed in the towns. Richly decorated tapa, often bearing clan *evovi* design, was still worn on ceremonial occasions. Beyond this, we had learned of distinct types of tapa that used to be prepared for widows and widowers, to cover the heads of girls undergoing tattooing, and for other special occasions. The Maisin also used to make large sheets of tapa to use as blankets during the cold nights of the dry season and as shawls to keep off the rain. In the past and to a lesser extent today, the Maisin traded tapa with neighbouring groups for cooking pots, pigs, and sea-going canoes. Tapa was a major item of wealth in formal exchanges. Finally, Roland demonstrated for me how useful the tough strips of old tapa can be when one needs to tie up a bundle or lash sticks together to make a temporary shelter in the bush.

I was delighted with this catalogue of uses as it provided an excellent check list for proceeding with the research. My main job, from now on, would be to fill out these categories and perhaps add a few more. Or so I thought.

Armed with the list, I now began a second, more leisurely swing through the village, casually visiting households in the evenings and setting up longer interviews during the day. Things began in a promising way. People happily confirmed that tapa had a wide variety of uses and meanings. Among other things, I learned that most clans owned several named designs, not just the most prominent ones that I had seen people wearing on ceremonial occasions. This led me to visit each named descent group to record systematically the names of the designs they owned. Here I hit a roadblock. More often than not, all people could remember were the names. Sometimes an elderly woman was able to trace a design for me on a blank strip of tapa or in the sand for me to photograph, but on other occasions people told me that while they had once possessed more tapa *evovi*, they had forgotten the patterns and even sometimes the names. Documenting the older uses also proved frustrating. Elders could provide descriptions of a variety of abandoned customs, but their information was often vague, and there were many contradictions.

Helpful as they were in filling out my survey, it was clear that most people had other concerns with regards to tapa. Once my questions were answered, conversations quickly moved to money matters. The Maisin had exchanged tapa with outsiders for as long as anyone could remember. Towards the end of the colonial period, however, a market developed in Papua New Guinea for artifacts marketed to the (then) large number of expatriates working in the country and increasingly to tourists and overseas collectors of "primitive art." Maisin tapa quickly found a niche and by the early 1980s, apart from the rare sale of copra, had become the only local product people could reliably sell for cash or, in the case of the Anglican Church, for credit towards school fees and transportation costs for students heading back and forth to the high schools.

Times had changed from the days of the ancestors, people told me. Now you needed cash to survive: to purchase basic necessities like clothing, medicines, and fish hooks; to pay ever-rising schools fees and transportation costs for students fortunate enough to attend one of the residential high schools; and for a few simple pleasures like tobacco or sugar. So villagers were relieved that a market had emerged for tapa. Success, however, came with new anxieties. These could be sorted into two types. First, villagers were keenly aware that they had very little influence over the market. One could go to a great deal of expense paying for an airplane ticket and the high freight costs to have a relative take a box of tapa to Port Moresby to sell, only to find that the shop owners were not interested. When they were, people had little choice but to accept the prices they set for the cloth. It wasn't long before the Maisin in town reported that the shops sold tapa for far higher prices than they paid the makers. Even Sister Helen Roberts in Wanigela, I was told by a few villagers, was making "millions" for the tapa she purchased on behalf of the Anglican Church.[1] It was unfair, but what could people do?

The second complaint turned inward. Over and over again, I was told that tapa "belonged to all the Maisin people." Yet some women managed to sell more and sometimes to fetch higher prices than their neighbours, usually because they had relatives in town willing to sell on their behalf but also, in a few cases, because they produced cloths that outsiders considered especially fine and beautiful. Even women who I knew were doing better than others joined the chorus: all Maisin women should be able to sell the same amount of cloth for the same price. Anything short of this struck everyone as terribly unfair.

Reading through my notes on these interviews for this book, I am struck by their moralism. Frustrated as they might feel with the outsiders who set arbitrary prices and bought tapa if and when they chose, villagers saved most of their criticisms for themselves. "The problem is," I was told, that people are too "lazy" to get busy finding purchasers for cloth, that they have allowed the quality of the cloth to slide, that those who have found success are too greedy to share their contacts with others, and that village leaders who should be working for everyone quietly make deals that benefit their own kin. Whatever success people enjoyed in selling tapa was matched by a keen sense of inadequacy. "We are poor," people insisted. "Look at how dirty the village is. We have no shops, no good roads."

In previous chapters, we have seen how tapa provides a material reminder for the Maisin of the continuing importance of their ancestral culture. Each piece of *wuwusi* a woman gathers from the garden, pounds into cloth, and decorates recapitulates basic and largely enduring aspects of life: the daily requirements of subsistence, the importance of kin, and the shadowy presence of spiritual forces and entities. Tapa, however, is also situated in the interface between the Maisin and the outside world. The focus of this chapter and the next shifts to this interface, to the ways the Maisin have adapted as their communities become increasingly integrated within wider regional and international political and economic orders. Compared to many places in the world, this process has, so far at least, progressed fairly smoothly for the Maisin. The people have not been deprived of their lands, sold off their resources for quick exploitation, or allowed their community to feel the scourge of alcohol abuse or gang violence. Yet, as my interviews concerning tapa reveal, the Maisin have often experienced this incorporation as a crisis of values requiring them to confront the very basis of their lives together as a community. This chapter, then, focusses on how the Maisin collectively manage the choices they face as members of a community. In particular, we look at two overlapping concerns — maintaining social order and making collective choices for action — concerns of law and politics respectively.

VILLAGER, CITIZEN, AND CHRISTIAN: THE CHANGING NATURE OF COMMUNITY

The problems the Maisin contend with these days are particular to their situation but far from unique in rural Papua New Guinea. The country as a whole faces severe challenges due to rising economic inequality, massive movements of people into the urban centres, and a steady decline in government services in the wake of a string of financial and political crises (Dorney 2000). To date, Uiaku and Collingwood Bay as a whole have been sheltered from the worst of the problems, but they increasingly impinge upon people's lives. Everyone is very concerned about the future. Even in the best of times, however, the Maisin face challenges from within and without. Conflicts and disputes periodically disrupt the peace in the villages and need to be dealt with. Challenges and opportunities arise that affect the entire community and demand attention and decisions. All societies face such challenges in distinctive ways that reflect their cultural orientations and historical experience. The Maisin, of course, are no exception.

Anthropologists typically distinguish between problems of maintaining social order and making collective decisions affecting the whole community as "legal" and "political" respectively, although there is considerable overlap between the two domains. I follow that practice here. In this chapter, we will look at the ways the Maisin typically deal with disputes within the community — the legal sphere — before turning to a discussion of leadership and politics. First, however, we need to consider the context within which both legal and political processes take place — that of the community.

There is no equivalent in the Maisin language for the English word "community," yet it is clear that most people today think of their villages as communities, that is to say, as moral and political unities. This is a modern development (Barker 1996). People lived in villages long before the arrival of the Europeans, but they did not form communities. Instead they were aggregates of interacting clan-based hamlets allied with various "war" and "peace" leaders, the *Sabu* and *Kawo* of old. The Maisin clans were recent migrants into the area, and both oral and archival evidence strongly suggests that large villages like Uiaku were temporary arrangements for defence against enemy tribes. Abandoned village sites along the coast, marked by groves of tall coconuts, stand in mute testimony to the ease by which villages split up or were abandoned.

The work of both the mission and the government relied upon the existence of stable populations in permanent villages. The Administration appointed village constables, took censuses, and applied regulations, all of which assumed sedentary populations. The Anglicans also paid little heed to Indigenous forms of political organization and leadership. They built their churches and schools in the centre of existing villages to serve the whole population and in the process created, for the first time, village-wide institutions. Remaking villages into communities was a foundational project of the colonial era. They were the key units both for the regulation of local populations and for the incorporation of formerly autonomous local societies into the colonial system as a whole.

By the time that Anne and I arrived in Uiaku in 1981, more than six years after Papua New Guinea had achieved Independence, the foreign missionaries and patrol officers were a quickly receding memory. Yet their efforts had left a deep and lasting imprint both in the ways that the Maisin organized and perceived their community and their place in the world. A few days after I arrived, I had a long discussion with Gideon Ifoki about the way Uiaku was organized. The community, he told me, had three "sides" (*yovei*) — the village, government, and mission, each with distinct responsibilities, organizations, and leaders. Village activities included such things as making gardens, arranging work parties to build houses, and planning for major ceremonials, all directed by *Kawo* leaders and clan elders. Government activities focussed on public works, such as the construction of medical aid posts, and undertaking economic initiatives for the benefit of the community. Two village councillors, who also represented Uiaku and Ganjiga at periodic meetings of a regional Local Government Council[2] based at Tufi, provided leadership in the government sphere of interest with the help of committees made up of representatives from across their respective villages. Finally, mission activities included providing support for the priest and teachers and keeping the church and classrooms in good repair. The primary mission leaders were members of the church council, with representatives from across Uiaku and Ganjiga.

Gideon elaborated further. Village activities were organized as need demanded, but government and mission projects unfolded according to a regularized schedule with two days a week set aside for all members of the community to pitch in. Further, the government and mission "sides" included a number of voluntary associations. The former included a youth club, which organized sports meets and dance parties for young people, and business associations. The most active mission group was the Mothers Union, a church women's group that met weekly for a prayer service and assisted the priest in preparing the church for regular services. The Maisin had also formed a Parents and Citizenship Association chapter, which aided the school by purchasing badly needed supplies, as well as a Board of Management to assist the headmaster in policy decisions affecting the school.[3]

It didn't take long to realize that Gideon's portrait of how the village worked was rather idealistic. Some of the organizations existed in name only, while membership in others waxed and waned. The distinctions between the categories of leaders and many of the activities often dissolved upon closer inspection. The "mission leaders" who organized church festivals, for instance, were at the same time "village" leaders who drew upon their kin networks to provide the needed food and labour. While there was always talk about the need for the village as a whole to undertake various projects, no person or organization possessed the authority on their own to plan or to order people to work. Everything depended upon people's willingness to participate. If they were unhappy with the organizers of some project or merely had more important things to attend to, they simply didn't show up on the community work days. It was not uncommon for weeks to pass without any community work taking place.

Despite what appeared to me to be obvious contradictions, I found that many Maisin talked about the village in the same terms as Gideon. It was an accurate model of how most Maisin thought the village *ought* to work. This is by no means unimportant. In Uiaku like most places, the heart of politics lies in the gap between what people think ought to be and what they actually experience. Keeping in mind that it is an idealization, we need to dwell a little longer on the three-sided picture of the village.

Taken at face value, the model appears a direct legacy of the colonial period, a time when the Maisin like most Melanesians found themselves as

one side of a triangular relationship with missionaries and government officers (Burridge 1960). As the mission and government turned over their powers to Papua New Guineans during the late colonial period, many of the
functions formerly exercised by European officials were passed on to local
villagers. The modern village councillor, for instance, combines in his person
some of the legal authority of the native village constables and white patrol
officers that preceded him. Yet more is at work here than simple substitution.
The various offices and associations on the government and mission side also
reflect the growing integration of Maisin society into wider social, political,
and economic networks. Most if not all have counterparts in hundreds of
other villages where they were introduced around the same time. Members
of the Mothers Union and delegates from the youth club regularly travel to
the provincial capital for district meetings and socials, forming a sense of
belonging to organizations that span local identities. Provincial and national
bodies set down rules of organization for their village counterparts and periodically provide small grants and training programs. In turn, the village committees, business associations, and school organizations take as their chief
mandates the improvement of the village according to standards established
on the outside: rationalized planning and sound fiscal management. For the
Maisin, then, the former colonial triangle has expanded outwards from its
local setting to bring them into a much wider set of relationships.

Hence, in speaking of the three sides of the village, the Maisin acknowledge
their participation in these encompassing networks. They are not only villagers,
they are also citizens of Papua New Guinea and, as Christians, members of a
global church. The community — identified generally with the village as a
whole — is the meeting place of these three networks and identities.

The three-sided model that Gideon and others described suggests that the
three networks and types of identity ideally are distinct and balanced. The
basic assumption is that the village, government, and mission "sides" deal
with different types of concerns. At a deeper level, however, I suspect that the
distinction also derives from a sense that the three sides imply distinctive
moral orientations. Morality on the village-side is relational, defined in terms
of reciprocal exchanges that ideally lead towards balance and amity.
Citizens, on the other hand, are thought of as individuals who pursue their
own self-interests within a free marketplace that determines their value
according to absolute measures, the most basic being money. Their behaviour is ultimately constrained by a legal code that (in principle) applies
equally to everyone. The mission-side presents yet another view of personal
morality. While the Anglican Church promotes a strongly communitarian
understanding of Christianity that contrasts with the individualism of citizenship, ultimately it too endorses a notion of individualism radically at odds

with the exchange ethic. People should treat each other kindly and generously because, as children of God, their personal salvation depends upon it and not merely because of more immediate obligations or advantages.

The idealized model suggests that the three sides with their distinctive concerns and moral orientations should somehow come into balance in the body of the community. Yet this is clearly impossible if for no other reason than the fact that rural Maisin do not participate equally in each of the three domains. The actual situation in Uiaku resembles less a triangle with three equal parts than a hierarchy of spheres. The village sphere is by far the most significant for the Maisin. The past century has introduced a new conception of community and an unheralded degree of specialized roles and forms of association. All the same, the degree of specialization is quite limited. People spend the vast majority of their time engaged in subsistence activities and meeting their obligations to kin and exchange partners. While they regard them as very important, villagers have only limited time left over for mission and government activities. Inevitably, the reciprocal values that are constantly reaffirmed in the village sphere tend to colour, although not determine, the ways people think about their roles as citizens and Christians.

In the final analysis, "community" for the Maisin is better understood as a project rather than as a place, one which has as its final goal the reconciliation of their identities as villagers, citizens, and Christians. The project reflects the changed conditions of Maisin existence since European contact, their incorporation into wider regional and international systems. That incorporation, however, is far from complete. To a degree unimaginable in industrialized countries, the Maisin remain largely self-sufficient, as much by necessity as choice. While people take their identities as citizens and Christians seriously, their assumptions about the nature of community continue to be informed primarily through their links with each other and thus largely in terms of reciprocity. Reciprocal values are especially central to the ways the Maisin talk about and deal with conflicts and social disruptions, that is to say, in the legal domain of community, to which we now turn.

THE LEGAL SYSTEM

The legal and political systems that exist in Uiaku today are hybrids of Western and Indigenous forms. Papua New Guinea is formally a modern democratic state with a constitution, an elected parliament, legal code, courts, and prisons. Every five years, the Maisin vote for a district and a provincial representative to the national Parliament. Also, like other citizens, they are subject to the laws of the land. In principle, any adult villager who refuses to pay taxes or violently attacks another can be arrested and punished to the full extent of the law.

147

Practice, however, is another matter. From the earliest days of the colonial regime, it was recognized that Indigenous societies operated according to conceptions of justice that were often at odds with formal Western notions.[4] Few if any local people, for instance, considered it a crime to raid enemy villages, killing not just the men but anyone they happened across. Generally, the notion of committing a crime stopped at the boundaries of a person's kin and exchange networks. An additional complexity was that local societies often had very different notions of the types of behaviour that constituted crimes among their own members. Premarital sex, for instance, was perfectly permissible and even encouraged in some places and punishable by death in others. At the deepest level of difference, Western and Indigenous justice systems worked towards fundamentally different goals. The Western system operates on the basis of a formal code that defines offensive behaviour and sets punishments accordingly. If you commit a crime, you are (in principle) punished with a fine or imprisonment established by law, regardless of who you are or your relationship to the victim of your crime. Melanesian systems, in contrast, place relationships above individual behaviour. The breaching of social relationships is usually of more concern than the particulars of the crime. Retaliation or attempts to heal the breach usually follow, but very often the individual who caused the trouble in the first place — other than feeling some shame, perhaps — goes unpunished.

The colonial regime put an end, at least temporarily, to most tribal warfare and established a legal system that embraced all Papua New Guinea.[5] From the start, however, allowance was made for Indigenous legal systems. This was formalized in the constitution, which gives equal weight to Western and Indigenous legal systems. Despite some important experiments,[6] however, the national system remains fundamentally Western in its assumptions and procedures. The degree to which the formal Western legal system has penetrated down to the local level varies, but it is safe to say that in most rural villages, including Uiaku, people are left to deal as best they can with most disputes, conflicts, and crimes. Up until the late colonial period, patrol officers held local court in Uiaku at least once a year, and the police detachment based at Tufi stood ready to deal with major disturbances (at least those brought to their attention). However, the patrols ended in the mid-1960s, and the police today rarely have the means to travel to the villages. Instead, villagers have to bring miscreants or disputes to Tufi and then wait weeks or even months for a hearing before a magistrate. Not surprisingly, this doesn't happen very often. In some parts of the country, village courts have filled the gap between the national and Indigenous legal systems. Uiaku, however, lacks a court just as it lacks a formal village government capable of passing by-laws. Legal as well as most political issues thus get worked out on a more fluid, informal basis that gives plenty of play to cultural conceptions of fairness.

To be good in Maisin society is to share. People experience enormous pressure to conform. From the time they can toddle, children are warmly praised for sharing food and scolded when they are selfish. The nearly incessant gossip that forms a background buzz to village life provides another effective sanction. Except when they are in their gardens or the bush, the Maisin live their lives in full view of their neighbours. While people are very careful not to directly accuse someone of bad behaviour, which would in itself mark a breach of moral behaviour, gossip has a way of getting back to its subjects, forming a powerful check. Little rituals of etiquette also convey moral expectations. If you visit someone, you should bring with you a small gift of betelnut or tobacco; if you pass a group of seated elders, you should bow your head slightly in a token of respect; if you are standing in your canoe using a pole, you should place your feet in the hollowed centre of the log when passing near a village so as to not put yourself higher than others. Not to conform to these behaviours brings gossip, and gossip, in turn, causes one to feel ashamed.

These kinds of sanctions are powerful not least because they form a kind of common sense, not open to critique. Consider another custom that I think of as the "falling down rule." I had heard of this rule but was still very surprised to witness it in action. One day I was standing at the bank of the river when a young man poling a canoe lost his balance and flipped over. Because he had his feet positioned in the narrow slit of the hollowed-out log, he was trapped and in danger of drowning. Before I quite knew what was happening, the people around me flung themselves violently face down into the water. Only then did a few young men swim out to make a rescue. A few weeks later, the rescued man put on a lavish feast for those who had mimicked his fall. (Since I had not fallen, I was not included). This all made perfect sense to everyone but me. When I asked my friends to explain the custom, I drew a blank. "It's just the correct thing to do," they told me, obviously puzzled by my simple-mindedness. Such everyday behaviours silently and efficiently reinforce the expectation of reciprocity.

All the same, conflicts do periodically break out. Neighbours sometimes quarrel over ownership of a piece of land; couples get discovered in adulterous relationships; or villagers accuse others of stealing food from their gardens or houses. The Maisin repertory of wrongs includes much that Westerners would recognize as crimes in their own society because they cause damage to persons and property. A full listing of the triggers for conflicts, however, would include many actions that few North Americans, for instance, would regard as crimes in any sense: neglecting to share one's food with sufficient generosity, making a show of one's material advantages, ordering others about, and so forth. At their heart, conflicts in Uiaku turn on a denial of reciprocity. Most conflicts get resolved quickly — the aggrieved parties talk out their differences; elders get involved and arrange for an exchange of food; or else one or the other disputant decides to back off, and the trouble gradually gets forgotten. Occasionally, however, the offence is simply too large to permit a ready solution, or the parties simply cannot let the matter rest and tempers continue to flare. The danger then is that the people who feel wronged may take matters into their own hands and retaliate, setting off a chain reaction of tit for tat that can threaten to turn a small dispute into a full-blown crisis.

Such a crisis threatened community peace towards the end of our first stint of fieldwork in 1983. One night, a boy from Ganjiga slipped into a house in Uiaku apparently to make a liaison with a girlfriend. Unfortunately for him, he went to the bed of the girl's mother, who raised the alarm. The boy was badly beaten by the girl's male relatives before escaping back across the river. A week later, an elder from the girl's clan, accompanied by his infant granddaughter, was sailing on his outrigger canoe past Ganjiga. One of the boy's uncles sped out in a motorized dinghy and cut the ropes holding the canoe together with a machete, causing it to capsize. Fortunately, the old man and little girl were rescued, but they could have easily drowned. In the aftermath, rumours spread that the young men on both sides of the river were pulling down spears and war clubs from the rafters of their houses in preparation for battle.

Lacking police or courts, the Maisin have two options when serious trouble breaks out: they can attempt to resolve the matter on their own or take it to an outside authority. Resolving a conflict internally requires the establishment of a new balance between aggrieved parties to end the cycle of escalating retaliation. Big men usually take a leading role. Immediately after the boy was beaten in the case related above, the village councillor from Ganjiga, who was also a senior member of a *Kawo* clan, visited the elders of the clans involved in an attempt to organize an exchange of food. Following the attack on the canoe, his efforts went into high gear to stave off another round of attacks. Another option would have been to convene a village meeting like that described in the previous chapter to deal with the sorcery rumours that spread after Mona became seriously ill. The aim of such meetings is to allow a full airing of tensions in the community in an effort to repair past wrongs and attain a new consensus. While the main players in a conflict are often subjected to public criticism, they are not punished. Indeed, to punish them would be counter-productive as it would likely be seen as a form of retaliation and thus escalate the conflict rather than resolve it.

Plate 1 Marua beach facing towards Airara village with the heavily forested Mount Suckling (Goropi) rising behind. The two women approaching are carrying clay pots filled with cooked food for a feast. (Photo by J. Barker)

Plate 2 Crossing the river from Ganjiga to Uiaku village. (Photo by J. Barker)

Plate 3 Applying the *dun* (red dye), Ganjiga village, 1982. Prisca Rairiga, in the centre of the photograph, received her tattoo a few months earlier. (Photo by A.M. Tietjen)

Plate 4 Part of a bride-price gift. A live pig is trussed beneath the decorative tapa cloth. The bananas are a special gift, known as *tonton*. At the time of the marriage, the bride's male relatives promise to give three types of food to the groom's people — this was the third and final installment. The presentation is meant to impress viewers with the generosity of the bride's family. (Photo by J. Barker)

Plate 5 Iris Bogu (Photo by A.M. Tietjen)

Plate 6 Deacon Russell Maikin (Photo by A.M. Tietjen)

Plate 7 St. Thomas Day dancers, December 1981. The man with the cassette radio in the background is on holidays from his job in Port Moresby. Maisin living in the towns often exchange cassettes of traditional music from home. (Photo by A.M. Tietjen)

Plate 8 A new generation of dancers prepares to greet the Stó:lō delegates, June 2000. (Photo by J. Barker)

People are apt to appeal to extra-village authorities in the case of major disputes. Elders will often remind other villagers that as Christians people shouldn't fight; they should support one another and trust that God will see that justice is done. It is very difficult to tell how effective appeals to Christian values are. I suspect that on occasion they do give people a way to back down from further confrontations. Yet, when tempers run high, I doubt that people pay much heed. Appeals to the "law" are different because there is always a possibility that someone will brave the long voyage up to Tufi to involve the police and court in a local dispute. People admire the supposed efficiencies of the Western legal system. There is something very attractive in the neatness of clearly defined crimes and ready punishments as opposed to the seemingly endless back-and-forth of the Indigenous system. People also agree that some crimes, like murder, are so heinous that they can only be handled by the court. All the same, crossing the line from threatening to take a matter to court and actually doing so is fraught with risk. From the village perspective, involving the police and court may well be seen as in itself a form of retaliation, thus escalating a conflict rather than bringing it to a close.

This is basically what happened in the crisis between Uiaku and Ganjiga. Following the attack on the canoe, the Uiaku village councillor sent up a request to the police. For once, the police boat had petrol, and so two police-man motored down to Ganjiga to make an arrest. People in Uiaku strongly supported the action. After all, the Ganjiga man had attempted murder, which was a crime in anyone's book. The Ganjiga councillor and his sup-porters saw matters differently. Having worked behind the scenes to recon-cile the parties to the dispute, they felt nothing short of betrayed. The matter was further complicated by other tensions over the village cooperative store and a rivalry between the two councillors (discussed in the last section of this chapter). By the time Anne and I left the village, a few weeks later, tempers were still running high. Fortunately, however, the rumours of preparations for warfare turned out to be idle speculation. The Ganjiga man who cut the canoe ropes paid a fine and returned to the village. A few weeks later, the long-planned food exchange took place, and the tensions gradually eased.[7]

Given distance and poor financing, the police and court at Tufi remain mostly theoretical sanctions for the Maisin. Still, my impression during my trips in the 1990s is that the Maisin have become more comfortable with the *idea* of Western law. This shift in attitude is occurring in part because a growing percentage of the local population is made up of people who have lived for extended periods in the towns where reliance upon police and courts is much greater. It is also possible that the Maisin's success in fending off loggers in the national court has increased their regard for the system, at least as a means of dealing with outsiders (see Chapter 6). In other words, as people have become more familiar with the national legal system, they have become more willing to take it seriously. I suspect, however, that the shift also reflects deeper changes within the community that are weakening the bonds of reciprocity. Many of the people retiring to the village after decades of working in the town have been less willing to share out their possessions and wealth than in the past. Just as importantly, their children who have grown up in the urban areas often have a difficult time adjusting to village life. Because their ties to kin are weaker, the newcomers are less reluctant to threaten to call in the police when a dispute breaks out. For their part, villagers complain of a rise in petty theft on the part of the alienated youth returning from the towns. They have no objections when the councillor takes them up to the Tufi court.

Uiaku is by and large a peaceful and safe community. With no easy access to alcohol and far removed from the towns, it has been largely spared the domestic violence and gang-related crime that have become enormous problems in Port Moresby and other urban areas. Yet people are anxious. They worry that outsiders wish to steal their resources while leaving them poor. They worry that the social problems in the towns will eventually migrate to the villages. However, their greatest concern is about their own weaknesses. The good person is one who is generous, who willingly shares all she or he has in support of the community. Yet modern conditions make it increasingly easy for people to avoid their reciprocal obligations. Opting out of modernity is not an option. Villagers are keen to improve their material conditions with better schools, ready access to mass-manufactured commodities, and good medical facilities. How to achieve a better material life without forsaking the reciprocal values that provide security and equality is perhaps the most urgent question the Maisin face today. It is at heart a moral question, one that is most vividly exemplified in the person and actions of community leaders.

LEADERS

The Maisin recognize several types of leaders, but their most general term for prominent people is *tamati bejji*, "big man." Maisin big men bear little obvious resemblance to their famous counterparts in the heavily populated New Guinea highlands. They do not own or manage huge pig herds, organize massive ceremonial exchanges, or boast of their achievements in swaggering orations on public occasions. In fact, there is considerable diversity in the forms that leadership takes across Melanesia (Chowning 1979). Still, beneath that diversity one can detect some common principles. The key one is a pattern of political egalitarianism.

Maisin big men are like everyone else — only more so. When you walk through Uiaku, you see few if any signs of status. Some of the *Kawo* hamlets have large plazas and houses with trimmed thatch (a privilege enjoyed exclusively by ritually superior clans), but otherwise they look the same as their neighbours. Most of the time, people go about the same subsistence tasks as everyone else. Apart from traditional ceremonial occasions when *Kawo* leaders dress in their finery, there is no clearly visible difference between the leaders and the led. Leadership emerges when circumstances require or invite it, and those circumstances, in turn, shape the nature and extent that leadership actually gets exercised. There are endless gradations in which virtually any person may be considered "big" for a time, including women. This became clear to me when I conducted a small and quite unsystematic experiment. I took a stroll along the entire length of Uiaku and Ganjiga, stopping to chat with every adult I encountered and asking them who they considered to be the "big people" of the village. Around a quarter of the 30 or so people I spoke with mentioned the village councillor and church deacon. That was the extent of any agreement. Most of my informants named people they turned to for advice, usually elders in their own clans. Several people nominated themselves. At the end of my stroll, none of the lists matched.

The term "political egalitarianism" is obviously relative. Clearly not all things are equal in Maisin society. Women are politically subordinated to men. Senior men and women likewise enjoy authority over their juniors. The most influential leaders emerge from a small subset of the society: middle-aged but still physically vigorous men. Further, belonging to a senior lineage within a *Kawo* clan allows a well-organized and connected man to organize large ceremonies within his own hamlet and thus demonstrate his managerial ability. Finally, men who have been to high school and worked for a time in professional careers tend to be favoured for positions as "government" and "mission" leaders. Thus, the Maisin political system appears egalitarian mainly in contrast to more hierarchical systems such as chieftainships or states, which possess formal offices that define leaders' powers and authority.

To a limited extent, Uiaku today has a hybrid system. While clan leaders more or less define their roles depending on circumstances and their own abilities, the village councillor occupies an official position with formal responsibilities and authority set by national law. Yet the degree of actual specialization is in practice very limited, even in the case of village councillors, who are part-time volunteers. They receive no salary or other support that might give them an independent platform for action. Their effectiveness depends largely upon people's willingness to listen to them. Their connection to the "law" and regional political system gives those who want to use it a bully pulpit from which to lecture and harangue villagers to follow certain courses of action. But few councillors actually do this. Those who try quickly find that people only follow them to the extent that they wish to. They cannot compel people to obey them. The same is true for leaders working within village or mission spheres of action. The political process in Uiaku relies largely upon consensus. Leaders, whatever their position within the community, are best regarded as managers of consensus rather than as officials.

The influence that Maisin big men enjoy comes very much from the people, not through periodic elections but rather a constant process of scrutiny and evaluation. It is reputation more than anything else that counts. People are willing to listen to big men and follow their lead because they have proven themselves exceptionally capable of doing the same things as everyone else. They are better gardeners or hunters, more generous in sharing food or pitching in when a new house needs to be constructed, and consistent in offering sound advice in planning for major events like a bride-price payment. This is not to say that men who are exceptionally skilled automatically become leaders. I know of several superb gardeners, for instance, who are content merely to meet their obligations to their kin and otherwise remain out of the limelight. The people who become big men are partially thrust into their roles, but they also include ambitious individuals who take pride in their influence and achievements. Just as reputation can lift up a big man, it can just as easily take him down. There are always rivals waiting in the wings to move in if a big man's powers flag or if he slips up and annoys his followers.

The Maisin say of their most outstanding big men that they are "good" and "strong." While people recognize that being a village, government, or mission leader requires different skills, they expect their leaders to be "good men" who meet their exchange obligations, readily helping out their equals and giving sound advice and other aid to their juniors. They also expect leaders to be "strong" men who make sound decisions on behalf of their followers and manage situations well so those decisions work to everyone's benefit. Big men thus exemplify a dynamic that lies at the very heart of reciprocal morality (Burridge 1975; Read 1959). To be good requires that a person be selfless. Big men are generous to a fault. They are usually among the first to bring food to a feast or to pitch in on a community project. They make themselves available to offer sage advice for those who seek it, and they consult respectfully with other leading men before advocating a position at a village meeting. But life requires more than goodness. Even the most moral of persons must make choices that contradict the ethics of reciprocity. This calls for "strength." Big men are considered strong because they are the ones who urge others to take new courses of action. To do this, they need to be willing to stand outside the constraints of reciprocal morality, to take in the big picture, to make decisions — in short, to act like individuals.

Ordinary villagers admire and, indeed, are grateful for big men's willing-ness to assume the challenges and risks associated with making major deci-sions and pulling people along. At the same time, it also worries them. The non-reciprocal element in the big man's makeup puts him in the same cate-gory as sorcerers or spirits, entities that operate largely outside the moral constraints of community. Big men assume an oversized presence in ceremo-nial exchanges and other public occasions in part to put these concerns to rest. Still, the more influential a big man becomes, the more intense the scrutiny of his activities and the accompanying gossip. People become con-cerned that he is using his position to benefit himself and his close relatives or that he is becoming a "big head" who makes decisions without consulting others. There may even be suspicion, especially in the case of older men, that they are resorting to sorcery to eliminate their rivals. Ironically, even hosting an especially generous ceremony may backfire on a big man if people feel that he is acting overly proud. The political system thus possesses an internal logic that limits the amount of power any individual can accrue. Many fac-tors come into play, but gossip is the greatest leveller.

Modern circumstances make this contradiction between goodness and strength, reciprocity and individuality, especially acute. Since the time of the founding of the Christian cooperatives in the late 1940s, the chief political goal of Maisin leaders has been to improve the material conditions of village life. Three generations of leaders have now worked to get government grants and other forms of aid to improve the schools and provide basic services such as health care. They have also initiated a succession of local economic projects ranging from the planting of cash crops like cocoa and coffee to the establishment of tapa cloth cooperatives to bring money into the commu-nity. Because such projects require some knowledge of government bureau-cracy, business organization, and financial management, villagers have tended to promote and follow the lead of men with at least high school education and who have worked for a time in professional capacities prior to returning to the village. People very much want money and the things money can buy. Yet they know that money and the white men they assume control it operate according to a moral logic largely at odds with reciprocity. People are well aware of the ease with which money can be siphoned off by their leaders or how projects can be manipulated to benefit leaders' families over everyone else. It is universally assumed by villagers that national politi-cians are corrupt, and they fret about whether their own leaders can resist temptation. For their part, to have any effectiveness at all, village big men today must participate in the world of money. Whatever their stance in the village, working with outside agencies gives them benefits and opportuni-ties denied to others. Their predicament exemplifies a persistent tension in contemporary village politics between the reciprocal morality that dominates village affairs and the individualistic ethic of modernity, especially as it is manifested in the growing market economy.

THE POLITICS OF CONSENSUS

Politics, so the old saying goes, is the "art of the possible."[8] In Uiaku political possibilities are constrained by the ways power is aligned inside and outside the community, by accepted decision-making procedures, and by what people perceive as the pressing issues of the day. In this section, we will consider the first two of these factors, saving the last for the conclusion of the chapter.

The Maisin participate in two political domains: the national electoral system and the village. Every five years villagers vote for a regional and a provincial representative to the National Parliament who since 1995 have also formed a provincial assembly with other members of Parliament from ridings in Oro Province. The Maisin are also represented by three councillors on the Local Government Council based in Tufi. While the local schools and hospital at Wanigela remain under the formal control of the Anglican Church, the national government is responsible for most of the funding and for setting standards. The government also provides policing and various infrastructural and economic development programs. As we've seen, however, the police actually have a very weak presence in the area, and funding for most other programs has steadily declined since Independence in 1975. This is a source of great frustration for the Maisin. A common complaint is that as soon as the election cycle is over, members of Parliament forget the people who voted for them, preferring to enjoy the easy life of Port Moresby rather than work to improve the living conditions of their poorer rural brothers and sisters. The Local Government Council is also regarded as largely irrelevant, despite the direct involvement of the village councillors and occasional small development grant.

The national political system thus touches lightly upon villagers. In theory, a council made up of the representative to the Local Government Council and a small committee representing different parts of the community forms a kind of village government. In practice, however, such councils have virtually no authority and often do not effectively exist. Whatever influence village councillors enjoy tends to come from their standing in the community rather than participation in the Local Government Council. Actual political power in the village is shared mostly between adult married men. Women and younger men are not without influence. They make their opinions known behind the scenes and resist decisions if they feel they are unreasonable or unfair, but they have no formal vote or means of setting political agendas. The important political decisions are made in public where senior men hold a near monopoly on talk.

The political process in Uiaku is focussed mostly upon the creation of consensus, especially among senior men. Sometimes agreement comes quickly; a course of action seems so obvious or urgent that people have little difficulty arriving at a decision. Most of the time, however, consensus building takes time and much talk. It is not a process that encourages snap decisions. Even once a decision has been reached, a consensus can easily be undermined if one or another of the parties involved changes their minds or new circumstances arise. Finding and maintaining a consensus, then, can be agonizingly slow and, once found, can disappear overnight. The Maisin are well aware of this. Over the years, I have often heard people express envy for what they perceive as the efficiency of decision-making among Europeans where lines of authority tend to be clearly established. Yet among themselves, the Maisin strongly resent any suggestion that an individual has the right to make decisions affecting others without their consent. If someone becomes a bit too pushy, others are likely to respond with the put down "You are not the boss of me!" (always delivered in English). Even as they complain about the effort required to build and maintain consensus, people also recognize that the system possesses certain advantages. This recognition is partly pragmatic: courses of action backed by strong public approval are far more likely to be achieved than those imposed from above. There is also a near mystical faith that consensus in itself is a good that brings both social and material benefits. In the Maisin view, consensus represents a state of being, the elusive condition of social amity.

There is no clear line between the personal and the political in Maisin society. Most decisions beyond the level of the household require negotiations. Big events like bride-price or end-of-mourning ceremonies usually involve years of careful coordination between clan elders. It is in such ordinary circumstances that aspiring big men first demonstrate their ability to manage the delicate process of finding and maintaining consensus. Leaders draw upon the same skills and, indeed, their own kin and exchange networks when addressing political matters at the village level, such as decisions on whether to build a new classroom or where to locate a public building, such as an aid post. However, there are crucial differences between the ways Maisin handle "village-side" affairs between the clans and those that concern the community as a whole. This is partly a matter of scale. With the rare exception of initiation ceremonies for first-borns, "village-side" activities involve far fewer people than projects or other issues at the community level. More significantly, there is a shift in the way that consensus is perceived. The most significant commitments are no longer to one's own clan or kin. Indeed, clan loyalty is an obstacle. Political action at the community level depends on the forging of a consensus that appeals to sources of identity that transcend personal kin and exchange networks.

The actual means by which people attempt to reach a consensus varies greatly according to the circumstances, the goal, and the people involved. In general, however, consensus building moves through two phases or, if a matter is especially contentious, back and forth between them. The first phase is one of semi-private negotiations between the parties most involved. These usually occur in the evening after people have finished their suppers and the village is quiet. Although the conversations are private, there is no secrecy about who is visiting whom, and usually people have a pretty good idea why. The aim of these discussions is to reach common positions before moving to a second public phase. If the matter under consideration is fairly routine—like planning a bride-price ceremony—then the leaders of the groups involved will simply announce the decision to their clans. More contentious matters, however, require the convening of a village meeting to which all of the public is invited. Village meetings may also be called by village councillors or the church council to discuss community-level projects and concerns.

In general, village assemblies are not occasions for making decisions. That should happen well before people start gathering. Instead, they are forums in which positions get challenged and refined with the aim of affirming a final consensus. Above all, they are moments of social theatre in which consensus is not only made but is *seen* to be made. The main protagonists in this theatre are the senior men who usually do all of the talking. They occupy a central place well in view of other villagers, usually on the raised platform of a shelter. Younger married men sit close by or lean against the side of the platform, sometimes quietly conferring with one of the "big people" on top. Elderly men sit a bit further out on the ground but close enough to hear the conversation and to volunteer an opinion if asked or if they feel the need. Further out again, women, young men, and children find whatever shade they can beneath nearby trees and strain to hear the discussion. A good turnout is considered critically important, even if most people do not speak. The more witnesses there are, the firmer the demonstration that there really is consensus.

Village meetings proceed at a leisurely pace. In my experience, they never start at the announced time. People slowly drift in, chew betelnut, smoke, and engage in casual conversation. At some point, one of the leaders will gauge that enough people have assembled and begin to talk. While there often are moments of drama—of energetic back-and-forth debate—most of the talk takes the form of speeches, often quite lengthy. I find these quite fascinating. Often as not, the speaker does not directly address the matter at hand but instead contextualizes it in terms of local history and the condition of social relations in the village. (We'll look at an example in the next section.) Often a speaker will preface his remarks by urging everyone on the platform to speak up in turn. The surrounding audience nods or murmurs when moved by a speaker's oratory or agreeing with his opinions. The talk proceeds at a gradual pace as speaker succeeds speaker. There is a great deal of repetition, but this is good because it demonstrates consensus. If all goes well, by the late afternoon all of the "big people" will have spoken, and the meeting will end with sugared tea and a small meal.

Although all of the men on the platform should and usually do speak, their words are by no means equally influential. People listen most closely to those men they consider to be "big." For their part, big men are masters of consensus politics. They have their own opinions and agendas, to be sure, but they are careful not to appear to be imposing these on others. They cultivate their relationships with other villagers, spending many of their evenings sitting on friends' verandahs quietly discussing the problems of the day. By the time an issue gets to a village meeting, big men are careful not to dominate the talk. They instead rely on their associates not just to back them up but to speak for a position as if it were their own, thus contributing to the appearance of agreement between equals.

The political process of consensus building is inherently fragile. It is often difficult to reach agreement and even harder to keep people on board once they do. Yet, for all the challenges, Maisin leaders have a remarkable ability to orchestrate consensus when the stakes are high enough. To do so requires them to appeal to all aspects of people's identities, as villagers, citizens, and Christians. This became quite apparent to me while observing meetings during the early 1980s.

A VILLAGE MEETING

On the 28 June 1983, the Uiaku councillor called a meeting. The purpose was to discuss the floundering operation of the village cooperative store, the last remaining legacy of the cooperative movement that had started more than 40 years earlier. Although little more than a hut on high posts, the store was one of the few buildings in the area built almost entirely of imported materials, including expensive finished wood flooring and iron sheeting for the walls and roof. As a sign of their modernity, it gave the Maisin enormous pride, but it was also a constant cause for concern. The store was supposed to earn a profit that could be used for other local projects; however, no matter how high the managers jacked up prices for supplies of rice, matches, kerosene, and other basic goods, the store steadily lost money and much of the time remained closed. The Uiaku councillor was a middle-aged man who had worked for some years in the cooperative development office of the former colonial government. When he took an early retirement to return to the village and care for his aging parents, he took a personal interest in the

Figure 5.2 A village meeting, Uiaku 1983. The councillor is making a point using the large blackboard propped up by the palm tree behind him. The senior men of the village are sitting on the shelter platform to his left. (Photo by J. Barker)

cooperative store and had made its success one of his top priorities upon becoming councillor.

The meeting took place in the midst of the festering conflict between Uiaku and Ganjiga described in the previous section. The Ganjiga councillor had played a key role in organizing a food exchange to end the crisis. When the Uiaku councillor called in the police to arrest the Ganjiga man who had attempted to drown the Uiaku elder, the Ganjiga councillor and his followers took personal offence. The conflict between the councillors spilled over into the management of the cooperative store, to which both men had keys. Checking the books one day, the Uiaku councillor was alarmed to find that Ganjiga customers were receiving a dangerous amount of credit. To prevent further depletion of the stock, he changed the lock and called for a meeting. It occurred the next day in a cleared area in front of the store. Most Ganjiga people, including the councillor, stayed away. While the focus of the meeting was the cooperative store, talk inevitably spilled over into the rivalry between the two leaders.

During the 18 months I had lived in Uiaku, I had heard a great deal of talk about the store, both in casual conversations and in meetings like this one. It was quite clear that people saw it as something much more than a

convenient place to shop. To begin with, villagers often spoke as if the cooperative store were the only possible economic option open to them. When I
would remind them of tapa sales or remittances from working relatives, they
readily agreed that these were important sources of money. And then the talk
would return to the cooperative store and its troubles. That talk entailed
intense criticism of the young men who sold the goods, of the councillors
who managed the business, and of the villagers who depended upon the store
for basic necessities. When I mentioned the practical difficulties of running
any business in a remote village like Uiaku, people again readily agreed. They
were keenly aware of their isolation from markets, of unreliable transportation, and of the very high prices charged by coastal boats when they did
show up. Yet, again, talk easily slid back to self-criticism.

I was fascinated by the quality of the talk. It closely resembled what I
heard privately and at meetings concerning sorcery and followed the same
basic logic. Villagers had an emotional investment in that small steel shack.
Like the body of a loved one, its health reflected the degree of solidarity in
the surrounding society.[9] People spoke nostalgically of earlier days when
people worked closely together, church services were well-attended, and
everyone pitched in to make formal exchanges exciting and successful. The
floundering cooperative society of the present represented not simply an economic failure but a moral one. It was an outward sign of inward divisions, of
rivalries, gossip, greed, and other weaknesses. Much of the time at meetings
was, in fact, taken up in condemnations of such moral failings.

The meeting of 28 June was typical in this respect, if somewhat more
intense than usual because of the tensions between the two villages and their
councillors' rivalry. Speaker after speaker denounced the social divisions they
saw undermining the store's success. While some of the talk became heated,
as we'll see below, the "big people" worked hardest at finding a point of consensus not just to defuse the tensions or plan future actions but more basically to restore the condition of social amity that the Maisin assume is a
necessary condition for prosperity. The politics of consensus, as reflected in
their speeches, relied on a strategy of blending the three orientations to community discussed earlier in this chapter by appealing to listeners as fellow villagers, citizens, and Christians.

Near the beginning of this meeting, a man who had served as the first
manager in 1965 reminded villagers of the history of the cooperative society:

> Our traditions say we must listen to what elders say and do it. Do it! Do it! The
> ancestors who came here worked together and made Uiaku's name good. Yet these
> young ones have not left it in good shape. The ancestors brought their *kawo* [i.e.,
> traditional rights and privileges]. They were strong and fought a lot. When the

missionaries came, they gave their traditions to God. They gave everything. That was a sign that they retain the traditions. The young ones are growing and we need to teach them what our ancestors did. If you elders had died and we spoilt [the cooperative], it would only be our fault. I am unhappy that you have to see what is happening.... Use your good sense (*mon seramon*)! God told us that things will happen. The strong wind will blow. The famine will come. If the flood must come to spoil the village, it will. If the fight comes, it will. We will argue and stay apart from each other. We know these things happen. So when someone does something bad, don't talk about it. We are Christians, so we shouldn't gossip. When we do bad things, we must go straight to that person and make amends (*marawa-wawe*).

Teach the young ones to speak Maisin properly so they won't get confused when they make speeches. Don't let them spoil this building you started. My fathers, you made this building for us. We have intelligence and education, so must look after it. Now it is not only the *Kawo* [leaders of the high-ranking clans] who talk. The spear *Sabu* [leaders of the low-ranking clans] may talk. You went to the big schools, so you may talk. All the *Kawo* must help each other and work together. I shouldn't say this, but I'm sad so I am reminding you. We should not forget these things. So my talk is finished.

Although obscure to outsiders, the audience had no trouble understanding the speaker's references to the ancestors and the coming of Christianity. His words reminded them of the founding of the cooperative store in the aftermath of the building of the first iron-roofed church in Uiaku in 1962. When the bishop arrived to consecrate the church, he found it surrounded on three sides by a special kind of fence made up of criss-crossed branches called an *oraa*. Each of the major clans donated trees they owned as *kawo* emblems. Thus, the clans gave their "traditions to God." When the bishop blessed the church, in effect he blessed those same emblems and thus the "traditions were retained." The clans thus symbolized their new Christian unity and their enduring traditions (Barker 1993). Around the same time, individuals (who by 1983 had become elders) gave money to initiate the cooperative store. The speaker next asserted that God will send disasters to test the people, with a clear allusion to the flood that had recently damaged Ganjiga. As Christians, the people must resist the urge to quarrel; they must make peace with each other. The main thrust of his speech came at the end. Uiaku has become a new kind of place where clan leaders should cooperate instead of competing. Today, education and experience count more than clan status in establishing leadership.

Other men echoed these sentiments and built upon them. The Uiaku councillor then stood up, pointing out that he was not a *Kawo* man but belonged to a ritually subservient *Sabu* clan and thus in the old days would not have been allowed to talk. However, "I have been elected as councillor, so I look after this place. We are all like that; when we have responsibility for the church or government-sides, we must do our work." Turning to the problem at hand, he said:

> GC [the Ganjiga councillor] says that I went over him. How? Ganjiga people did not tell me what to do. The trouble was in my Ward so I wrote the note and sent it to [the police].... If this problem goes on all will be spoiled. If we solve it, all will be well. GC says I went over him. I have that right on the Government-side, so he shouldn't complain. I don't like how my mother's brother[10] has responded to this. We are adults. We are no longer small boys! We mustn't act like that when we are men and spoil things. We must only do good. That's why I put a lock.... As a man representing the government I have the right to do it! I am the only one. Don't talk about my children or my wives.[11] I am the councillor and you should come straight to me.

The councillor claimed a special governmental authority in this speech. Mission and government leaders should work towards village cooperation and unity; to do so they must sometimes make independent decisions for the good of the village. It is inappropriate to gossip about their kin, as one might about a traditional village leader, because they act on a higher authority — that of the central government and its laws from outside the village. If people want to complain about how government-side leaders are doing their job, they should confront them directly.

The Uiaku councillor, however, did not argue that government rules must replace traditional values and institutions. Later in his speech, he suggested that village and government leadership should work hand-in-hand. He argued that GC failed to act when feelings began to be worked up over the tryst between the Ganjiga boy and Uiaku girl:

> GC was here when that happened. He is *Kawo*, so he should have taken his string bag across [i.e., gone to Uiaku with gifts and sat down in a friendly manner with the aggrieved parents].... What was he doing? He was there when it happened. He is a *Kawo* man and a councillor. If he had solved this problem, these rumours would not go around. It is spoilt because one person is playing. When you split up you will fight with spears again, and it is one person's fault.

In other words, as a traditional village leader, GC had the responsibility and authority to keep order among his people. Because he did not act quickly enough, the conflict spread. By implication, the Uiaku councillor said that he

163

had no choice but to call in the police because villagers themselves could no longer contain the violence.

Both of these speakers affirmed a government-side notion of the village as a single polity under the constituted rule of the councillors and "educated men." They also expressed ambivalent assessments of Maisin traditions and of the changes the community had experienced. Beneath these similarities, however, were differences in emphasis and nuance reflecting each man's political situation and personal experience. The first speaker was a founder of the cooperative store, but he had long before withdrawn from direct participation in the running of the business.[12] His speech begins with an allusion to the conversion of the Maisin, to their movement from division and fighting to unity and peace under God. The provision of Western education and other changes have further undermined divisions: all may now talk openly, all should work together. Nevertheless, he asserts that these innovations are based upon the work of the ancestors and village values. By not respecting the elders and traditions, the young people are abusing their new freedoms and thus undoing the good work of those who established the store. The speaker thus implied that it is the younger men who are undermining the store and causing trouble in the community. The criticism was directed towards the Ganjiga councillor, but it could have just as easily been addressed to his Uiaku counterpart. Village values form the touchstone in this imagined social order.

The Uiaku councillor had quite different concerns. His actions had contributed to divisions within the community, and much of the thrust of his speech was to justify them. His speech strongly attacked the Ganjiga councillor in personal terms, referring to him as "childish" and disrespectful of the peace-making role of senior *Kawo* clans. The touchstone here, however, is clearly government-side values. The Uiaku councillor attempted to legitimate his role as a representative of the government who maintains law and order in the village. He presented village values positively as the first resort for keeping peace. However, misplaced egalitarianism and gossip may also generate dissension. Distancing himself from the village order, the Uiaku councillor warned darkly that the community could go back to the bad old days when "you will fight with spears again."

The difficulties remained unresolved, eventually put aside with the final closing of the cooperative society store. Yet the larger theme remained. These two speakers, like others I heard, accepted that the community needed to unite if there were to be any hope of material advancement. All villagers needed to work together. All three of the discourses offered alternate conceptions of moral unity and cooperative labour, whether based upon village traditions, the love of God, or the rule of the law. As we see in the words of the two speakers above, leaders worked hard to merge the three discourses but leaned, often subtly, toward one side or another. This is the work of big men and the central goal of political discourse in Maisin villages today: finding common ground around consensus and the values of community. It is not easy.

THE MORAL POLITICS OF "DEVELOPMENT"

I was often struck by the passion with which the Maisin discussed the cooperative store. There was no denying that the store was a problem. In the early 1980s, it was the only local source for basic goods such as rice, sugar, tea, matches, and kerosene upon which villagers had become dependent. People griped but tolerated the high prices set by the managers to cover transport costs. They appreciated the convenience of the store and felt pride that it was owned by the entire community. They even put up stoically with extended and frequent closings when storemen failed to show up for work or the stocks ran low. Such inconveniences were frustrating, but what was truly intolerable was that the store had always lost money. Periodically, people would invest funds raised through copra or tapa sales or a small government grant to restock the store. Villagers crushed through the door on the opening day, grateful not only for the goods on sale but for the sense that this time for sure the store would fill its full mandate: providing profits that would be invested in other local businesses. People regarded the store as their best shot at generating money that could be used to buy goods, pay school fees, purchase medicines, and, most general, create a more comfortable and secure material existence. When the store closed, as it inevitably did, a few months or a year later, its finances in complete disarray, there was a tangible sense of disappointment verging on despair.

I spent many hours listening to people talk about the store and other cooperative economic ventures which had also started with high hopes before floundering and failing. The tone of these conversations and speeches was often emotional and moralistic. While villagers castigated working relatives and politicians for failing to support community projects, they saved their harshest criticisms for themselves. The projects failed because people gossiped too much, because the young people no longer respected their elders, because members of clans thought only of themselves instead of pitching in to help the community as a whole. Left unmentioned was the fact that the lack of ready access to markets made it next to impossible for any local economic venture to succeed and that the mass exodus of young people to the towns made it impossible for households to devote as much time and labour to community ventures as in the past. My friends readily agreed that these were important factors when I brought them up — and then they returned to what was for them the salient point: the community was to blame for the failures.

165

Similar attitudes have been reported from across rural Papua New Guinea, including areas that have enjoyed considerably more success with cash cropping or which have economically benefited from the presence of factories, mines, and other projects (e.g., Errington and Gewertz 2004). Villagers often feel intense shame concerning their "poverty," as reflected in their continued reliance on subsistence agriculture, residence in bush houses without modern conveniences like electricity, and limited access to cash and the many things that cash buys. The sense of shame is powerfully mixed with a complex attitude of admiration, envy, and resentment towards Europeans and fellow citizens who have had the opportunity to embrace a European lifestyle (Bashkow 2006).[13] Villagers attribute Europeans' economic successes to their supposed superior virtues of organization, self-discipline, hard work, and advanced technical skills (Smith 1994). At the same time, Europeans as imagined by Papua New Guineans evoke disturbing feelings because they appear to operate individually, without regard to kin folk, and they refuse to share their good fortune without any apparent consequences. These are traits, as we have seen, shared by sorcerers.

In North America, people tend to think of politics as largely a pragmatic business. At best, it is a process by which contending interests debate, modify, and commit to various policies; at worse, it is a contest played out by factions and individuals pursuing their own self-interests. This is also true in Maisin society, but as an outside observer one can't help but notice the powerful ways that deeply held moral assumptions condition political discussions. The intense shame many Maisin felt about their standard of living in the 1980s was profoundly shaped by their assumptions about reciprocal virtues. When villagers told me that they were "poor" and that the village was "dirty" and "backwards," they were referring not only to a lack of material development—important as this was to them—but, at a deeper level, moral integrity. As we've seen, the Maisin equate moral uprightness with the pursuit of balanced exchange. The key concept of *marawa-wawe* entails an idealized state in which people transcend their obligations to each other by achieving a perfect state of balance that is at once material, moral, and spiritual. Despite their best efforts, however, the people were not materially the equals of Europeans (as they imagined Europeans to be) and thus were morally inferior as well. In an ideal world, the rich Europeans would be obliged to share their wealth, to bring the relationship into equivalence. This did not happen, and people strongly suspected that the problem lay within themselves.

Politics in Uiaku and other Maisin villages in the 1980s revolved around the conundrums of development as it was locally understood. In the meetings I attended, most of the focus was directed at the failings of the community.

The moral tone of the speeches, stressing endlessly the need for mutual support, resonated powerfully with speeches I heard at meetings dealing with sorcery accusations: much in the way that social amity produced good health, Maisin supposed that unity provided the essential foundation for prosperity. Political efforts, however, were also directed outwards. Villager councillors spent weeks at a time in the provincial capital of Popondetta petitioning politicians and bureaucrats to release funds to support local development projects. Despite promises made by politicians around election time, steady government support for development work failed to materialize, and many people were convinced that the government actually intended to leave them mired in poverty. This seemed to leave only a single option: enticing a foreign businessman to visit and take pity upon the Maisin. He would then offer to help the Maisin develop their lands as an equal partner.[14] When a representative of a logging company came to Uiaku in 1982 to pitch a scheme to replace the rainforest behind the villages with a massive oil palm scheme, villagers were ecstatic. Development was about to arrive, and integrity would at last be restored.

Notes

1. Sister Helen lived in a modest house near the airstrip and church at Wanigela. When I told her about the rumours, she laughed. She'd heard it all before. It was clear from her meticulous records, which she kindly allowed me to copy, that she was barely breaking even. When she died in the early 1990s, Wanigela ceased to be an outlet for tapa.

2. Local Government Councils were introduced by the Australian colonial government beginning in the 1950s to provide a degree of self-governance to local communities and to encourage village-level economic development. The Maisin received a few small grants from the Local Government Council during the 1980s for water tanks to supply village medical aid posts in Uiaku and Airara. Otherwise, the Council appears to have been largely ignored.

3. Strictly speaking, the community school could be regarded as belonging to the government side, as since the early 1970s the national government had set the curriculum and trained and paid the teachers. Formally, however, the schools remain the property of the Anglican Church, and a class of religious instruction taught by the priest remains part of the curriculum. More importantly, the Maisin strongly associate schools with the church and Christianity more generally because of the long mission involvement during the colonial era. In rural Papua New Guinea today approximately 40 per cent of the schools are at least partially funded and controlled by churches and missions as is one of the universities (Gibbs 2005).

4. The word "formal" needs to be stressed here, as there is abundant evidence,

despite the efforts to create international legal accords such as the Geneva Conventions, that members of modern nation-states often find it difficult to consider those they regard as enemies as moral beings to be accorded the same rights and considerations as fellow members of their own communities.

5. Given the thinness of the police force on the ground, it is doubtful that warfare was completely brought under control, and some acts of violence within communities certainly went undetected and unpunished. There is also evidence of police committing their own crimes, sometimes with the knowledge of patrol officers (Kituai 1998). Sadly, since Independence, Papua New Guinea has struggled with a resumption of tribal fighting in much of the Highlands, increasingly with imported and homemade guns, and gang violence in the towns and along the road systems (Dinnen 2001; Gordon and Meggitt 1985).

6. According to Scaglion (2004), "Papua New Guinea has been one of the more progressive of the Pacific nations in pursuing law reform," that is to say, in attempting to mesh Indigenous and Western legal systems. Efforts have included detailed research on legal proceedings in local communities, much of it carried out by anthropologists, and the introduction of new legislation and legal forms that recognize customary law, the most successful of which have been village courts.

7. At least this is how people recalled the matter when I returned in October 1986.

8. The quote is attributed to the famed nineteenth-century German Chancellor, Otto von Bismarck. Bismarck also once remarked, "Politics is not an exact science." (*Oxford Dictionary of Quotations*, 3rd ed., 1979).

9. Indeed, at one meeting, a big man opened his speech by proclaiming that the cooperative society store was "sick," a condition he attributed to the incessant gossiping and sniping around the village about the storemen.

10. The Ganjiga councillor was a classificatory mother's brother to the speaker.

11. The Uiaku councillor had two wives, the Ganjiga councillor had three. The allusion here is to sorcerers, who were known to thrive upon rumour-mongering and gossip.

12. It is of interest to note that this speaker and both of the councillors came from similar backgrounds. All had been in the first cohort of Maisin boys to attend high school, and all were about the same age. Only the Uiaku councillor, however, had taken up (and later left) a career outside the village.

13. It is important to stress that most Papua New Guineans have had very limited experience of Europeans and other foreigners. Throughout the colonial period, the only European the Maisin saw with any regularity was the priest stationed at Wanigela when he visited the villages for a few hours once a month to celebration the Communion service. The number of expatriates living today in the country is far less than prior to 1975, and very few visit Collingwood Bay. The Maisin's notions about Europeans have been built from their historical experiences, from mostly fleeting per-

sonal observations of and encounters with foreigners in the towns and villages, and from what they hear from other Papua New Guineans. From these perspectives, Europeans stand in sharp contrast to local peoples not only because of their light skins but because they appear so wealthy and powerful, yet never seem to work very hard. They thus present a challenging puzzle that has long preoccupied rural Papua New Guineans (e.g., Burridge 1960). The Maisin commonly refer to Europeans as *bariyawa*, a loan word from the Wedau language to the east (the direction from which Europeans arrived) which translates as "spirit." They also know them as "whitemen." Their notions about the *bariyawa* are best understood as constructions built partially from experience and partially from Indigenous assumptions about human nature. As Ira Bashkow notes of the Orokaiva who live in the central part of Oro Province, "[they] project onto their whitemen, from their own evaluative viewpoint, their most pressing moral concerns" (2006: 9). This is a kind of Indigenous anthropology, the equivalent of centuries of Western constructions of "primitive" peoples held up as the moral opposite of European "civilization" (Lutz and Collins 1993; Pagden 1982). In the end, both types of projections tell us at least as much about their authors as the people they aim to depict.

14. I first learned of this hopeful fantasy about a month after arriving in Uiaku when the village council appointed a man to approach me to see if I would use my supposed connections to American businessmen to entice them to visit and work with the Maisin. A year later, when *Anthropology on Trial* was being shot, villagers were invited to suggest subjects for filming. After conferring with others, the village councillor asked that the film include a segment following the entire 12 kilometre route from the Wanigela airstrip, across seven crocodile-infested rivers, to Uiaku so that American audiences would see how poor the Maisin were and take pity. The director instead elected to film an elderly woman, Nita Keru, telling a traditional folk tale.

CHAPTER SIX

Culture Change: Tapa and the Rainforest

Early in 1995, I received a letter from Franklin Seri, then the village councillor for Uiaku and an old friend. After updating me on recent births and deaths, Franklin ended by mentioning he would be visiting Berkeley, California in a few months as part of a delegation of four Maisin men to promote tapa cloth.

Needless to say, I was electrified. I hadn't been back to Papua New Guinea for more than eight years and had heard nothing about a visit to the United States in the infrequent letters I had received from villagers. Franklin's letter gave few clues as to what this visit was about, but he did mention that it had been organized by Lafcadio Cortesi, who was a representative of Greenpeace International. I quickly found Cortesi's phone number through directory assistance and called him. I don't quite know what I expected, but not the effusive response I received when I got him on the line. He was delighted that I had called! He had heard many good things about Anne and me from the Maisin and very much wanted us to be part of the current project he was coordinating. That project was to mount a major exhibition of Maisin tapa cloth at the Berkeley Art Museum in collaboration with Larry Rinder, the Curator for Contemporary Art.

The exhibition was to be highly innovative in several ways. First, it would showcase tapa as a modern art form on a par with the Western art that filled most of the galleries of modern museums. Second, the tapa display would be tied to the theme of preserving the rainforest of Papua New Guinea from commercial exploitation. The Maisin would be presented as Indigenous stewards of their ancestral lands. Finally, the exhibition would make use of the most modern multimedia facilities both to tell the story of the Maisin in the most vivid way possible and to reach a wider "virtual" audience. A special website was prepared, full of colourful photographs and detailed articles concerning the Maisin and their tapa. In addition, Nick Bowness, another close friend of Cortesi's, prepared a computer kiosk featuring a "virtual village" that allowed visitors to tour parts of Uiaku and to learn about the process of making tapa.

I was asked to write a commentary on Maisin culture for the website and to give a public lecture at the opening of the exhibition. In April, Anne, Jake, and I travelled down to Berkeley. We were delighted to be reunited with Franklin. The other Maisin greeted us as family. Literally. John Ferguson Kasona had been one of the children Anne studied back in 1981-83. He and Ronald Ross Kania were members of the Jogun clan and thus Anne's "brothers." The senior member of the group, Sylvester Moi, belonged to a junior lineage of my clan, Gafi, and was thus my younger brother (although older than me; see Chapter 3).

The opening was impressive. A large number of people came — artists and environmental activists, owners of local galleries, and others. The Papua New Guinea ambassador flew in from New York to give a speech, praising the exhibition and declaring his country's dedication to conserving its rich cultural heritage and natural environment. The delegation, garbed in shells, feathers, and tapa, gave a brief performance of traditional dances and spoke about the importance of tapa and the rainforest for the community. The highlight was the tapa itself, beautifully displayed around the walls of a large room. The individual cloths were lovely, but everything was overshadowed by a spectacular piece taking up an entire wall, composed of 16 individual large *embobi* surrounded by a designed fringe. I had never seen anything like it. It had been specially commissioned for the exhibition as a material representation of the solidarity of the Maisin community.

This was not the first time Maisin tapa had been displayed in a Western museum nor even that a Maisin had travelled overseas to display and demonstrate the making of the cloth. In 1985, the Papua New Guinea government had sent Franklin along with a non-Maisin artist to represent the country in a cultural festival in Scotland, and in 1986 Anne and I had mounted a small exhibition on Maisin tapa at the Burke Museum at the University of Washington.[1] The Berkeley show, however, was a watershed moment. For the first time, tapa cloth was identified with the hot topic of conserving the world's rapidly diminishing tropical rainforests.

In 1997, I returned for a month's stay in Uiaku after a ten-year absence. The village looked much the same. Even some of the buildings had survived the decade, although they were now in advanced stages of decay, some tilting dangerously. The first thing that struck me was that the population was considerably larger and younger. Some families had returned from the towns to raise their children in the safer environment of the village, but most of the

Figure 6.1 Sylvester Moi and Franklin Seri in front of the big tapa, Berkeley, 1995. The rooster plumes in Sylvester's headdress and the cut of his loin cloth indicate that his clan belongs to the higher *Kawo* rank. Franklin's clan is *Sabu*, but he was at the time village councillor for Uiaku. (Photo by A.M. Tietjen)

increase was due to the fact that fewer children now got into high school, and even those who did often couldn't find jobs and so returned home. The place also looked a little wealthier. People wore better clothes than before, and most households seemed to possess new steel cookware, plates, and utensils. The casual daily exchange of food, betelnut, and tobacco had been at least partially superseded by a twice-weekly market at which villagers paid each other small amounts of cash for garden produce. Finally, I heard more English and *Tok Pisin* (neo-Melanesian pidgin English) than in earlier years, although people of all ages preferred to converse in Maisin.

The biggest visible change had to do with the near constant coming and going of foreign visitors. By Papua New Guinean standards, Uiaku is not a remote place. If you can catch a flight to Wanigela, you can reach it within a half-day of leaving Port Moresby.[2] In the past, however, few outsiders had any reason to go there. In the two years I lived in the village during the 1980s, the very few Europeans who visited did so at the invitation of villagers or myself for short casual stays or to watch church celebrations. During April and early May 1997, however, it was clear that Uiaku had become a destination. Every week brought new visitors from Port Moresby. Village leaders spent much of their time arranging and attending meetings with the visitors while households found a welcome source of income by putting them up. Indeed, hoping to cash in on this unexpected boom, one family was building a very lovely guesthouse to cater to visitors. This was a good investment, at least in the short term. Over the next few years, the Maisin continued to draw a steady stream of consultants working on land and conservation issues, activists providing workshops on small-scale economic development, and museum curators and researchers interested in tapa cloth. In 1998, the Uiaku mission station had become home for an American couple from the Peace Corps, who spent the next two years helping the Maisin organize the purchase and marketing of tapa, and two young European volunteers with the Summer Institute of Linguistics,[3] who had come to aid in the creation of a Maisin-language Bible. More delegations of Maisin travelled to Australia, the United States, Japan, and Canada. Within a 12-month period in 1999-2000, three foreign film crews visited the Maisin to shoot news pieces and documentaries for the Australian Broadcasting Corporation, the Canadian Broadcasting Corporation (CBC), and CNN.

The immediate cause for all of this interest and support was a decision made by the Maisin in the early 1990s not to allow commercial logging on their ancestral lands and a continuing struggle to keep loggers out that has periodically occupied the community ever since. The first part of this chapter explores the reasons why they made this decision and the larger political context that made it so significant for outsiders. The second part deals with internal changes to Maisin society over the past decade, partly in response to the struggle over logging and the relationship with outside organizations and activists.

THE CHOICE

Most of the developments I discuss in this chapter stem from a choice the Maisin made in the early 1990s to oppose the industrial logging of the rainforests that form the hinterland of the Collingwood Bay villages. All across Papua New Guinea as well as the neighbouring Melanesian nations of the Solomon Islands and Vanuatu, local landowners were making similar choices around the same time. These choices had dramatic effects: a frenzy of highly destructive logging in some areas that, according to the critics, could entirely deplete the commercially viable rainforests within a decade or less; and the almost instantaneous appearance of a wide array of local, national, and international non-governmental organizations (NGOs) in vigorous opposition.

I use the word "choice" in describing the actions of local people in these developments to draw attention to their importance as historical actors. In similar circumstances elsewhere, like the Canadian north or Indonesia, Indigenous people have usually been allowed little choice. Decisions on the fate of their lands have been made largely by powerful outsiders — national governments, commercial companies, or hordes of invading settlers. The Melanesian situation is different in that most people — even those in the towns — retain legal ownership to customary lands. Papua New Guinea has been described as a "nation of landowners" (Filer 1998a). Some 97 per cent of the land belongs to local corporate kin groups, like the Maisin clans. Local people are keenly protective of their right to dispose of the resources found on those lands as they see fit. As a consequence, the local populations of Papua New Guinea enjoy an influence over the fate of their lands that can scarcely be imagined by formerly colonized Indigenous peoples elsewhere.

Behind the clean simplicity of people making a choice, however, lie many complexities. In the early 1990s the Maisin reached a consensus that industrial logging of their lands would do them more harm than good and decided to oppose such initiatives. This is accurate enough, but it tells us nothing of their motivations or understanding. Nor does it tell us why they had to make the choice in the first place or the struggles they have had to force powerful outside interests (and some insiders as well) to respect it. To understand the choice and its implications, we need to first consider the wider contexts in which hundreds of local communities in the Melanesian world are struggling with similar decisions.

Let's begin with the rainforest. Much of the lowland region of Papua New

Guinea is covered by a dense carpet of rainforest, which provides a home for an astonishing diversity of species; there are at least 9,000 types of plants and 700 birds, including the spectacular birds of paradise that provide the country with its national symbol, and untold varieties of insects. Flying over the mountainous terrain, much of Papua New Guinea appears to be virgin forest, untouched by humans. Population density in the lowlands is, in fact, quite light compared to neighbouring Asian countries. Still, humans have been settled in New Guinea for at least 50,000 years and have had a profound impact upon the environment. This is most visible in the densely populated highlands regions, where intensive cultivation resulted in the replacement of most of the forest cover by grasslands long before the colonial period. Elsewhere, villages like Uiaku are surrounded by broad areas of secondary jungle where people make their gardens. More remote forests are less touched but still periodically visited by hunters following game and by villagers seeking medicines.

Tropical rainforests are biologically diverse. For centuries, forest products have circulated widely as commodities: rubber from the Amazon, bird of paradise plumes from New Guinea (for a time widely sought in the West for women's hats), medicines, and building materials. The very diversity of the forests, however, until recently discouraged large-scale industrial logging. As Anna Tsing (2005: 14) notes for Borneo, the big logging companies "prefer forests in which one valuable species predominates." Although the Australians recognized the commercial potential of logging in Papua New Guinea as early as the 1930s, logging operations almost up to the time of Independence remained small in scale. The situation changed dramatically, however, over the next two decades. The trigger, according to most analysts, was the movement of powerful Japanese general trading companies, the *sogo shosha*, into the international timber market. The companies provided loans and trading contracts to Southeast Asian countries, particularly Indonesia, to stimulate the production of large quantities of cheaply produced logs, most of which were used to produce plywood in Japan. This stimulated the emergence of Asian logging companies with a strong inducement to maximize the rate at which trees were felled and the valuable logs extracted from rainforests in Malaysia and Indonesia. The rapid growth of the new market and the equally rapid depletion of the more accessible rainforests in Southeast Asia led the more successful companies to seek out new areas to exploit in the Pacific Islands and Latin America. Thus the Malaysian company, Rimbunan Hijau, became the dominant player in the forestry sector in Papua New Guinea in the 1980s, providing the bulk of equipment and expertise in partnerships formed with local start-up companies.

The new international market for logs encouraged a perception of tropical forests that ignored their biological diversity. Non-commercial trees, plants, animals, birds, and even humans tended to be viewed as, at best, obstacles and, at worst, waste. Inevitably, this encouraged a frightening degree of environmental damage as giant bulldozers gouged out roads along ecologically sensitive streams and giant trees were hauled by chains to the roads, flattening everything in their path. The jumble of broken trees, gouged earth, and eroded roadbeds left behind by the loggers inhibited the recovery of the forest and, in many case, the conversion of the land for other purposes, like plantations. The immediate commercial returns, however, were spectacular. The volume of logs exported from Papua New Guinea rose from less than 500,000 cubic metres per year in 1978 to a peak of 3 million cubic metres in 1994 with an estimated market value of around US$410 million (Filer 1998a: 49). These numbers underestimate the actual rate of the cut as there is evidence of substantial illegal smuggling of logs during this same period. It is generally believed that the situation was even more out of control in the neighbouring Solomon Islands. Alarmed, some environmentalists warned that were this rate of cut to continue, the rainforests of Melanesia would disappear within a decade. This was an exaggeration, but there is little doubt that much of the logging was (and continues to be) unregulated, very damaging to the environment, and unsustainable.

From the outside, the near instant appearance of a massive logging industry in Papua New Guinea looks like a textbook example of globalization, the embrace of even the most remote areas of the world within a single economic and communication system. However, it is important to bear in mind that global trends and connections always take shape and have effects within localities. These localities, in turn, exert their own influences. In the case of Papua New Guinea, these influences kick in at two levels: the government and local landowners. Both provide a legal and political context within which the companies must operate.

In general, the government is the more powerful of the two. It establishes national policies guiding development strategies, reviews projects and issues permits, creates the regulatory and enforcement frameworks within which companies operate, and collects taxes and redistributes royalties to landowners. Since 1975, Papua New Guinea has relied primarily upon the exploitation of its abundant natural resources in its development strategy. Papua New Guinea is home to some of the largest open pit gold and copper mines in the world, and these have provided it with the lion's share of national revenue. National planners have also encouraged large-scale development of oil and gas reserves, fisheries, oil palm plantations, and timber. The Parliament has enacted many regulations meant to assure that taxes and royalties generated by the projects flow back into government coffers, that Papua New

Guinea citizens rather than foreigners receive job training and employment whenever feasible, and that the environment is protected. Unfortunately, the government has a very limited ability to monitor companies and enforce regulations once projects receive approval. The revenues generated by the projects have yet to be balanced against often substantial environmental damage, the underpayment of royalties, and theft of resources, especially in the fisheries and timber sectors (Kirsch 2006; Zimmer-Tamakoshi 1998).

Resource development in Papua New Guinea is hugely complicated by the fact that projects require the approval of landowners before they can proceed. Since land tends to be owned communally, it is often difficult to determine who has the local authority to approve a project. Even when a consensus is forged by a majority, it can be effectively challenged by disgruntled individuals before and after a project has begun (Filer 1998b). In the early years of independence, the government and resource companies learned a hard lesson when a simmering dispute between villagers situated near the giant Panguna copper mine on Bougainville Island blew up into a disastrous rebellion that took a decade to settle (Dorney 2000). The ability of rural villagers to sabotage and close the mine—at the time, one of the largest in the world—and then fend off of the national army chastened the government and resource companies. Companies seeking to start up new projects elsewhere in Papua New Guinea not only increased their royalty payments to landowners but promised significant investments in roads, schools, medical facilities, local development initiatives, and other services in order to win and maintain support—in effect, taking over government services even as they were declining elsewhere in the country. This has resulted in a very uneven pattern of economic development, with booms occurring near mines and other large projects and deterioration in government and other services almost everywhere else (Jorgensen 2006).

The enormous profits to be made from Papua New Guinea's rich natural resources on the world market, the complexities of getting legal access to them, and the lax controls over companies once they begin operation all but guarantee abuses, largely in the form of bribes to pliant politicians, bureaucrats, and village leaders to encourage approval or to look the other way when a company fails to meet its promises. It is tempting to see rural folk like the Maisin as innocent victims whose powerful desire to improve their material conditions is exploited by unscrupulous national politicians and foreign entrepreneurs. There is truth to this. Rural villagers often have only a dim understanding of how companies work or of the environmental and other effects of a mine or logging project and get taken in by often inflated promises made by promoters. Yet Papua New Guineans all have very strong attachments to their lands. Even when they are desperate for development, they insist on exercising control over how it will proceed.

I was a witness to this in May 1982. From the time we arrived, six months earlier, Anne and I had heard rumours that a major logging operation was scheduled to commence within 18 months. Once the land was cleared, the forest would be replaced with groves of oil palms, similar to a massive commercial plantation of the trees near the provincial capital of Popondetta (Newton 1982). On 18 May, villagers from several Maisin villages gathered in Uiaku to hear two officials employed by the national and provincial forestry departments outline the proposed project. The national officer did most of the talking. He told how he had been approached by a lawyer for a Philippine company who had heard of the desperate economic straits of the area and wanted to help. Good news was on the way! All the people had to do was form a local company in partnership with the Philippine company to sublet the land, and they would bring in the workers, clear away the trees, and set up the plantation. "It will not cost you a penny," he concluded. "And profits will come to the government, the company, and the people." The Uiaku village councillor spoke next, his voice cracking with emotion as he described his efforts over the years to convince the provincial government to promote logging in the area. At last it was going to happen. The meeting had the feel of a gospel revival with people emotionally murmuring their agreement, sometimes repeating the phrases of the officers and councillor as they delivered the good news. Salvation — "development" — was at last coming!

One person asked whether any logging would take place in the gardening zone around the villages. After being assured that logs would only be removed from the deep forest, discussion shifted to the two topics most on peoples' minds. They were outraged that 75 per cent of the royalties would go to the provincial and national governments. A number of men spoke eloquently of how their ancestors had conquered the land. They didn't see why the governments should receive more in royalties than the owners. The second issue had to do with the ownership of the lands and whether the clans owning specific areas of forests or the Maisin as a whole would be compensated. An elder spoke up: "When the Australian government came, they asked questions about the land. They asked whether we would separate into clans or look after it as one Maisin land. People said, 'All Maisin fought for this land so we could have the land as Maisin. Whatever happens in future, we will use it as one land for all Maisin.'" There was general agreement that the royalties must be equally distributed among the villagers, but the overall share going to the people remained a sticking point.

Over the next few days, I visited friends and privately asked them about the project. Given the certain disruptions, including the appearance of a large expatriate workforce, was it really worth the risk? People assured me that it was. The village was mired in "poverty" with no products of interest to the outside world. Logging presented the one and probably only chance of "development" that would bring decent houses, access for medicine, and schooling for the children. I pushed a little harder. What if the loggers damage gardens, scare away the game, or pollute the rivers and reefs? "We will stop them," people said confidently. "We'll make them leave." Some people had relatives in town who had expressed similar concerns. These city folk, I was told, did not have the true interest of their rural kin in mind.

Ironically, given later developments, the project was blocked by the national Forestry Department which reprimanded the officer for his extra-curricular activities on behalf of foreign loggers. Around this time, some of the lustre was wearing off logging projects elsewhere in the country. A small but vocal group of conservationists, some of them in the government, were expressing alarm over some of the operations, but the main opposition came from disillusioned landowners who had signed on as partners. They complained of promised royalties and infrastructure such as all-weather roads and permanent bridges that had not been delivered, of damaged gardens, and of mysterious barges removing logs at the dead of night. The national government had its own complaints about companies that avoided paying taxes by underestimating the value of the logs they exported or even declaring losses. Politicians joined the chorus of criticisms, demanding the government enforce its own laws. Unfortunately, the government simply did not possess the means (nor, too often, the will) to do so. There were increasing incidents of local people blocking or sabotaging logging operations and demanding compensation for the damaged environment.

In 1989 after two years of research, Judge Thomas Barnett, an Australian member of the Papua New Guinea judiciary, released a detailed report on the logging industry. He then promptly left the country, fearing for his life. Conducted over two years and resulting in 20 volumes of findings, the inquiry painstakingly documented a "forest industry out of control." This was the direct result, in Barnett's view, of collusion between foreign investors and corrupt officials and politicians out to make a quick return by exporting commercially valuable rough logs as quickly as possible. He recommended the government cut back on timber harvesting, promote local processing of logs to retain more of the value, and adopt a new national policy aimed at curtailing corruption and building an environmentally sensitive and sustainable industry (Filer 1998a: 92-97).

The Barnett Inquiry unleashed a fierce debate within Papua New Guinea over the future of industrial logging. The government made substantive changes in its forestry policies, mostly voluntary but to some extent under the forceful prodding of its main financial donors, particularly the World

Bank. A rapidly growing number of local and international environmental NGOs took it upon themselves to work with the government in developing conservation programs and low-impact development projects while also serving as watchdogs against abuses. At the same time, the larger logging companies formed a national lobbying group, started up a new newspaper, and vigorously promoted an image of themselves as good corporate citizens. The basic problems, however, did not disappear. The government still lacked the ability to monitor companies, let alone enforce its laws in the field. Those companies in the log export business still faced the challenge of getting legal access to the forests at the cheapest possible price. It was (and remains) a situation that invites dodgy backroom deal-making to give the appearance of meeting requirements without incurring the cost.

This brings us back to the Maisin. In 1986, I found that people remained committed to selling off their trees, but some doubts had settled in about the trustworthiness of the logging companies. I think that much of this came by word of mouth. There are Maisin employed right across Papua New Guinea in a wide variety of jobs; some had personally witnessed the damage caused by logging and urged their relatives to be careful. By 1994 at the latest, the consensus had swung to oppose any industrial logging. The shift in opinion may have been partially due to the types of scandals revealed by the Barnett inquiry, but the main precipitating factor was more direct. Rumours had been circulating for some time that a group of men who had left Collingwood Bay as children to live in the cities had secretly signed an agreement with a logging company giving it access to the Maisin rainforest. A photocopy of the document, complete with signatures, then showed up. People were outraged. Meetings were held in the villages denouncing the scheme, and village leaders were given permission to run full-page ads in the *Post-Courier* newspaper declaring Collingwood Bay the property of the local landowners. Two years later, the scenario was replayed when another secret contract appeared, this time bearing the signature of the then provincial premier, approving a bizarre scheme to clear-cut the rainforest and replace it with plantations of an experimental sap-producing palm for a new health drink. The proposal promised millions of US dollars each year to the landowners who would set up family farms alongside 50,000 Philippine migrant farmers. The contract was said to have gotten as far as the Prime Minister's Office and was awaiting final approval when it was leaked. Again, there were meetings and full-page ads placed in the press. The government denied any involvement.

The biggest threat came in 1998 when a "Keroro Development Corporation" secured recognition from the national government as a "Representative Landowner Body." (It later was revealed that many if not most of the men listed as partners had never been approached for permission.) In its supposed

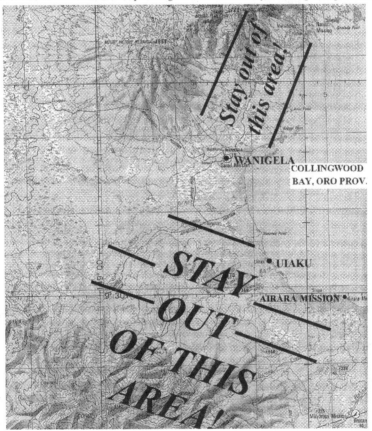

TO: LOGGING, AGROFORESTRY & MINING COMPANIES...
F.I.A., PNG Forest Authority, PNG Dept. Mining & Petroleum....
Cut this out and save for your future reference!

We Maisin leaders are tired of being the LAST ones to be asked to 'okay' projects proposed for our land. If you want to do *anything* on our land, FIRST get the approval of Maisin traditional leaders who live in the villages. State your business and speak in front of all the Maisin villagers. No dealmaking in Waigani, Popondetta, Asia or Australia. *Come to Collingwood Bay.* If that is not your style, then go 'help' people somewhere else in PNG. **WARNING:** The Maisin people don't want ANY projects where you buy our timber or minerals with no downstream processing. If that is what is on your mind, go someplace else.

Figure 6.2 An anti-logging newspaper ad, 1996. Sponsored in part by Greenpeace International, this ad took up a full page of the *Post-Courier* following the Maisin's discovery that the government was on the verge of approving a logging concession on their lands. (Reproduced with permission of MICAD)

capacity as a landowner association, Keroro invited the government to remove the land from customary ownership and then leased back 38,000 hectares of prime forest land to itself and a partner company, Deegold (PNG), for 50 years. The partners contracted with a Malaysian firm to clear-cut the forest with plans to develop an oil palm plantation later. Word leaked out in June 1999 just as bulldozers and other heavy equipment were being prepared to be shipped by barge to Collingwood Bay. The Maisin immediately sent a delegation to Port Moresby and managed to get the leases suspended. A complicated and expensive legal battle followed in the National Court with suits and countersuits between the landowners, Deegold, and the government. In 2002, the National Court ruled that the government had acted illegally, cancelled all leases, and forbade the companies involved from entering Maisin territory without the prior written approval of the people (Barker 2004b).

There was much talk in Uiaku about the looming court battle during my visit in June 2000. People kept returning to a point that I had also heard during the 1982 meeting when everyone was eager for logging to commence, that is "Our ancestors conquered this land." The move by Deegold, Keroro, and the unnamed logging company amounted to "theft." The choice the Maisin made to oppose logging, then, rested on the same principle that motivated their earlier desire to allow it. They own the land. It is their right to decide how it should be used, nobody else's. They are unified on that.

This is, however, by no means the whole story. While I believe that the Maisin independently reached a consensus on the fate of the rainforest in the early 1990s, their choice was certainly made more attractive by the active support of NGOs. The Maisin did not see their decision to block logging as a decision to opt out of economic development as critics in the national government and the companies claimed. Instead, with the assistance of their new partners, they would seek out alternative, less environmentally destructive ways to improve their material life. And these efforts, in turn, would stimulate a debate on customary ways, a revolution in local governance, and a heightened engagement with the outside world.

THE PARTNERS

News of the Maisin's victory in the National Court in 2002 was disseminated around the globe within hours. Congratulations poured in from environmental organizations far and wide. To the outside world, this was a David versus Goliath story, an instance of a small and vulnerable Indigenous group taking on a powerful modern company, which had all of the advantages of lawyers and friends in high places, and winning. And so it was. Yet such victories are not quite as rare as one might suppose. Many Papua New Guineans have become fed up with promises of easy wealth that never materializes and have effectively slowed or halted logging operations by blockading roads, sabo-taging machinery, and chasing away workers. Their stories rarely garner international attention. We know of David's battle against the giant because the tale is recounted in the Bible. To the extent that the outside world knows about the Maisin, it is through their alliance with various, mostly Western-based individuals and groups who have likewise publicized their story. While the Maisin deserve the most credit for their victory, their wide circle of allies also played a critical role.

Environmentalists concerned with conserving the remaining rainforests of Southeast Asia form the core of these alliances. They make up the largest part of a burgeoning group of NGOs that have grown in tandem with the expansion of industrial mining and logging in Papua New Guinea in the post-Independence period. Colin Filer (1998: 264) estimates that as of 1996 somewhere between 100 and 150 NGOs were operating in the country, a third to a half concerned with forest policy. These NGOs range from organi-zations with a global reach, like Greenpeace and the World Wildlife Fund, to village-based associations. They are mostly staffed by Papua New Guineans, but most receive (or hope to receive) much of their funding from interna-tional environmental organizations, foreign government aid agencies, and national and international church groups and development organizations, as well as individual donors. The largest employ expatriates in senior staff posi-tions and as consultants.

In their publicity, environmental activists like to portray themselves as opponents of "globalization," which they identify with the activities of multinational corporations. Yet the enormous expansion of environmental NGOs in the late twentieth century must also be understood as a facet of globalization. While tiny compared to international corporations, the NGOs work within a comparable global network that also depends upon modern means of mass communication, forms of bureaucratic organization, and funding. They also rationalize their efforts in terms of universal values: the human rights of local peoples, the need to preserve pristine environments for the benefit of all humankind, and so forth. These are worthy aims, but they require as much international agreement and coordination as the commercial networks of companies that transfer logs from Papua New Guinea to Japan and Korea. The key difference has to do with their vision of what is in the best interests of the world's population—unfettered development driven by capital markets seeking new sources of profit, or regulation with the aim of restoring a sustainable balance between the earth's environment and the needs of its human and nonhuman inhabitants.

Eleven years after the representative of a logging company visited Uiaku, Lafcadio Cortesi, who then worked for Greenpeace International, came to the village on the recommendation of a friend who had visited the area as a tourist earlier in 1993. For some time, Greenpeace had been expanding from its earlier role as a radical environmental protest organization to promote "green" development projects, especially among Indigenous peoples. Cortesi saw that Maisin tapa cloth was exactly the sort of thing Greenpeace would be interested in supporting. Cortesi's offer to help create an overseas market for tapa was eagerly accepted by the Maisin. A few months later, in 1994, the other shoe dropped when villagers discovered that the National Forest Board had placed Collingwood Bay among priority areas for logging without first consulting them. Maisin leaders organized meetings and compiled a petition in protest. Cortesi facilitated these efforts, putting the leaders in touch with a lawyer in Port Moresby and with national journalists who could report the story from the Maisin point of view. He also helped to secure funds to place full-page advertisements in the national newspaper, the *Post-Courier*, to protest the project, actions that would be repeated in 1996 and 2000 in response to renewed threats.

The Maisin, via Cortesi, put out a call for help. The response was impressive. Within a year, the Maisin went from a situation of political isolation to partnership with a bewildering array of outside organizations and individuals. The help offered and accepted by the people worked in three overlapping directions: publicizing the Maisin's situation to the outside world, securing legal protection of the rainforest, and enhancing the local economy and governance.

Although many of these interventions required a great deal of consultation and planning, the Maisin's sudden and unexpected engagement with anti-logging forces was anything but preplanned and only loosely coordinated, more or less on the fly. Instead there was something of a chain reaction as a project with one group led to involvement with another. Larry Rinder, the curator of the successful 1995 tapa exhibition at the Berkeley Art Museum, for instance, helped develop a project with the Fabric Workshop, an independent museum in Philadelphia. Three Maisin women spent an extended period of time at the Workshop, creating innovative tapa designs on various types of media for a major exhibition. Fabric Workshop staff, in turn, visited the Maisin villages twice to confer on the project and to film in the communities. A larger Maisin delegation travelled to Philadelphia for the grand opening. John Wesley Vaso, who once enjoyed a short stint as an announcer on the Papua New Guinea radio service before returning to Uiaku, was interviewed on the "Fresh Air" show on National Public Radio in the United States. During this time, one of the Maisin women visiting Philadelphia expressed regrets that there had been no opportunity to meet Indigenous people in North America. This provided the seed for another project, in which I played a leading role, of setting up an exchange between the Maisin and the Stó:lō First Nation of British Columbia. In June 2000, a delegation of five members of the Stó:lō Nation visited the Maisin villages to discuss issues of mutual concern, and the next year seven Maisin came to Canada. These exchanges were the subject of two documentaries, aired on the CBC's flagship science program, *The Nature of Things*, hosted by David Suzuki.[4] Maisin delegations also visited New Zealand, Australia, and Japan.

Meanwhile back in Papua New Guinea, steps were being taken to enhance legal protection of Maisin lands. Representatives of the Individual and Community Rights Forum (ICRAF), a national NGO, held a workshop to inform people of their legal rights under Papua New Guinea law as landowners. Papua New Guinea officially protects only a tiny portion of its territory in the form of national parks, wildlife management areas, and wildlife sanctuaries. This is not so much the result of a lack of interest or determination as the fact that the vast majority of land remains under customary tenure. The same factors that make it difficult to alienate land for commercial development militates against putting it aside to be protected. Once they learned that having their lands declared a Wildlife Management Area would involve ceding some control to the government, most Maisin lost interest. By the early 1990s, however, the national government developed new policies that would recognize and protect conservation areas from uncontrolled logging. These policies were backed by the commitment of funds by outsider donors to identify areas for conservation and by the government's signing, in 1993, of the International Convention on Biological Diversity. These conditions, in turn, gave the environmental NGO community more influence and encouraged the emergence of new organizations focussed around specific areas and projects. One of these organizations, Conservation Melanesia, made Collingwood Bay its first project and for the first five or so years of its existence remained almost exclusively concerned with the Maisin. In 1996, Conservation Melanesia coordinated an inventory of the marine and forest resources of all the Maisin villages, including the Cape Nelson outlier of Uwe, and provided a number of educational workshops on conservation values.

This brings us to a third set of interventions intended to enhance the local economy and system of governance. In 1995, the leaders of the petition drive against the first logging proposal drafted a "Maisin Declaration" in support of their ancestral lands that was widely broadcast by Greenpeace in brochures and on the Internet (reproduced in full at the end of this chapter). While acknowledging the sustaining values of the forest for the community, the Declaration states clearly:

> ...we do not only wish to live as our ancestors did. We seek to maintain our heritage but also to improve our lives and the lives of our future generations. We

therefore require better opportunities for education, health and transportation, to name a few. The Government has failed to adequately assist us in developing these opportunities. We require money, information, training and technical support to develop them ourselves.

The various NGOs and other partners, under this scenario, would fill the breach left by the steady decline in government services. A number of workshops were held in the villages to provide basic training in small-scale development in areas such as insect farming and eco-tourism, but almost all the effort focussed on the expansion of a market for tapa cloth. Delegates on the overseas trips spent part of their time meeting with "ethnic arts" dealers and shopowners, hoping to establish business partnerships. Several environmental NGOs began marketing tapa on their websites, accompanied with colourful pictures of the villagers and brief descriptions of the "Maisin story." Cortesi also worked closely with village leaders to start up a tapa cloth cooperative, described in the next section.

These various projects all required some form of official approval from the community. This posed an immediate problem. Although the Maisin had come together to resist the illegal sale of their forest in 1994, they possessed no overarching form of governance. A solution came, ironically enough, via policy initiatives occurring at the national level. In the early 1990s, the Department of Environment and Conservation secured US$5 million to begin experiments with locally based "integrated conservation and development" (ICAD) projects (Filer 1998a: 246). Several of these were set up around the country (e.g., West 2006), but a number of other communities, including the Maisin, independently adopted the model for themselves. In 1996, the Maisin Integrated Conservation and Development association, MICAD (pronounced "My-Cad"), came into existence with formal representation from all of the Maisin villages, although dominated in practice by Uiaku. In principle, MICAD coordinated the work of the various partners, such as Conservation Melanesia and Greenpeace. Its leaders, however, had greater ambitions for it, seeing it as a kind of Maisin government that would give each of the villages a political voice in future developments and provide a range of services. One of the first orders of business after its formation was MICAD's decision that profits from the tapa business and hospitality charges to visitors would go towards the purchase of medicines for the community aid posts. We'll look more closely at MICAD towards the end of this chapter.

Cortesi's efforts and the establishment of Conservation Melanesia and MICAD provided a certain degree of coherence to these developments. Yet there was never a master plan. The various groups and individuals who became involved with the Maisin, mostly for short periods of time, had few if any organizational links with each other. They are autonomous, with their own goals, funding sources, and requirements. Thus, the Maisin in the 1990s became a focus for a loose and shifting coalition of sympathetic outsiders whose notions of how to help sometimes clashed. Greenpeace's policies during the 1990s had moved from purely confrontational tactics to encouraging small-scale sustainable local economic development, a goal that required wary cooperation with the Papua New Guinea government and occasionally traditional adversaries like the World Bank. During this same period, the Maisin were visited by more radical activists who urged a return to "traditional" values and rejection of most forms of modern economic development. The most influential of this group was the remarkable Sister Yasuko Shimizu, a member of the Mercendarian Missionaries of Berriz in Tokyo and founder of her own NGO dedicated to ending destructive logging in Melanesia. Forceful and energetic, this diminutive nun attracted a great deal of interest whenever she visited the area, often with Japanese biologists in tow, lecturing the people on the need to preserve their ancient culture and to reject grants and aid from the outside, which might make them too dependent. Ironically, Sister Yasuko is also an ardent feminist who does not hesitate to protest the subservience of women in Maisin society. Equally ironically, despite her opposition to outsiders helping Indigenous people materially, she provided the Maisin with an enormously useful and well-received gift—a satellite telephone which, for the first time, provided them with fairly reliable means of communication with the outside world.

It is impossible to say with any precision just why the Maisin attracted so much attention and help during this brief period of time. Many factors were at work: sheer happenstance, the initiative taken by resourceful activists, the receptiveness of the Maisin to their new partners, the emergence of a political space in Papua New Guinea for NGOs like Conservation Melanesia, and so forth. What can be said with certainty is that the developments in Collingwood Bay in the 1990s amounted to a sign of the times with both the massive expansion of a global market for tropical wood and the emergence of a loose global network of environmental NGOs dedicated to conservation of the rainforests.[5] While not everything, timing is important. The Maisin were the beneficiaries of the explosion of NGOs in Papua New Guinea, many of which were searching for worthy projects. More generally, the Maisin also benefited from other well-publicized campaigns occurring in the 1980s and early 1990s in which international environmental activists had teamed up with Indigenous peoples like the Haida of British Columbia, the Kayapo of Brazil, and the Penan of Malaysia to block industrial logging and mining projects (Brosius 2003; Turner 1993). While on a much smaller scale, the Maisin rejection of commercial logging fit neatly into a scenario of an

Indigenous people defending their lands, to which NGOs could respond quickly with money, advice, and international publicity.

The unusual political clout of NGOs in Papua New Guinea is also an important contextual factor. Although politicians and civil servants often react angrily to the complaints of activists or simply ignore them, the NGOs are mostly tolerated and often even encouraged. Part of the reason for this is that the organizations have strong support in the rural communities where most people live. However, it is also the case that many politicians share at least some of the concerns raised by the NGOs about deforestation. In addition, the NGOs fulfill some important needs. Despite its rich endowment of natural resources, Papua New Guinea is greatly dependent upon foreign aid, particularly from Australia and the World Bank, which have long insisted on more sustainable forestry practices. This has encouraged the government to bring in experts from some of the NGOs to help develop policies and to carry out projects. Finally, the NGOs have come to occupy a small but significant niche in the country as years of economic shortfalls made worse by mismanagement and widespread corruption have contributed to a weakening of state-provided services in most rural areas. In the late 1990s, for instance, Conservation Melanesia became a major conduit for mail and medical supplies to Maisin villages years after local government services had completely broken down. Some politicians praise resident NGOs as examples of "self-reliance." For their part, NGOs echo the dissatisfactions of their local supporters with the failures of social services and a perceived lack of interest or will on the part of politicians to respond to their needs.

A final important factor attracting the NGOs to the Maisin has to do with their basic funding requirements. NGOs are voluntary organizations that rely upon donors to pay their salaries and carry out their work. Typically a great deal of fundraising is required, as well as writing project proposals and reports on progress. Collingwood Bay was by no means the largest or most significant project undertaken by environmental NGOs in Papua New Guinea during the 1990s (Filer 1997). Yet, apart from Greenpeace and Conservation Melanesia, it attracted an extraordinary number of organizations and individuals who made short visits and provided limited consultations. The core attraction, of course, was the David and Goliath story of fighting off loggers along with the presence of what could easily be portrayed as a suitable, sustainable economic alternative: tapa cloth. There were also other practical advantages. The setting of the Maisin villages makes for vibrant publicity materials—"unspoiled" thatched huts surrounded by lush tropical jungles backed by dramatic mountains, the tapa cloth itself, and the women with their exotic facial tattoos. Such images speak compellingly of a world that would soon be lost without outside help.

What the images don't convey is equally important. Collingwood Bay is within a relatively easy half-day's journey from Port Moresby. It is cheap to stay there, there is no danger from crime as in the cities or tribal warfare as in the Highlands, and many people speak fluent English. It was simply much easier to visit, consult, and initiate projects with the Maisin than many other places in the country, and as more groups did so, something of a snowball effect took place.

None of the groups coming to the aid of the Maisin sought to change the community in any significant way. While their familiarity with the culture generally was not very deep and was based upon impressions (often romantic), they liked the people and admired what they perceived as a "traditional" way of life. Their purpose was to help the Maisin sustain their way of life by providing them with the tools to protect their lands and to develop sustainable alternatives to logging, particularly the development of a market for tapa cloth. Yet such a sudden and large influx of outsiders with ideas, projects, money, and powerful outside connections was bound to have a major impact on a small, formerly remote community. Much of this impact focussed on tapa and around MICAD.

TAPA CLOTH AND WOMEN
From the start, it was clear that tapa would figure centrally in the effort to foster integrated conservation and development. The decision to block logging did nothing to alleviate the practical difficulties of starting most other businesses in the Collingwood Bay region. The lack of regular shipping along the coast and absence of good harbours had defeated innumerable earlier attempts to develop copra, cocoa, coffee, and other cash crops. There was at first much talk about other possibilities such as insect farming or eco-tourism, but the main hope rested with tapa. After all, the Maisin had long enjoyed a small but fairly steady market for the cloth in Papua New Guinea, having captured a small niche in the artifact trade.

Tapa had additional attractions for the Maisin's partners and sponsors. All of the work that has been carried out in Collingwood Bay depends upon the financial support of donors in distant countries whose knowledge of Papua New Guinea, let alone the Maisin, is minimal. In appealing to them for funds, the partners have to sell an attractive if generic picture of the people and the cause. The cause, of course, is rainforest conservation, a global campaign that got its start in the highly publicized efforts to save the great Amazon forest in the 1980s. This generated a new political model of collaboration between environmentalists and Indigenous peoples that was quickly transferred to other parts of the globe. Thus, Indigenous "rights became entangled with conservation initiatives" (Tsing 2005: 159). Tapa was ideal for this purpose. It was a sustainable product with a low environmental impact; it was easy to ship out of the villages to both national and international markets; and it was an iconic form of Oceanic art, a symbol of the continuing viability of an Indigenous culture. Purchasers of tapa could feel that they are supporting not only rainforest conservation and the rights of Indigenous people but also, more directly, the advancement of the economic position of "Third World" women who, in general, have fared worse under globalization than men.

Early in their relationship with the Maisin, Greenpeace initiated a "Painting a Sustainable Future" campaign to foster the development of a stable market for tapa. Locally, village leaders formed a new economic cooperative with a governing council made up of two representatives (one male, one female) from each of the tapa-producing villages. Maisin Tapa Enterprises did not hold a monopoly. Villagers agreed that individuals should be free to sell their tapa directly to artifact shops if they wished. Still, the hope was that the cooperative would capture most of the trade and, on that basis, be able to secure better prices for the producers and generate a steady profit to pay overhead and invest in new projects. Maisin Tapa Enterprises was by no means an entirely new creation; the Maisin had created a similar cooperative, Haus Tapa, back in 1982. It had floundered, most people thought, because the young men running it had mishandled the funds. Greenpeace organized a workshop on financial management for the staff of the new cooperative. More importantly, it convinced the Peace Corps, a voluntary organization funded by the American government, to place Kerry and Kate Sullivan in Uiaku for two years to assist the tapa business. Trained accountants, the Sullivans provided Maisin Tapa Enterprises with a stability that would have been nearly impossible for villagers to achieve on their own.

Meanwhile, Cortesi orchestrated a major publicity campaign overseas through Greenpeace and his own extensive network of activists to promote tapa and the Maisin cause. This involved the arrangement of museum exhibits in Berkeley, Philadelphia, and New York; marketing research; and establishing connections between Maisin Tapa Enterprises and overseas buyers. Maisin tapa was featured in brochures, catalogues, and websites, usually accompanied by a capsule description of the people and their battle against loggers.[6] Worried that the market for tapa wall-hangings would be too limited, Cortesi and his allies (including myself) conferred with various businesses to consider spin-offs such as tapa hats, handbags, and book covers. This met with limited success, but Cortesi pursued another possibility that might prove more lucrative in the future: the licensing of Maisin tapa designs. In 1997, Greenpeace Germany licensed a design to use on coffee mugs and t-shirts. For a time, Cortesi was involved in hot negotiations with the clothing giant Patagonia to license tapa designs for a new fashion line, but unfortunately this fell through.

It was very clear on my visits in 1997 and 1998 that a great deal of tapa was being produced in the villages. There was also an impressive degree of innovation. Much of this was subtle, involving small design changes, a tendency to produce small one-panel tapas that were easier to market, and experimentation with dyes to produce sharper blacks and reds. Other changes, however, were more radical. A number of men now designed tapa, although none seemed willing to undertake the hard labour of beating. My old language teacher, Gideon Ifoki, had developed not only into a fine artist but a skilled innovator, producing attractive tapa cloth hats and ties. Some Maisin were developing ways of rationalizing the process of producing tapa to make it more efficient. One household in Ganjiga, for instance, created a kind of factory line, with different people assigned to beating, drawing the design, and filling in the red on a steady flow of tapa cloths. People were vigorously debating whether designs were straying too far from traditional norms as some tapa makers combed through magazines and even design books for ideas. A number of people had used crayons to design cartoon-like figures on tapa, usually accompanied by political slogans and biblical quotations. These were not for sale but adorned the walls of the MICAD building and some houses. Upon my departure in April 1997, Gideon surprised me with a beautiful tapa with a bright cartoon of Bart Simpson on a skate board surrounded by traditional tapa designs to give to my son Jake on his upcoming seventh birthday.

While the tapa promotion campaign along with the cash injected by visitors resulted in a sudden rise in the prosperity of the Maisin villages, particularly Uiaku, no one became wealthy. Most of the money was quickly dispersed along exchange networks and spent on store-bought food, clothing, transportation fees, and other consumables rather than put in bank accounts. In any case, the surge didn't last long. By the time of my visit in June and July 2000, the Painting a Sustainable Future campaign had petered out, with Cortesi leaving Greenpeace and working full time on environmental issues in Indonesia and with the departure of the Peace Corps volunteers. The fundamentals kicked back in. Faced by the problems of irregular and expensive transportation, no control over market prices, and the failure of some purchasers to pay for the tapa they received, Maisin Tapa Enterprises was moribund, and individual tapa sales, mostly to artifact shops in the towns, had slowed to a trickle.

Demand for tapa has waxed and waned over the past 30 years. The market will likely pick up again. In any case, the Maisin will continue to pursue ways of making money with or without outside assistance. Although unusually intense, the short-lived tapa project is very instructive not just of the challenges of integrating conservation with sustainable development in peripheral areas but of reconciling the demands of the market economy with deeply held Melanesian values. Every villager I spoke to was delighted by the money that outsiders brought to the community, either directly or through tapa sales. However, this was coupled by strong discontent with how things were actually working out. Many people harboured deep suspicions that some partners were getting far more out of the arrangement than others, pocketing more than their fair share of the profits that the cloth fetched overseas. Most partners, it was thought, were good and working selflessly on behalf of the people, but perhaps not all. Much of the discontent, however, was directed inwards, upon the Maisin themselves. Each time that the cooperative made the rounds of the villages to purchase tapa, complaints arose in its wake that people were not being treated fairly. Many felt that they were not given as much opportunity to sell their cloth as others. Rumours spread that the managers of the cooperative tended to favour their own relatives and perhaps had sticky fingers, skimming off profits for their own use. At times the griping and gossip grew so intense, I felt that the main accomplishment of the tapa initiative had been to stir up a hornets' nest. This was perhaps unfair. Gossip and complaint are normal in the context of a political system based on consensus. Everyone agreed that the cooperative was a good thing. However, the inflow of cash brought by tapa sales directly challenged deeply engrained notions of fairness because it proved impossible to guarantee an equitable share across the villages and among tapa makers.

The tapa project stirred up another conflict of values that proved just as stubbornly difficult. As I noted earlier, outside sponsors were attracted to tapa cloth not only because it was clearly "Indigenous" but also because it was produced mainly by women. Around the same time as the collaborative model between environmentalists and Indigenous peoples emerged, development agencies ranging from small NGOs to the giant World Bank increasingly earmarked funds to promote "women and development." In part, this initiative was motivated by a sense of justice. It was widely held that women held subservient positions in "traditional" societies, and there was lots of evidence that men were usually the main beneficiaries of development projects. There were additional pragmatic considerations. In most developing countries, women provide the glue holding families together. Very often they contribute more labour than men do in support of their households. Beyond this, they are considered to be more responsible and more likely to use scant financial resources to further their children's education or purchase medicine, while many men would use the same funds for gambling or to purchase alcohol or hire prostitutes. In Melanesia, the most stable and effective community organizations tend to be women's church groups like the Anglican Mothers Union. Hence, a number of experts have argued that rather than channelling money and projects through men, who tend to fritter away the proceeds or use them to advance their own political careers, a better strategy would be to work directly with women who are much more likely to use the resources to the betterment of their communities (Dickson-Waiko 2003).

Unfailingly respectful and polite, the partners working with the Maisin on various tapa projects insisted that women have a prominent place not only in the making of the cloth but in making decisions and enjoying the benefits. Just as politely, Maisin male leaders resisted. The delegation to Berkeley, for instance, was originally supposed to include two women and two men. When four men showed up, the inevitable question from the audience was, "Where are the women?" Leaders protested that women were unable or unwilling to take leading roles in the tapa initiative, yet they had little choice but to compromise if they wished further cooperation from the partners. Future delegations included women, although usually in the minority. Women were formally, although not effectively, given equal control over Maisin Tapa Enterprises, and women's councils were formed in Uiaku and Airara to meet with partners when they came into the area to discuss tapa-related projects. In 1997, I was amazed to find senior women sitting *upon* (rather than below and beside) the shelters with their male counterparts during the various meetings I attended. They sat apart and sat quietly unless prompted by the men to speak, but a number made eloquent speeches not only about tapa but about the need for the Maisin to preserve the rainforest. This state of affairs didn't last long. By 2000, senior men again sat alone on the shelters. I was then working on the early stages of organizing a delegation to visit Canada. When I told people it had to be half women, a number of men complained bitterly to me that I and the other partners were "interfering with the culture."

It was harder for me to get a sense of what the women thought. A few younger women (and men as well) were clearly happy about the changes, but most women, uncomfortable talking about political matters or just shy, refused to share their opinion. It was clear that Uiaku was not on the brink of a feminist revolution. The women's council only convened when visitors requested a meeting. The Mothers Union remained the only viable women's group. It had grown greatly in popularity since the 1980s, but it still included only a small minority of the women (mostly older) and limited its activities to shared meals and services and pastoral care for the sick and infirm. Whether because of jealousy or notions of appropriate behaviour, senior women were among the most adamantly opposed to women joining delegations, and those who managed to go overseas could count upon tongue-lashings, particularly from their female in-laws. The main problem, I suspect, was that despite all the good intentions, the tapa projects did not do much in a practical sense to support women. Indeed, they added considerably to their burden (cf. Douglas 2003). Women still remained responsible for most daily subsistence tasks. The increased pressure to beat and design tapa added to their already heavy workloads, as did visits from activists, museum curators, and film crews who needed to be housed, fed, and entertained. In many cases, their husbands, brothers, and fathers appropriated any cash earned from tapa, so women often saw few of the benefits. This all suggests to me that their resistance had less to do with cultural conservatism or a reluctance to upset the men as resistance to being burdened with additional work. As we saw in Chapter 3, Maisin women are not drudges who merely obey their husbands. While they do not usually speak out in public, they do let the men know their opinions. Thus, I was not entirely surprised when an old friend shared with me her hope that the next development project for the Maisin would for once require the men to do "real work" rather than just sit around and talk, as they did incessantly about MICAD.

MICAD

What began as a normal market day on the Uiaku mission station in March 1997 broke out into a flurry of activity as men began to converge on the area, some carrying heavy hardwood logs and others a large portable winch. Under the careful supervision of Sylvester Moi, MICAD's chairman and the owner of the winch, teams of young men dug deep holes and then manoeuvered the winch to lift and set the massive posts down. The atmosphere was festive, with the working men singing and trading sexual barbs with each other and the women standing in the market stalls. It was indeed a moment for celebration. The Maisin were erecting their very first two-storey building. Once completed, it would house the satellite telephone just donated by Sister Yasuko and powered by a solar panel contributed by another NGO. It would also serve as the headquarters for MICAD itself. There was one sour note. People from other villages had been invited to contribute materials and labour for the new office building. Sylvester became increasingly worried when they failed to show up. The splendid new office building and phone had been located in Uiaku by agreement of all the village representatives on MICAD, he told me. It was the most central location and, with Ganjiga, the largest of the communities. Everyone had agreed, but now it appeared he had more work to do to convince leaders in the other villages that it really had been the right choice.

MICAD was the joint creation of Maisin leaders and outside partners, in particular Greenpeace and Conservation Melanesia. Its immediate origins lay in the landowners' refusal to cede control over the forest in the mid-1990s. The emergency, perhaps for the first time, brought together all of the Maisin villages in large political rallies, including even remote Uwe, lying far to the north and possessing no commercially valuable stands of timber.[7] The model of integrated conservation and development being introduced nationally around the same time gave this political movement form. That form was recognizably Western and democratic. Working closely with Conservation Melanesia, MICAD developed a constitution laying out procedures for electing officers and their duties and responsibilities to the community. While the Maisin saw the need for a unified front to stave off attempts by individuals or whole villages from signing contracts with loggers, the partners perhaps had the greater need for a formally constituted political organization. Indeed, it is hard to see how the partnerships could have continued without the invention of MICAD or something similar. MICAD's constituted authority included the power to negotiate projects with outsiders, make arrangements for food and accommodation for visitors, and handle profits from tapa sales and the telephone, along with direct grants, for the benefit of the Maisin people as a whole. Without MICAD, the partners would have had to negotiate virtually everything they did directly with individual villages, adding enormously to their expenses as well as the difficulty of getting projects up and running.

During my fieldwork in the late 1990s, I was very curious to learn more about MICAD. The various partners I had spoken to for the most part dealt only with the MICAD leadership and talked about the organization as a kind of government, albeit one that was still finding its feet. My curiosity stemmed in part from my historical research into the cooperative movement of the 1950s and 1960s. How did the Maisin view MICAD? Did they see it as a return of the old cooperative movement, only now on a much greater scale? Or did it represent something entirely new, a true break from the past? Because I had "family" in Uiaku, I was treated somewhat differently than other partners. I arrived in 1997 and 1998 with places to stay. Still, I now paid an accommodation fee that had been set by MICAD for visitors. I found, in Uiaku at least, MICAD had a large presence. I attended workshops and meetings and interviewed the leaders at length. I also spent much of my time with people in several villages, getting their views on the organization and listening to the gossip.

I came away from my research convinced that MICAD really does mark a major change in Maisin society. While the organization itself is shaky — perhaps more an idea than established reality — it has provided the Maisin with a new way of thinking of themselves, more as a kind of nation than as individual communities or simply as members of clans. This kind of development is by no means unique to the Maisin. "Micro-nationalist" movements have been common across Melanesia as people rethink and rework their notions of cultural and linguistic identity in the context of the multicultural states of which they are citizens (Foster 1995b). At their more heady moments, some Maisin — particularly young men — talked defiantly of the Maisin as rejecting the authority of the Papua New Guinea government entirely, of building up local businesses and infrastructures that would allow them complete autonomy. I doubt that many Maisin share this illusion, but certainly the integrated conservation and development movement has contributed to a new sense of their identity as Maisin and increasingly fostered a politics focussed upon unity across the region rather than based at the village level.

Important as such changes were, I also found much that was familiar in the ways the Maisin actually thought about and dealt with MICAD. This is perhaps inevitable when you consider that MICAD was and remains essentially a volunteer, part-time organization. It has no paid staff and through most of its years has lacked the budget even to hold the twice-yearly meetings of the board as required by its constitution. All of the leaders and village representatives in MICAD are at the same time "ordinary" villagers in the sense that they spend most of their days engaged in subsistence activities, taking care of their households, and meeting their obligations to extended kin and exchange partners. Much of the time, the office building on the Uiaku mission station is locked and empty. MICAD only comes into being when there is a need, such as a request from an outside partner or in response to a threat to Maisin lands.

What I have found on my visits is that there is lots of talk about MICAD, talk that follows the patterns of political discourse we examined in the last chapter. Assessments are deeply informed by the key value of equivalence. While villagers I spoke to clearly took great pride in forming MICAD and in its accomplishments, it did not take long before the talk became critical. People everywhere (including some MICAD leaders) complained that the organization did not fairly share projects and the money they brought in. Such criticisms were especially acute the further one moved from Uiaku, which was widely perceived as receiving the lion's share of benefits. For Maisin living in Sinapa or Airara, the MICAD office building was proof of their subservient role in the organization, and, from time to time, they let it be known that unless things improved they might pull out. Within Uiaku and Ganjiga, criticisms focussed more on the leaders who were widely suspected of taking advantage of their positions to skim money or secure other benefits. Such suspicions were not misplaced. MICAD leaders tended to be heavily represented on overseas delegations, to visit Port Moresby frequently, and to take other perks.

MICAD exists in the tension between the need for an authority that can speak for all of the Maisin and the cultural expectation of equivalence. In its formative years, it was the work of big men to navigate that space, to build and maintain consensus despite the contradictions. No one played a more significant role than Sylvester Moi, who until his death in 2003 served as the director of MICAD. Sylvester's life reads like a history of the Maisin in the twentieth century. His father had been a mission teacher and founder of the first cooperative in Uiaku. As an infant, Sylvester was fostered to the Jogun clan in Ganjiga, who are *Sabu*. When his adopted parents died, he returned to his own *Kawo* clan of Gafi but retained ties to Jogun. He was among the first generation of Maisin to go to high school. After receiving medical training in Papua New Guinea and New Zealand, he worked as a medical orderly at the giant Panguna copper mine on Bougainville Island until fighting broke out, leading to a ten-year civil war. Sylvester's family settled with him in Uiaku, quickly establishing gardens and contributing to exchanges, thus establishing him as a generous man. He was also a powerful orator. However, his greatest skill lay in quiet diplomacy. Making use of his split identity as *Sabu* and *Kawo*, belonging to two villages, Sylvester spent most of his evenings quietly visiting other elders, making use of his extended kin networks to establish bonds in all of the Maisin communities. He was also effective as a cultural broker, equally comfortable with Westerners and his own people. No one worked harder to convince partners to visit and engage with people in all of the communities or to make sure that the benefits of MICAD were shared equally. It is a measure of Sylvester's understanding and commitment that he declined to join overseas delegations after the first trip to Berkeley.

Building and maintaining consensus in a politically egalitarian society is enormously difficult even when limited to a single village. The ambitions of MICAD, of course, are much greater. Like any big man, Sylvester was subjected to constant scrutiny and gossip. He was an obvious target for sorcery attack from a jealous rival. Although he joked about this with me, he did leave the village for extended periods of time when the pressure got too intense. I have no doubt that many Maisin attribute his early death to sorcery. MICAD, however, has survived him. The need for a Maisin-wide political alliance has not disappeared even in the aftermath of the successful win in the National Court. A consensus in favour of unity remains. MICAD is perhaps the most impressive testimony to the Maisin's faith that solidarity and social amity provides the foundation for health and prosperity, for it continues to operate despite the gossip, the disappointments, and the death of its major founder. Drawing on the image of the traditional *Kawo* leader, Sylvester reminded anyone who would listen that the people's success in the past rested not just on their prowess as warriors but on their ability to make alliances. The Maisin have again demonstrated warrior unity when they faced off against a giant logging company and its partners in the government. MICAD represents the alliance side of their nature, the ability to build networks of friends.

FRIENDSHIP

> March 1, 1997. I have just arrived in Uiaku yesterday and am now sitting in the shade under Sylvester Moi's house, very sweaty but happy. I was worried about my reception. For the past three or four years, a large number of national and foreign activists have worked closely with the Maisin to support their efforts to stop logging in the rainforest and to promote small-scale development. I had helped a little when the delegation visited the United States, but I had been away from the village for more than a decade. Many of the people I knew had died and a very large number of adults were mere kids or had been living in the towns ten years earlier and so wouldn't know me. I've been fretting that those who do will feel that I haven't done enough to help the village. Yet I needn't have worried as it turns out. I received a very warm welcome — not the lavish ceremonial put on for visiting dignitaries, but more low-key, just like people would give for one of their own. Earlier today, a young man from the Maume Rerebin clan came to chat. "Older brother," he told me smiling, "you made us famous. Now all of these people are coming here. We have many friends."

I can hardly take responsibility for making the Maisin famous, but certainly I have become friends with many people. During my years working in Uiaku, I have heard much talk about friends. I am pleased that many Maisin consider me a friend, as I do them. As my Rerebin companion said, the Maisin have also made friends with the many activists, museum curators, film makers, delegations, and others who have visited and stayed for short periods with them over the past few years. The productive alliances the Maisin have formed with various outsiders pivot on "friendship" in that they have been entirely voluntary, as opposed to relationships with government workers, nurses, teachers, police, politicians, and others who are obliged by the nature of their jobs to work with rural folk like the Maisin. While everyone knows that the partners are not entirely selfless, that they gain benefits from working with the Maisin, the fact that they do so freely and at little cost to the community makes them appear relatively altruistic. In fact, both the partners and the Maisin praise each other for their graciousness and generosity. That is what friendship is about.

Yet, like most things, understandings of friendship are conditioned by cultural assumptions and values. It doesn't take long when living with the

Maisin to realize that friendship means something quite distinct from the usual Western understanding. Western assumptions about friendship assume individual volition. One chooses to become friends because of common interests and experiences. Part of the test of friendship has to do with coming to each other's aid when times are tough, even or especially if to do so comes at a personal cost. People believe that they do this through independent choice based upon empathy. Maisin friendship — the *toma* relationship — is based on quite a different premise — that of exchange. In brief, friends should be in a situation of generalized reciprocity, exchanging regularly and freely with each other. This is tied in with a presumption of equivalence. If your friend has more things than you, she or he should be willing to "help you out" by sharing their good fortune generously, balancing out the relationship. I thus found out quite early on that the villagers who called me "friend" tended to be quite forthright and persistent in their requests for rice, tobacco, money, and the rest of my possessions. These two notions of friendship are by no means mutually exclusive. We help out our friends in need, and the Maisin are quite aware that their friends may be unwilling to impoverish themselves so as to make everything equal. Still, the premises are quite different and provide the main source, I think, of some of the tensions and misunderstandings that arise between the Maisin and their new friends.

Melanesians can appear to be very materialistic to outsiders. You are chatting with someone, feeling a warm bond of friendship, comfortable and relaxed, and then they come out with a blunt request for money or some item that they covet. I have never gotten quite used to this, but it helps to understand that in Melanesian cultures the exchange of material items forms the basic language of sociality. Not just the acts of giving and receiving but the objects exchanged communicate messages about the state of relationships. I had a nice lesson about this in 1997. I was visiting an old friend of Anne and mine, a woman with a delightful sense of humour who had often helped us out with gifts of food. We were sitting on her verandah, enjoying a cup of tea (a gift from me), when she asked me to wait a minute. She went into the house and returned carrying a cheap plastic bucket. It had my last name on it and had been part of the gear we gave away upon our departure in 1983. "I still have your bucket," she said with a huge smile as if it were the most valuable keepsake in the world. I was surprised by how moved I felt.

The Melanesian conception of friendship is not entirely foreign to members of other cultures. Gift-giving is an essential part of friendship everywhere. In the short term, visitors to Uiaku and other Maisin villages are impressed by the expressions of friendship, not least because they are often accompanied by generous gifts of food and aid. I was amazed when several villagers hosting the Stó:lō First Nation delegation I had brought to the area

Figure 6.3 Stó:lō-Maisin exchange, June 2000. As their dinghy approaches Ganjiga beach, the Stó:lō delegation receives a traditional welcome from dancing "warriors." Sonny McHalsie (standing) responds with a Stó:lō gesture of peace. (Photo by J. Barker)

in 2000 gave their new friends extremely rare shell ornaments that were clearly heirlooms. In return, most visitors want to be equally generous. Thus the Stó:lō provided their hosts with additional cash, clothing, and other items and sent back gifts after their return to Canada, including soccer balls and uniforms for the youth. Tensions only emerge when the relationship is continuous because for Maisin the point of the exchange is achieving balance. The requests for help become more persistent and lavish. One begins to feel discomfort in the knowledge that in material terms you as the outsider have most of the advantages and so things can never be fair. However, given our conceptions of friendship, based on a notion of individualism, you begin to suspect you are being manipulated, that maybe this never was about "real" friendship.

The longer partners work with the Maisin, the more likely they feel discomforted. They fret about what their relationship means. Hence, some activists I spoke to in the late 1990s told me that one of their biggest concerns was that most Maisin were not hearing the conservation message but were seeing organizations like Greenpeace and Conservation Melanesia as cash cows to be milked for immediate benefits. Some speculated that many villagers were engaging in "cargoist" thinking, believing that the mere appearance of the NGOs and others would magically bring about a new era of prosperity with no additional efforts on their part. Others interpreted Maisin requests for ever more compensation as a type of extortion, a thinly veiled threat that unless the partners anteed up, villagers would change their minds and invite in the loggers. This was of great concern. Supporting the Maisin, for the partners, meant providing them with tools to better adjust to the challenges of globalization. This was supposed to be a short-term intervention with the aim of increasing autonomy and not creating a new dependency. Many Maisin professed to be committed to conserving the rainforest. Yet in light of their demands, how deep did this commitment go? What would happen in a few short years when the NGOs and others shifted their attention and efforts to other places?

These concerns are not unrealistic. There is a strong element of coercion in the ways that Maisin and other Melanesians insist upon "balance" in their relationships. I attended many meetings in which some villagers, in the absence of the partners, angrily denounced their "friends" for secretly pocketing the bulk of profits from overseas sales of tapa and for not adequately compensating people for their time and efforts. Such talk tends to get around and eventually back to its target. It helps to realize that the Maisin often speak of their own leaders in the same harsh terms. It also helps to know that such statements are as often as not a form of testing, to see how far one can go to get the other side to share out its good fortune. The Maisin even have a name for this: "trying luck," an English phrase for which, as far as I'm aware, there is no Maisin language equivalent. Still, the words sting. They feel unfair, although at the same time one senses their ethical truth. Equivalence can never be attained, and true friendship, in the Melanesian sense, remains at best tentative, although no less real for that.

What then of the rainforest? One of my main tasks during my fieldwork in 1997 was to study villagers' perceptions and motivations. Unlike my initial research project in the early 1980s, this was an exercise in applied anthropology. I agreed to write up a report for MICAD and Conservation Melanesia on my findings and to make recommendations. The research entailed attending meetings, especially those with visiting partners, administering a simple questionnaire, and conducting hours of both formal and casual interviews in several villages. As I anticipated, many people told me that they would agree to some limited logging but objected to the secrecy of the projects that had been foisted upon them without their consent. Others, however, also expressed a love of the forest and the need to conserve it. Such sentiments were especially common among women and younger people, although I also heard them from adult males. This marked quite a difference from a decade earlier, when the forest was rarely mentioned and then mostly as a source of danger from enemies, human and spiritual. Yet now school children were drawing lovely pictures of the animals found there. Most impressive to me, I heard very little talk about poverty compared to a decade earlier. Instead, many people talked of the wealth they possessed in the rainforest and about the fact that no one went hungry and everyone had shelter. These findings held consistently through my three visits between 1997 and 2000.

The bigger test rests with what happens after the partners move on. Even by July 2000, the number of visitors and projects had declined dramatically. Lafcadio Cortesi and Greenpeace were gone, and Conservation Melanesia was busy trying to bring its projects in Collingwood Bay to a conclusion. With the win at the National Court against the government and Deegold in 2002, other partners shifted their attention to other parts of the country in more immediate need of support. The determination to conserve the rainforest and other natural resources, however, remains strong. The movement is spreading. A news item from the online edition of the *Post-Courier* newspaper, dated 19 April 2006, reports a massive meeting attended by delegates from across southern Collingwood Bay, spanning five language groups, to form a new association, the Collingwood Bay Conservation and Development Authority. According to spokesman Kingston Kamurar, the Authority will "oversee the implementation of a process that will form the basis of a guideline by which the Collingwood Bay people will conserve their rich marine and terrestrial resources while ensuring these resources are developed in environmentally friendly and sustainable ways."

Despite their relative poverty, the Maisin and their neighbours are fortunate compared to many Indigenous peoples. So far at least, they have retained control over their lands and ability to make choices about how it should be treated and about their own futures. And they have been mostly fortunate in their friends. Despite the missteps, misunderstandings, and occasional bursts of frustrated anger, the collaboration has been remarkably productive and positive. In our increasingly globalized impersonal world, it presents an imperfect but still inspirational example of the power of friendships that reach across cultural, ethnic, and economic barriers.

THE MAISIN DECLARATION (1995)

WE, THE LEADERS OF THE CLANS AND SUBCLANS of the Maisin-speaking people of Collingwood Bay, Oro Province, Papua New Guinea, hereby declare:

That, we enjoy plentiful food and materials for shelter that nature provides from the land and the sea;

That, we take strength from and enjoy great pride in our traditional culture including the clan structure, traditional medicines, ceremonies, and the tapa art form unique to our people;

However, we do not only wish to live as our ancestors did. We seek to maintain our heritage but also to improve our lives and the lives of future generations. We therefore require better opportunities for education, health care, and transportation to name a few. The Government has failed adequately to assist us in developing these opportunities. We require money, information, training, and technical support to develop ourselves.

THEREFORE, WE DECLARE:

That, because we understand that large-scale logging and agriculture will not assist the Maisin people in realizing their aspirations but on the contrary undermine them;

That, in order to assure a source of cash income which will benefit the entire Maisin community and assure the protection of our natural and cultural resources;

That, to maintain control of our destiny in the hands of our own people;

The community will explore, and invites the collaboration of interested parties in supporting, appropriate alternative sources of income such as expanded markets for tapa, village-based tourism, and community-based sustainable forest management.

FURTHERMORE, WE DECLARE:

That, insofar as the forest environment of the traditional Maisin lands provides a home for the game that is our food, a source for the pure water that we drink, a site for the cultivation of our gardens including the tapa trees uniquely suited to the soils of our region, and protection against the ravages of flooding;

That, insofar as this land was inherited from our ancestors and that we intend to pass it on to future generations;

That, insofar as we are aware of how other peoples of Papua New Guinea have been taken advantage of by logging interests, who have repeatedly exploited landholders' ignorance, taking all the goodness out of their place and leaving it barren;

We firmly and unanimously stand opposed to destructive large-scale industrial logging, and to agricultural activity that entails the clearing of large areas of forest, in any part of the lands traditionally held by the Maisin people.

Notes

1. It is not unlikely that Maisin tapa had previously been displayed in museum exhibitions. During the early colonial period, government officers, missionaries, and visiting scientists acquired Maisin tapa, which now resides in the collections of museums around the world. Given the fragility of the cloth when exposed to light, the older pieces are rarely displayed. In catalogues I have seen, the cloth is rarely specifically identified as Maisin and instead attributed to the region (Tufi or Collingwood Bay). The exhibit that Anne and I mounted, like that at Berkeley, was made up of cloth acquired specifically for that purpose. For an excellent account of artifact collecting in Uiaku and Wanigela, see Bonshek (1989) and Hermkens (2005).

2. The key word here is "if." The grass strip at Wanigela has been served over the years by a string of short-lived local airlines. As often as not, the planes overfly Wanigela these days either because the grass has not been cut, the plane is full, or the airline has pulled its planes to fulfill a more lucrative charter. The erratic and expensive service is a matter of great frustration locally, but there is little people can do but complain. During 1997 and 1998, the flights seemed more reliable than usual. My understanding is that today most people need to go the extra distance to Tufi to catch flights.

3. The Summer Institute of Linguistics (SIL) is a branch of the Wycliffe Bible Translators International, one of the largest missionary organizations in the world. The SIL works cooperatively with established churches and local people to provide basic linguistic research on unwritten languages with the aim of furthering biblical translation. Given its vast number of vernacular languages, Papua New Guinea has long been a primary target for the SIL. While its volunteers receive advanced training in linguistics, their aim is to organize and provide expert advice to local people ("national translators") who eventually carry out the actual work of writing Bibles in their own languages.

4. See Chapter 1, note 5.

5. Had the Maisin decided back in 1982 to reject industrial logging, they would not have received anything like the attention and support they did a decade later because at that earlier time the global environmentalist network was just coming into existence and only a handful of NGOs worked in Papua New Guinea.

6. Many of these remain on the web and can be discovered by typing "Maisin tapa" into any search engine.

7. When I asked about this, Sylvester Moi explained that the ancestors of the Uwe Maisin once lived in the Uiaku area and thus retain a claim to the land.

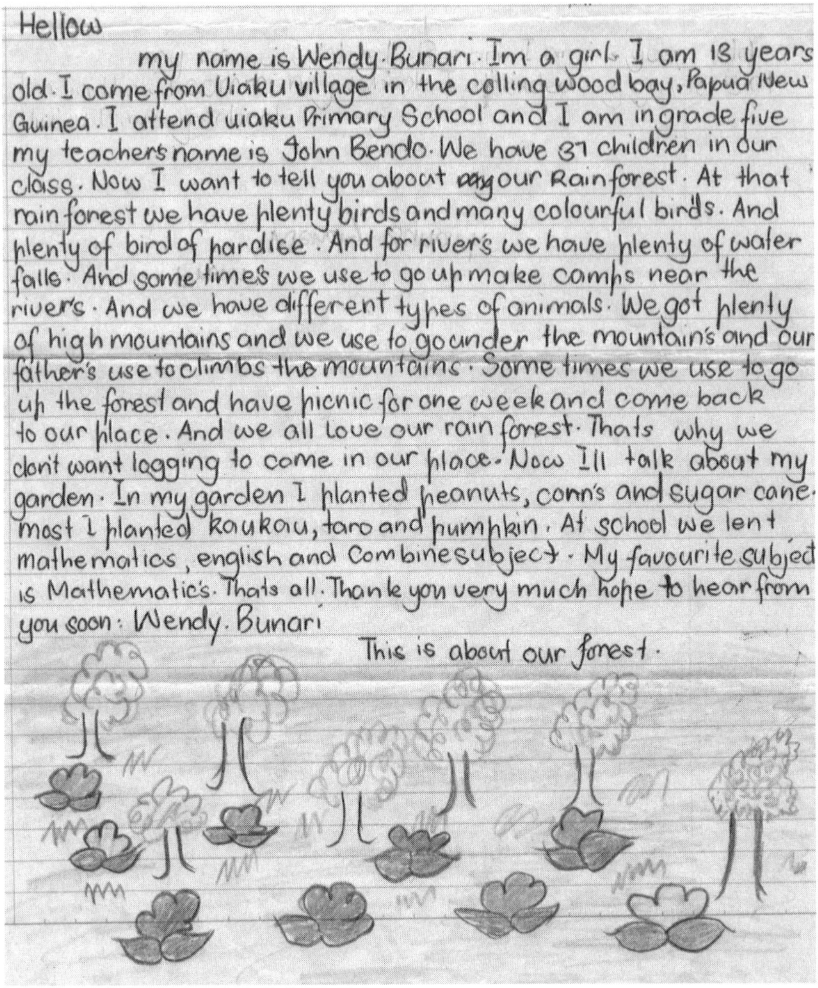

Hellow

my name is Wendy Bunari. Im a girl. I am 13 years old. I come from Uiaku village in the colling wood bay, Papua New Guinea. I attend uiaku Primary School and I am in grade five my teacher's name is John Bendo. We have 37 children in our class. Now I want to tell you about our Rainforest. At that rain forest we have plenty birds and many colourful birds. And plenty of bird of pardise. And for rivers we have plenty of water falls. And some times we use to go up make camps near the rivers. And we have different types of animals. We got plenty of high mountains and we use to go under the mountains and our father's use to climbs the mountains. Some times we use to go up the forest and have picnic for one week and come back to our place. And we all love our rain forest. Thats why we don't want logging to come in our place. Now Ill talk about my garden. In my garden I planted peanuts, conns and sugar cane. most I planted koukou, taro and pumpkin. At school we lent mathematics, english and Combine subject. My favourite subject is Mathematic's. Thats all. Thank you very much hope to hear from you soon: Wendy. Bunari

This is about our forest.

Figure 7.1 Wendy Bunari's letter, 2000. In July 2000, students at the Uiaku Community School wrote letters and drew pictures of their homes for Jake to share with his own classmates in the United States. Her comment about going under and over the mountains is a reference to the Maisin origin story. (Photo by J. Barker)

Conclusion:
Ancestral Lines

In May 1998, I walked into the upstairs office of the MICAD building in Uiaku, picked up the satellite phone, and called my wife in the United States. This very ordinary action would have been unimaginable only a year or two earlier. Although not without difficulties — much of the time, the phone failed to make connections and cost a small fortune to operate — it still struck me as a vivid illustration of globalization. We live in a time of unprecedented movement and integration of people, products, and ideas around the world. Even remote places like Uiaku are not untouched.

Western commentators, economists, and politicians tend to see globalization as an inexorable process that is steadily eroding cultural distinctiveness as more and more societies become integrated into a single, global, capitalist economy (Saul 2005). They acknowledge that the process creates victims of those impoverished by the concentration of wealth into an ever-smaller set of hands and that too often the environment is damaged in the search for quick profits. Finally, they also point out that a growing number of people are resisting globalization, both peacefully (in the case of most environmentalists) or violently (in the case of some religious nationalists). All the same, the advocates of globalization see it as inevitable and ultimately good; they believe that, in time, the rising tide of new wealth will raise the standard of living in even the poorest countries, that a technological fix will be found for the serious environmental challenges ahead, that religious and nationalist wars will fade away as people identify themselves as world citizens, and that democracy will flower in even the most repressive societies. In the words of *New York Times* columnist, Thomas Friedman, the world is becoming "flat" (Friedman 2005).

The utopian understanding of globalization promoted by the CEOs of giant international corporations and their fellow travellers in governments and the media has been strongly countered by the dystopian view of environmentalists and others who fear that the flattening process celebrated by Friedman is true only in the most literal sense: the crushing destruction of local communities accompanied by the theft of their resources and impoverishment of their people and, ultimately, the destruction of the planet in the mad rush for quick profits. In various forms and guises, these opposing views circulate widely across the globe, influencing policies and politics. As we've seen, the Maisin are familiar with both. They take these arguments very seriously, and we need to as well, for they form the outward parameters of debates over our collective future. All the same, we need to be careful not to assume that one or the other represents a "Truth" that transcends the messy realities of life. Both views are human creations, and both are products as well of the very globalization processes they seek to explain.

This is where ethnographic studies like this one come to the fore. By focussing on the experiences of actual people in localities, they reveal a number of smaller truths that challenge the big "Truths" of utopian and dystopian globalization models. Three are especially important. The first is that globalization has allowed the increasing circulation of many things: products, ideas, words, people, and so forth. Second, as a result, most people subjectively experience globalization as an increase in diversity rather than a flattening; it can seem both liberating and threatening to the local status quo. Third, people actively respond to the experiences and pressures of globalization according to their local situations and moral and cultural assumptions. In this process, local cultures do not disappear overnight except where whole communities are physically destroyed, which sadly is a too common event in the modern world. Most of the time, people engage in a kind of dialogue with global forces and entities, leading to changes and modification in local culture and, over the long term, changes and modifications to global culture as well.

The promoters of logging projects and environmental activists tend to subscribe to similar visions of globalization, although they evaluate the process in opposing ways. Ironically, this leads both sides to view Indigenous peoples like the Maisin in comparable ways: as tribesmen living in a timeless culture perched on the very edge of modernity. From such perspectives, southern Collingwood Bay appears as a battleground between two alternative futures, one headed for material prosperity based on "development" and the other contributing towards a sustainable global ecosystem. The Maisin appear either as partners in the global economic enterprise or as plucky traditional conservators of the rainforest. Neither image is entirely wrong, but they are both inadequate and misleading in their characterizations. The Maisin have a long history in the region. Their society experienced development and change long before the arrival of the first European colonialists. Just as important, the Maisin had been connected in various ways to regional and global networks and institutions for almost a century prior to the battle over their forests. While clear cultural continuities exist, especially in terms of subsistence activities, social organization, and moral orientations, the Maisin have incorporated schools, churches, trade stores, Western medicines, and many other modern features into their world. The society encountered by developers and environmentalists in the 1990s was not like that from their own home countries, but neither was it a primeval traditional culture untouched by the outside world.

By the same token, the challenges and choices the Maisin face today are not limited to the fate of the rainforest, important as this is. Nor is it between, in any simple sense, a modern or traditional way of life. Like people everywhere else, the Maisin respond to challenges sometimes through conscious choice but mainly in countless individual adjustments, compromises, and initiatives based on the options actually available to them. In so doing, they become, to use Bruce Knauft's (2002) useful phrase, "locally modern." Perhaps the most valuable contribution made today by ethnographic studies of local communities lies in documenting the many ways that people are creating new modernities on the ground by merging Indigenous ancestral ways with global trends.

TWO REVIVALS

Many examples from my studies of Maisin society could be given, but to conclude this chapter I want to focus upon two in particular. They appeal to me because both are dramatic expressions of identity clearly shaped by entanglements with outsiders. Taken at face value, they appear to embrace opposed solutions to the challenge of modernity, neither of which conform to the expectations of the standard model of globalization. They also appeal because they are embraced primarily by younger people, the future leaders of the Maisin community. They can both be described as revivals.

The first is a Christian revival. As we saw in Chapter 5, the Anglican Christianity practised by the Maisin in the 1980s accorded a passive role for members of the congregations. Church services followed a standard format, set out in a version of the *Book of Common Prayer,* with an invariable ordering of prayers, hymns, and the sharing of sacramental bread and wine. Only evangelists, deacons, and priests licensed by the bishop were allowed to deliver sermons. Other church offices, such as baptism or marriage, were similarly controlled by the clergy. Up until the late 1980s, the Anglicans held a religious monopoly in Collingwood Bay. Some migrants to the towns, however, converted to other sects, which they began to bring back into the villages around that time. In the mid-1990s, four families living in Uiaku erected a small Pentecostal chapel. A few years later, they were joined by a handful of other families and individuals belonging to other sects — Seventh-day Adventists, Jehovah's Witnesses, and Mormons — although a large majority of villagers remained faithful to the Anglican Church. There were some tensions, partly over theological differences but mostly from worries that members of the minority sects would separate themselves from village affairs in general. This didn't happen. Nor did members of the different churches try to convert their neighbours. Everyone adopted a live-and-let-live attitude.

All the same, it was very clear to me on my visit in March 1997 that younger Maisin were taking a much more active interest in Christianity than their elders had in the recent past. The church services were better attended than a decade earlier, a large number of hymns had been translated into Maisin, and people were very excited about the arrival of two volunteers from the Summer Institute of Linguistics who were just beginning the long process of translating the Bible into Maisin. For the first time, I saw people walking through the village carrying Bibles and other Christian works for personal study. The Mothers Union had grown from a small club for elders to a fairly large organization run by young to middle-aged women holding regular meetings and with a healthy bank account.

I was especially interested in the activities of a "youth fellowship" movement that had been underway for several months prior to my arrival (Barker 2003). During the weeks leading up to Easter, the youth held large rallies in each of the Maisin villages. Under palm leaf arches, richly festooned with flowers, young men and women joined in group dances and gospel singing, accompanied by guitars. The celebrations were followed by a meal and then hours of individual testimonials delivered by youth leaders, mainly males. Unlike the sermons given in church, the testimonials did not focus on biblical lessons but were highly personal accounts of the speakers' brushes with sin and their deliverance through faith in Jesus. The climax of the gatherings came in the early hours of the morning, when the youth leaders laid hands on their followers to bless them. Several adolescent girls fell back in a faint as they felt the Holy Ghost enter their bodies.[1]

This form of Christian worship was new to Uiaku but familiar to me. I had participated in similar services while studying Christianity among First Nations peoples on the northern coast of British Columbia where Pentecostal and Fundamentalist churches have a great appeal. Christian revivals of this sort have long been common elsewhere in Melanesia where the focus on individual salvation is usually tied to a strong rejection of local cultural traditions and an apocalyptic vision of the end of the world based upon the book of Revelations in the New Testament (Robbins *et al.* 2001). Indeed, similar movements have been sweeping much of the world, leading to a global reshaping of Christianity (Ernst 2006; Gifford 1998; Martin 2002). The youth fellowship movement was clearly inspired by the forms of Christian revivalism that its leaders had witnessed in the towns. The organizers thus brought something new to the villages that connected participants to a worldwide phenomenon.

Exciting and novel as it was, however, the youth fellowship movement did not imprint itself on a blank page when it arrived in Uiaku and other Maisin villages. Perhaps the most radical aspect of the fellowship meetings was the rhetoric used in the testimonials. Unlike the rather dull sermons heard in church, with their repetitive recitation of biblical stories and general admonitions to "obey Jesus," the young revivalists spoke emotionally of how faith in the Holy Spirit had transformed their personal lives. Their testimonials urged listeners towards a personal relationship with God. This was a far more individualist expression of Christianity than most villagers had encountered. Yet when I asked the young people who attended the rallies what they thought the main lessons were, they mostly stressed community-oriented values such as generosity, avoiding gossip, and listening respectfully to one's elders. The rallies, one of the organizers told me, provided a demonstration that by sharing a faith in Jesus and coming together as one, the Maisin people could overcome petty rivalries and divisions. Perhaps not entirely coincidentally, the youth fellowship movement occurred a few months after the sorcery purge mentioned in Chapter 4. The fellowship movement was something new, and yet in some ways it reminded me of earlier periods of religious excitement when the Maisin had tried to rid their communities of division associated with sorcery and illness to embrace instead a condition of social amity, balance, and prosperity. I was not entirely surprised to learn that each of the girls who had swooned when hands were laid upon them were known to have been suffering from mysterious, lingering sicknesses. As in the past, this new generation of Maisin was equating health with collective solidarity, the idealized condition of *marawa-wawe*.

Meanwhile, many of the same young people were throwing themselves into a very different kind of revival, this one focussed upon their cultural heritage. This was stimulated in the first instance by the sudden interest that outsiders were taking in Maisin culture as a result of the anti-logging campaign. In their travels overseas, Maisin delegations brought not only the materials to demonstrate the making of tapa but traditional costumes and drums to put on cultural performances. In turn, visits by the Greenpeace flagship, *The Rainbow Warrior*, in 1997 and the Stó:lō delegation in 2000 were occasions for large welcoming ceremonies marked by hours of traditional dancing, lavish feasts, and inspiring oratory by the *Kawo* leaders. The renewed interest in traditional customs, however, did not stop with performances for outsiders. Some people started to make body ornaments or revive dances that they had seen in their youth or only heard about; others encouraged the painting of half-forgotten *evovi* clan designs on tapa and criticized artists who wandered too far from traditional patterns; and there was talk of resuming the tattooing of girls' faces and even more ancient customs, like the building of specially designed "chiefly" (*Kawo*) houses, last seen in the late 1930s. A woman in Marua village wrote skits in which people performed long-abandoned customs connected to marriage and widowhood. Meanwhile, end-of-mourning ceremonies became more elaborate, with more individuals undertaking the mourning observations and consequently larger celebrations at the end.

The cultural revival built upon knowledge of Maisin customs. The whole business was taken very seriously, with elders critiquing ceremonies and customs for their authenticity and younger folk expressing awe at seeing ceremonies about which they had only heard in stories of the old days. Still, it was not occurring in a vacuum. As anthropologists have documented for many other people in the Pacific Islands, the Maisin revival was selective and creative — as much a matter of adjusting to modern conditions as resisting the homogenizing influences of globalization (Foster 1995a; Keesing 1992). The revival thus favoured customs that could be comfortably performed before audiences, whether Maisin or outsiders. In the 1980s, ceremonial dances usually began at dusk and carried on until dawn. Ten years later, the performances were much shorter and usually performed during the day. People were happy to perform skits about the traditional treatment of widows or dimly remembered marriage customs, but no one was advocating their re-adoption. The support of ancestral traditions was both selective and political. The revival drew from the reservoir of Maisin traditions to create a new message, one of unity based upon a common heritage. Thus, the performances played up customs, like dancing or the respect shown to *Kawo* leaders, that are generic to the Maisin rather than those that centred upon particular clans. Not surprisingly, MICAD played a leading role in organizing the largest ceremonies.

The two revivals I've discussed here are fascinating in that they appear to point towards different kinds of futures: one in which the Maisin merge into the global body of Christian believers and another in which they retain a clear cultural distinctiveness in a world of nations. They are indicative of the kinds of options many Indigenous peoples face as their lives become increasingly entangled with global institutions, agents, and ideas. This experience generates a kind of dialogue between local and global realities, resulting in often surprising compromises and innovations. Such compromises were embodied in both revivals. In subtle but powerful ways, the Christian revival resonated with deeply engrained Indigenous assumptions that illness has a moral cause. The cultural revival, despite its overt appearance, was strongly stimulated by the presence of foreign environmentalists and media working to produce a sympathetic image of the Maisin on the world stage. Both revivals, then, were more than they at first appeared to be.

That the two revivals occurred simultaneously and were broadly supported across the community is surprising only if one assumes that globalization permits only a single direction of change towards a market-driven world inhabited by consumers making individual choices. Neither of the revivals embraced that vision.

The Maisin experience is by no means unique. In fact, it is rather common as many people in different localities encounter and deal with similar global forces. The example suggests that globalization is not confined or even necessarily dominated by strictly economic concerns — both are secondary at best to both Christian revivalism and cultural nationalism. It suggests that there is no inevitable direction to globalization. In an increasingly integrated world, people do face similar challenges. Yet what is most interesting and telling, in the final analysis, is what people do with them in light of their own experiences and the possibilities of their lives. It is in that interface, between the global and the local, that history gets made.

ANCESTRAL LINES

The decision to reject commercial logging brought in its wake many changes to Uiaku and other Maisin communities: a deeper involvement in the cash economy, a changing sense of the value of the land and its resources, an awakened sense of cultural distinctiveness and political unity, a renewed commitment to Christianity, and much else. When I began my fieldwork in 1981, not a single villager had travelled outside of Papua New Guinea, and Maisin tapa cloth was known only to tourist shopowners in the towns. By 2000, delegations of Maisin villagers had visited an array of foreign countries, and tapa cloth along with the Maisin story was featured prominently on the Internet. These developments command our attention not because the Maisin have become major players on the world stage — clearly they have not — but because their sudden fame brings into focus in a particularly sharp way the local context in which globalization plays out and is limited.

Things could have been different. I have often wondered what would have happened to the Maisin had the rainforest been logged and replaced by commercial plantations in the 1980s, as the people wished at the time. I also wonder whether many of the changes brought by their sudden fame would have happened if the logging option had never existed, albeit at a slower pace. Across Melanesia, researchers, artists, poets, politicians, church leaders, and ordinary people alike have noticed the steady erosion of the reciprocal value systems so essential to village life in the face of increasing migration, exposure to global media, and dependence on money and commodities (Foster 2002; Smith 2002). The day Anne and I first arrived in Uiaku, we were told never to pay cash for the food and other sorts of help villagers brought to us. Today, visitors pay a modest fee set by MICAD for room and board, and when people have extra food from the garden they are as likely to sell it at the market as give it freely to a neighbour. The moral orientations of reciprocity embodied in the concept of *marawa-wawe* remain at the heart of Maisin culture, as does clan identity symbolized in the wearing of *kawo*. Yet the Maisin feel steady pressures and temptations to shift towards a more individualized ethic and away from the communal values of the past. They are engaged in a complex dance of experience, expectations, and aspirations that registers only dimly on the edge of consciousness. Viewed from the perspective of this small remote village, the outcome is far from certain.

From the distanced perspective of standard understandings of globalization, people like the Maisin appear either as stubborn traditionalists opposed to "progress" or as plucky natural conservators of the planet's environment. They are neither. They are ordinary human beings who have over many years developed certain ways of surviving in their environment, of associating with each other, of viewing the cosmos and its inhabitants, and of working out their differences. These deeply engrained cultural patterns did not determine the ways the Maisin responded to the challenges they faced in the late twentieth century, but they were highly formative. They are ancestral lines: at once ancient and modern, stable and innovative. Like the patterns on a tapa cloth, they are familiar and new, bold and faint, straight and curving. They draw from the deep well of historic and cultural experience, informing and shaping Maisin understandings of the challenges of their time.

In the 1980s, the Maisin tended to think of themselves as shamefully poor and of the rainforest as their last best hope of "development" and a more comfortable life. Such thoughts linger, but more and more people have come to think of themselves and the rainforest in a new light: as an immense gift, sustaining life and fending off the grinding poverty and violence many Maisin have heard about and witnessed in their travels to the towns and overseas. The Maisin villages are small and remote from the centres of global politics and business. Yet consider this: in an era of global climate change, the rapid destruction of the world's remaining rainforests threatens us all. The young Maisin girl who carefully designs a tapa cloth at home and lovingly draws pictures of the plants and animals of the forest at school may in the end have as much influence over the world's long-term survival as the richest and most powerful corporate executive in New York City or Tokyo. The fate of small remote peoples like the Maisin is ours as well. We have much to learn from them.

Note

1. In Pentecostal circles, this is known as being "slain in the spirit." At this time, however, the Maisin were not aware of the phrase and simply told me that the Holy Spirit had possessed their bodies.

References

Akin, David, and Joel Robbins (Eds.). 1999. *Money and Modernity: State and Local Currencies in Melanesia.* Pittsburgh: Pittsburgh University Press.

Barker, John. 1979. Papuans and Protestants. A Sociological Study of the London Missionary Society, Methodist, and Anglican Missions in Papua, 1870 to 1930. M.A. thesis. Victoria: University of Wellington.

——. 1985. Missionaries and Mourning: Continuity and Change in the Death Ceremonies of a Melanesian People. In *Anthropologists, Missionaries, and Cultural Change*, ed. Darrel L. Whiteman. 263-94. Williamsburg: College of William and Mary.

——. 1986. From Boy's House to Youth Club: A Case Study of the Youth Movement in Uiaku and Ganjiga Villages, Oro Province. In *Youth and Society: Perspectives from Papua New Guinea*, ed. Maev O'Collins. 81-107. Canberra: Department of Political and Social Change, Research School of Pacific Studies, Australian National University.

——. 1987. Optimistic Pragmatists: Anglican Missionaries among the Maisin of Collingwood Bay, Oro Province. *Journal of Pacific History* 22: 66-81.

——. 1990. Encounters with Evil: The Historical Construction of Sorcery in Maisin Society, Papua New Guinea. *Oceania* 61: 139-55.

——. 1992. Christianity in Western Melanesian Ethnography. In *History and Tradition in Melanesian Anthropology*, ed. James Carrier. 143-44. Berkeley: University of California Press.

——. 1993. We are "Ekelesia": Conversion in Uiaku, Papua New Guinea. In *Christian Conversion: Historical and Anthropological Perspectives on a Great Transformation*, ed. Robert Hefner. 199-230. Berkeley: University of California Press.

——. 1996. Village Inventions: Historical Variations upon a Regional Theme. *Oceania* 66: 211-29.

——. 2001. Dangerous Objects: Changing Indigenous Perceptions of Material Culture in a Papua New Guinea Society. *Pacific Science* 55: 359-75.

——. 2003. Christian Bodies: Dialectics of Sickness and Salvation Among the Maisin of Papua New Guinea. *Journal of Religious History* 27: 272-92.

——. 2004a. Films and Other Trials: Reflections on Fieldwork among the Maisin, Papua New Guinea. *Pacific Studies* 27: 81-106.

——. 2004b. Between Heaven and Earth: Missionaries, Environmentalists, and the Maisin. In *Pacific Island Societies in a Global World*, ed. Victoria Lockwood. 439-59. Englewood Cliffs: Prentice-Hall.

——. 2005. An Outpost in Papua: Anglican Missionaries and Melanesian Teachers among the Maisin, 1902-1934. In *Indigenous Peoples and Religious Change*, ed. Peggy Brock. 79-106. Leiden: Brill.

Barker, John, and Anne Marie Tietjen. 1990. Female Facial Tattooing among the Maisin of Oro Province, Papua New Guinea: The Changing Significance of an Ancient Custom. *Oceania* 60: 217-34.

Barton, F.R. 1918. Tattooing in South Eastern New Guinea. *Journal of the Royal Anthropological Institute* 48: 22-79.

Bashkow, Ira. 2006. *The Meaning of Whitemen: Race & Modernity in the Orokaiva Cultural World*. Chicago: Chicago University Press.

Bloch, Maurice, and Jonathan Parry (Eds.). 1989. *Money and the Morality of Exchange*. Cambridge: Cambridge University Press.

Bonshek, Elizabeth. 1989. Money, Pots and Patterns: The Percy Money Collection of Bark Cloth and Pottery Held at the Australian Museum. M.A. thesis. Brisbane: University of Queensland.

Brosius, J. Peter. 2003. Voices from the Borneo Rain Forest: Writing the History of an Environmental Campaign. In *Nature in the Global South*, ed. Paul Greenough and Anna Lowenhaupt Tsing. 319-46. Durham: Duke University Press.

Burridge, Kenelm. 1960. *Mambu: A Study of Melanesian Cargo Movements and their Social and Ideological Background*. New York: Harper and Row.

——. 1969. *New Heaven, New Earth: A Study of Millenarian Activities*. New York: Schocken.

——. 1975. The Melanesian Manager. In *Studies in Social Anthropology*, ed. J. Beattie and G. Lienhardt. 86-104. Oxford: Clarendon.

Carrier, James G. 1981. Labour Migration and Labour Export on Ponam Island. *Oceania* 51: 237-55.

Carrier, James G., and Achsah H. Carrier. 1989. *Wage, Trade, and Exchange in Melanesia: A Manus Society in the Modern State*. Berkeley: University of California Press.

Chignell, Arthur Kent. 1911. *An Outpost in Papua*. London: Murray.

Chowning, Ann. 1979. Leadership in Melanesia. *Journal of Pacific History* 14: 66-84.

Comaroff, Jean, and John Comaroff. 1991. *Of Revelation and Revolution:*

Christianity, Colonialism, and Consciousness in South Africa. Chicago: University of Chicago Press.

Comaroff, John L., and Jean Comaroff. 1997. *Of Revelation and Revolution: The Dialectics of Modernity on a South African Frontier.* Chicago: University of Chicago Press.

Dakeyne, R.B. 1966. Co-operatives at Yega. In *Orokaiva Papers.* New Guinea Research Bulletin No. 4. 53-68. Port Moresby and Canberra: New Guinea Research Unit.

Dickson-Waiko, Anne. 2003. The Missing Rib: Mobilizing Church Women for Change in Papua New Guinea. *Oceania* 74: 98-119.

Dinnen, Sinclair. 2001. *Law and Order in a Weak State: Crime and Politics in Papua New Guinea.* Honolulu: University of Hawai'i Press.

Dorney, Sean. 2000. *Papua New Guinea: People, Politics, and History Since 1975.* Sydney: ABC Books.

Douglas, Bronwen. 2003. Christianity, Tradition, and Everyday Modernity: Towards an Anatomy of Women's Groupings in Melanesia. *Oceania* 74: 6-23.

Egloff, Brian. 1979. *Recent Prehistory in Southeast Papua.* Canberra: Department of Prehistory, Research School of the Pacific, Australian National University.

Ernst, Manfred (Ed.). 2006. *Globalization and the Re-Shaping of Christianity in the Pacific Islands.* Suva: Pacific Theological College.

Errington, Frederick, and Deborah Gewertz. 1987. *Cultural Alternatives and a Feminist Anthropology: An Analysis of Culturally Constructed Gender Interests in Papua New Guinea.* Cambridge: Cambridge University Press.

———. 2004. *Yali's Question: Sugar, Culture, and History.* Chicago: University of Chicago Press.

Evans-Pritchard, E.E. 1937. *Witchcraft, Oracles, and Magic among the Azande.* Oxford: Clarendon.

Filer, Colin (Ed.). 1997. *The Political Economy of Forest Management in Papua New Guinea.* NRI Monograph 32. London and Port Moresby: International Institute for Environment and Development, National Research Institute.

———. 1998a. *Loggers, Donors, and Resource Owners.* Vol. 2. London and Port Moresby: International Institute for Environment and Development, National Research Institute.

———. 1998b. The Melanesian Way of Menacing the Mining Industry. In *Modern Papua New Guinea,* ed. Laura Zimmer-Tamakoshi. 147-78. Kirksville, Thomas Jefferson University Press.

Foster, Robert. 1995a. *Social Reproduction and History in Melanesia.* Cambridge: Cambridge University Press.

Foster, Robert J. (Ed.). 1995b. *Nation Making: Emergent Identities in Postcolonial Melanesia.* Ann Arbor: University of Michigan Press.

———. 2002. *Materializing the Nation: Commodities, Consumption, and Media in Papua New Guinea.* Bloomington: Indiana University Press.

Frankel, Stephen, and Gilbert Lewis (Eds.). 1989. *A Continuing Trial of Treatment: Medical Pluralism in Papua New Guinea.* Dordrecht/Boston/London: Kluwer.

Friedman, Thomas. 2005. *The World is Flat: A Brief History of the Twenty-First Century.* New York: Farrar, Straus and Giroux.

Geertz, Clifford. 1973. *The Interpretation of Cultures.* New York: Basic Books.

Gell, Alfred. 1993. *Wrapping in Images: Tattooing in Polynesia.* Oxford: Oxford University Press.

Gibbs, Philip. 2005. *Political Discourse and Religious Narratives of Church and State in Papua New Guinea.* State, Society, and Governance in Melanesia Project, Australian National University.

———. 2006. Papua New Guinea. In *Globalization and the Re-Shaping of Christianity in the Pacific Islands,* ed. Manfred Ernst. 81-158. Suva: The Pacific Theological College.

Gifford, Paul. 1998. *African Christianity: Its Public Role.* London: Hurst and Company.

Godelier, Maurice. 1986. *The Making of Great Men: Male Domination and Power among the New Guinea Baruya.* New York: Cambridge University Press.

———. 1999. *The Enigma of the Gift.* Chicago: University of Chicago Press.

Gordon, Robert, and Mervyn Meggitt. 1985. *Law and Order in the New Guinea Highlands.* Hanover: University Press of New England.

Gregory, C.A. 1982. *Gifts and Commodities.* London: Academic Press.

Haviland, William A., Gary W. Crawford, and Shirley A. Fedorak (Eds.). 2002. *Cultural Anthropology: First Canadian Edition.* Scarborough: Thompson Nelson.

Hefner, Robert W. (Ed.) 1993. *Conversion to Christianity: Historical and Anthropological Perspectives on a Great Transformation.* Berkeley: University of California Press.

Herdt, G.H. 1981. *Guardians of the Flutes: Idioms of Masculinity.* New York: McGraw-Hill.

Hermkens, Anna-Karina. 2005. Engendering Objects: Barkcloth and the Dynamics of Identity in Papua New Guinea. PhD dissertation. Nijmegen: Radboud Universiteit.

Jorgensen, Dan. 2006. Hinderland History: The Ok Tedi Mine and Its Cultural Consequences in Telefolmin. *The Contemporary Pacific* 18: 233-63.

Joyce, R.B. 1968. William MacGregor: The Role of the Individual. In *The History of Melanesia*, ed. K.S. Inglis. 33-45. Canberra and Port Moresby: Australian National University and University of Papua New Guinea.

Kahn, Miriam. 1983. Sunday Christians, Monday Sorcerers: Selective Adaptation to Missionization in Wamira. *Journal of Pacific History* 18: 96-112.

Keesing, Roger. 1975. *Kin Groups and Social Structure*. New York: Holt, Rinehart and Winston.

———. 1984. Rethinking Mana. *Journal of Anthropological Research* 40: 137-56.

———. 1992. *Custom and Confrontation: The Kwaio Struggle for Cultural Autonomy*. Chicago: University of Chicago Press.

Kirch, Patrick. 2000. *On The Road of the Winds: An Archaeological History of the Pacific Islands Before European Contact*. Berkeley: University of California Press.

Kirsch, Stuart. 2006. *Reverse Anthropology: Indigenous Analysis of Social and Environmental Relations in New Guinea*. Palo Alto: Stanford University Press.

Kituai, August Ibrum K. 1998. *My Gun, My Brother: The World of the Papua New Guinea Colonial Police, 1920-1960*. Honolulu: University of Hawai'i Press.

Knauft, Bruce M. 2002. *Exchanging the Past: A Rainforest World of Before and After*. Chicago: University of Chicago Press.

Kooijman, Simon. 1972. *Tapa in Polynesia*. Honolulu: Bishop Museum Press.

Lawrence, Peter. 1984. *The Garia: The Ethnography of a Traditional Cosmic System in Papua New Guinea*. Manchester: Manchester University Press.

Lepowsky, Maria. 1993. *Fruit of the Motherland: Gender in an Egalitarian Society*. New York: Columbia University Press.

Lohmann, Roger Ivar (Ed.). 2003. *Dream Travelers: Sleep Experiences and Culture in the Western Pacific*. New York: Palgrave Macmillan.

Lutz, Catherine, and Jane Lou Collins. 1993. *Reading National Geographic*. Chicago: University of Chicago Press.

Lynch, John. 1988. *Pacific Languages: An Introduction*. Honolulu: University of Hawai'i Press.

Malinowski, Bronislaw. 1922. *Argonauts of the Western Pacific*. New York: Dutton.

———. 1954. *Science, Magic, and Religion*. Garden City: Doubleday.

Martin, David. 2002. *Pentecostalism: The World Their Parish*. Oxford: Blackwell.

219

Mauss, Marcel. 1990 [1925]. *The Gift: The Form and Reason of Exchange in Primitive and Archaic Societies*. London: Routledge.

Mayo, Lida. 1974. *Bloody Buna*. Garden City: Doubleday.

Monckton, C.A.W. 1922. *Taming New Guinea*. New York: Dodd Mead and Company.

Moore, Clive. 2003. *New Guinea: Crossing Boundaries and History*. Honolulu: University of Hawai'i Press.

Moresby, John. 1876. *Discoveries and Surveys in New Guinea and the D'Entrecasteaux Islands*. London: Murray.

Morgan, Lewis Henry. 1877. *Ancient Society*. New York: Henry Holt.

Munroe, Doug, and Andrew Thornley (Eds.). 1996. *The Covenant Makers: Islander Missionaries in the Pacific*. Suva, Fiji: Pacific Theological College and the Institute of Pacific Studies, University of the South Pacific.

Narakobi, Bernard. 1980. *The Melanesian Way*. Boroko, Papua New Guinea. Suva, Fiji: Institute of Papua New Guinea Studies and Institute of Pacific Studies.

Neich, Roger, and Mick Prendergast. 2005. *Pacific Tapa*. Honolulu: University of Hawai'i Press.

Newton, Janice. 1982. Feasting for Oil Palm. *Social Analysis* 10: 63-78.

Pagden, Anthony. 1982. *The Fall of Natural Man: The American Indian and the Origins of Comparative Ethnology*. Cambridge: Cambridge University Press.

Ray, Sidney H. 1911. Comparative Notes on Maisin and Other Languages of Eastern Papua. *Journal of the Royal Anthropological Institute* 41.

Read, K.E. 1959. Leadership and Consensus in a New Guinea Society. *American Anthropologist* 61: 425-36.

Robbins, Joel, Pamela J. Stewart, and Andrew J. Strathern (Eds.). 2001. Charismatic and Pentecostal Christianity in Oceania (special issue). *Journal of Ritual Studies* 15(2).

Ross, Malcolm. 1984. *Maisin: A Preliminary Sketch, No. 23*. Pacific Linguistics, Series A, No. 69. Canberra: Australian National University.

Sahlins, Marshall. 1972. *Stone Age Economics*. Chicago: Aldine.

Saul, John Ralston. 2005. *The Collapse of Globalism and the Reinvention of the World*. Toronto: Viking Canada.

Scaglion, Richard. 2004. Legal Pluralism in Pacific Island Societies. In *Globalization and Culture Change in the Pacific Islands*, ed. Victoria S. Lockwood. 86-101. Upper Saddle River: Pearson/Prentice Hall.

Schieffelin, Edward L. 1976. *The Sorrow of the Lonely and the Burning of the Dancers*. New York: St. Martin's Press.

Schieffelin, Edward L., and Robert Crittenden. 1991. *Like People You See in a Dream: First Contact in Six Papuan Societies*. Stanford: Stanford University Press.

Schwimmer, Erik. 1969. *Cultural Consequences of a Volcanic Eruption Experienced by the Mount Lamington Orokaiva.* Eugene: Department of Anthropology, University of Oregon.

Schwimmer, Z. 1979. Tapa Cloths of the Northern District, Papua-New Guinea. *Pacific Arts Newsletter* 9: 6-11.

Small, Cathy. 1997. *Voyages: From Tongan Villages to American Suburbs.* Ithaca: Cornell University Press.

Smith, Michael French. 1994. *Hard Times on Kairiru Island: Poverty, Development, and Morality in a Papua New Guinea Village.* Honolulu: University of Hawai'i Press.

———. 2002. *Village on the Edge: Changing Times in Papua New Guinea.* Honolulu: University of Hawai'i Press.

Stephen, Michele. 1995. *A'aisa's Gifts: A Study of Magic and the Self.* Berkeley: University of California Press.

Strathern, Marilyn (Ed.). 1987. *Dealing with Inequality: Analyzing Gender Relations in Melanesia and Beyond.* Cambridge: Cambridge University Press.

Strong, Walter Mersh. 1911. The Maisin Language. *Journal of the Royal Anthropological Institute* 4: 381-96.

Suzuki, David, and Holly Dressel. 2002. *Good News for a Change: How Everyday People are Helping the Planet.* Toronto: Stoddart.

Sykes, Karen. 2005. *Arguing with Anthropology: An Introduction to Critical Theories of the Gift.* London: Routledge.

Synge, F.M. 1908. *Albert Maclaren, Pioneer Missionary in New Guinea.* London: Society for the Propagation of the Gospel.

Teilhet, Jehanne. 1983. The Role of Women Artists in Polynesia and Melanesia. In *Arts and Artists of Oceania,* ed. S.M. Mead and B. Kernot. 45-56. Palmerston North: Dunmore.

Tietjen, Anne Marie. 1985. Infant Care and Feeding Practices and the Beginnings of Socialization among the Maisin of Papua New Guinea. In *Infant Care and Feeding in the South Pacific,* ed. Leslie Marshall. 121-35. New York: Gordon and Breach.

———. 1986. Prosocial Reasoning among Children and Adults in a Papua New Guinea Society. *Developmental Psychology* 22: 861-68.

Trompf, G.W. 1994. *Payback: The Logic of Retribution in Melanesian Religions.* Cambridge: Cambridge University Press.

Tsing, Anna Lowenhaupt. 2005. *Friction: An Ethnography of Global Connection.* Princeton: Princeton University Press.

Turner, Terence. 1993. The Kayapo Resistance. *Perspectives in Biology and Medicine* 36: 526-45.

Turner, V.W. 1974. *Dramas, Fields, and Metaphors.* Ithaca: Cornell University Press.

Tuzin, Donald F. 1980. *The Voice of the Tambaran: Truth and Illusion in Ilahita Arapesh Religion*. Berkeley: University of California Press.

Wagner, Roy. 1967. *The Curse of Souw: Principles of Daribi Clan Definition and Alliance in New Guinea*. Chicago: University of Chicago Press.

Waiko, John Dademo. 1993. *A Short History of Papua New Guinea*. Melbourne: Oxford University Press.

Weiner, Annette B. 1988. *The Trobrianders of Papua New Guinea*. Fort Worth: Harcourt Brace Jovanovich.

West, Paige. 2006. *Conservation is Our Government Now: The Politics of Ecology in Papua New Guinea*. Durham: Duke University Press.

Wetherell, David. 1977. *Reluctant Mission: The Anglican Church in Papua New Guinea, 1891-1942*. St. Lucia: University of Queensland Press.

Williams, F.E. 1930. *Orokaiva Society*. London: Oxford University Press.

Worsley, Peter. 1968. *The Trumpet Shall Sound: A Study of "Cargo Cults" in Melanesia*. New York: Schocken Books.

Zimmer-Tamakoshi, L., (Ed.). 1998. *Modern Papua New Guinea*. Kirksville, Missouri: Thomas Jefferson University Press.

Index